BECOMING HUMAN BY DESIGN

BECOMING HUMAN BY DESIGN

Tony Fry

London • New York

English edition
First published in 2012 by
Berg
Editorial offices:
50 Bedford Square, London WC1B 3DP, UK
175 Fifth Avenue, New York, NY 10010, USA

© Tony Fry 2012

Berg is an imprint of Bloomsbury Publishing Plc.

Library of Congress Cataloging-in-Publication Data
A catalogue record for this book is available from the Library of Congress.

British Library Cataloguing-in-Publication Data
A catalogue record for this book is available from the British Library.

ISBN 978 0 85785 354 7 (Cloth)
978 0 85785 355 4 (Paper)
e-ISBN 978 0 85785 356 1 (epub)

Typeset by Apex CoVantage, LLC, Madison, WI, USA.

Printed in the UK by the MPG Books Group

www.bergpublishers.com

Contents

Preface

Ideas have their time. But, as Nietzsche's tragic life indicates, the author has no control over when or if this moment arrives or, equally, if she or he will have presence during it. Power, in the end, rests with the reader and events.

This book is about design, time, the past and the future in relation to the nature of the human species. While it asks, as others have before, where the species came from, how it was created, what it became and what its likely future will be, it also does something else. It puts design into the picture of our becoming. In doing this, it engages a good deal of the recent literature on the human-animal relation and the future form of 'the human', but from a new perspective that challenges existing accounts.

In many ways this book can be considered the last of a trilogy. The first book, *Design Futuring,* set out to pose design practice transformed against the forces of structural unsustainability. Book 2, *Design as Politics,* placed the activity of redirective design firmly in the domain of the political and, in so doing, exposed the impotence of democracy to confront and overcome the unsustainable. *Becoming Human by Design* has an even wider context. As such, it arrives as an extension and, in some ways, a culmination of work on the concepts of remaking, defuturing, futuring and Sustainment (as sovereign) undertaken over the past two decades.[1]

The three books of the trilogy actually fit into a large schema and unite with a good deal of writing that prefigured them. But, in all honesty, it has taken a long time to recognize this and to state what this schema adds up to. It reveals itself with two characteristics. The first exposes just how important design has been, in its every dimension, in the creation, nature and fate of the 'world-within-the-world' of human occupation. Yet, not only has the world at large, the humanities and science, not grasped the significance of design but neither has the professional and academic design community, which doggedly adheres to a myopic view of design, what constitutes design practices, what design objects and discourses are, what they have done and do. The second characteristic, shared by all three books, is captured by the bald statement 'we can only get to a future with a future (for us) by design'.

This book sets out to put what we actually are before ourselves. It exposes how design, in significant part, made us what we are. It also addresses the perplexing question 'what it is that we need to become?'

In varied ways, all three books confront the anthropocentric nature of human being as a fundamental and unavoidable issue. Likewise, the significance of ontological design is constantly explored and explicated. As with the prior books, this one is also a provocation. It invites us to radically think the fate of *Homo sapiens,* recognizing all species are finite and that 'we' have arrived at a decisive moment of our being—one wherein we face a stark choice: change or continue to rapidly negate our future. All three books recognize this situation and place humanity at the epicentre of the unsustainable. They also all affirm that our current understandings and practices of 'sustainability' are totally inadequate to deal with this problem.

Traversing boundaries that divide theory, analysis and speculation, the book's argument centres on the way that the historicity of ontological design revises the story of human 'evolution'. While not contesting Darwin's account and the sociocultural supplement to his thesis by Herbert Spencer, what the book will show is that the biological and social models of evolution are an insufficient explanation of how 'we humans' came to be what we are.

Books carry the name of an author, but in fact they are authored by many minds, as the selected readings of this work and all others confirms. Such token remarks belie the depth of real debts. And then there are other debts. Special thanks, as ever, goes to Anne-Marie Willis, but I would also like to especially acknowledge my friends who have been part of the journey: Clive Dilnot, Lisa Norton, Duncan Fairfax, Oliver Feltham, Abby Mellick Lopes, Cameron Tonkinwise and Will McNeill.

Introduction

My doctrine declares: the task is to live in such a way *that you must wish to live again.*

—Friedrich Nietzsche, 1881

Our story starts with accounts of two and a half million years ago, when our ancient hominoid ancestors first picked up stones and used them as tools. This action opens a pathway into the book's main narrative, which is the indivisible relation between the formation of the world of human fabrication and the making of mankind itself. Now, one might reasonably ask: how is it possible to comment on such events and, even more ambitiously, extrapolate from them? There are two answers to this question.

The first answer is straightforward and simply acknowledges the use made of the work of palaeontologists, especially the transdisciplinary work of André Leroi-Gourhan. The second answer is more complex. It involves narrative and bringing together two different ways of understanding 'the nature of things': the trace (not least as understood by Walter Benjamin and evidenced in his Arcades project) and ontological design.

Benjamin's revelatory mode of making the world of everyday objects appear strange and mythic brought everything associated with the origins and futuring of things to the present moment of *ur-historical* interrogation. This was not as transparent figures but as clues to be found, deciphered and read. His claim was that the materially present in any particular moment of history was a gathering buried in human (designed) artefacts or events that could be 'rescued'. These objects or events, as they arrived out of exposing the 'ever-lasting now', he named *Jetztzeit*.[1]

To Benjamin's method, we will add a second way of 'understanding the nature of things', which is to take up ontological design as a mode of historical back projection. Any particular thing delivers over to us a history of agency of what it does, as well as object transformation—the history of the thinging of the thing retraced back via the thinging of the thing in the present *as it is used*. Thus, all things that, for instance, cut, hammer, write, dig or engrave are performatively linked (this by cutting, hammering, writing, writing, digging and engraving). Essentially, all tools lead back to the first tools. Our mode of observation is therefore a tracing back accompanied by a tracing forward (which implies a denaturalization of history). This means that nothing is seen that is not present.

While a great deal of what will be engaged comes from tracing archaeological and contemporary material, mystery endures. Like a photographic image with a lost caption, there are signs that invite analysis and conjecture, but truth eludes. Likewise, and inevitably, there are absences and gaps—some will be discerned, yet others will be missed.

The Story Framed

The story to be told arrives where the past meets the future. As such, it contests dominant ways of understanding 'now'.

'Unsustainability' is an extremely ambiguous category. Notwithstanding an ability to identify its cause, what it names is a condition never adequately defined. The relational complexity of humanity's creation of means that negate both itself and other species is just not represented. Divisions of knowledge and the way issues are reported do not provide the means to assemble an adequate picture. More than this, the term travels with an assumption of worldly objectification, whereas unsustainability is an elemental feature of what we are and always have been—a fundamental condition that begs understanding.

Unsustainability will not destroy the planet—it may well do untold damage, but what is actually at risk is us—we are at risk of auto-destruction. In some form, the planet will recover from the damage we do after our demise. The evidence is in—it has been estimated that some 250 million years ago around 90 per cent of the planet's species were rendered extinct by a climatic disaster, yet the planet recovered to constitute what became the world we know. Just as worldly circumstances have redefined the meaning of unsustainability, so it is with Sustainment—specifically, it has to be understood well beyond the biological reductionism evoked by the term 'Sustainability'.

Sustainment in the face of the unsustainable is about time. It is the project of making time.

As a finite species, we are fated. But how we act upon the environmental conditions upon which we depend will determine whether our duration is short or long. Here it should be remembered that 'the environment' is not a location; rather, it is 'the everywhere'—the inner and outer; the earth, the sky and the ocean; the home as the world given and the world of our own creation. Sustainment is also a process as well as a conditional project that has to become sovereign—the value above all other values. This value is grounded in ontological conditions of necessity. It is a value that has to be in order for us to be. It is being itself. All values are, of course, perspectival—as Friedrich Nietzsche put it, 'values do not exist in the fabric of the world.'[2] Clearly, the world itself is framed by values vested in specific perspectives that constitute particular worldviews. These values overdetermine ideas and judgements that themselves conceptually objectify our experience of self and the world. As such, they carry an impositional power. The Eurocentric worldview has, for example, acted to negate the values of other cultures with greater sustaining ability than it had.

Insofar as unsustainability is intrinsic to the human ontology, we cannot overcome it without overcoming ourselves. 'We' have to become other than we are. Nietzsche's *Thus Spoke Zarathustra* was a provocation to radically rethink the 'nature', fate and future form of *Homo sapiens.* But the task still remains. Essentially, to be futural, the human has to become other than itself. 'It' has to self-re-create. Why is this re-creation not just needed but unavoidable? One answer comes from the human drive to dominance as a species.

The evidence suggests this drive seems to have been present from the very arrival of *Homo sapiens,* as seen in 'our' disposition and ability to surmount and extinguish competition from all other hominoid species and to become the ultimate predator on land and sea. This inherent quality of our being became amplified by the sheer growth in numbers of the human population combined with our 'gift' of developing extraordinary technologies of death (which, of course, we use to great effect upon our enemy selves). Alongside our ability to be deliberately destructive of human life and those species of immediate use to us is the accidental capability we have acquired to destroy life in general. A point has now been reached where the oceans have been depleted to a critical level and our terrestrial actions, combined with the damage done to the planet's atmosphere, constantly reduce planetary biodiversity. But, as already registered, now our destructive actions (at multiple levels of our social, economic and political existence) are putting our very own being at risk.

Being Here

In stark contrast to how we have been introduced to the idea of shelter and home, it can be said that ever since human beings started to make 'a world for themselves in the world', they put themselves on the path to homelessness. For all the attainments of human beings, the failure to live according to the recognition that, in the last instance, the world is our home is a manifestation of defuturing at its most fundamental.

As said, the unsustainable nature of human beings, past and present, is a structural condition of negation. Unsustainability essentially names human-initiated processes hostile to our future being and the being of many nonhuman others. Yet this continues to be ignored, including by the discourse of sustainability, which talks of unsustainability only as it applies to environmental phenomena.

The mantras of productivity, the necessity of continual economic growth and sustainable development all indicate a commitment to a mode of exchange that fails to recognize that both we (as a species) and the natural resources upon which we depend are finite. Misdirected by the allure of the production of wealth, a mode of objectified nihilism has been globalized. It goes by various names: development, the market, economics, progress. Of course, means of exchange are needed, but, for us to have a future, they must be integrated with means that naturally and artificially sustain life rather than negate it. That we have a future has become a psychologically inscribed given—salvation is through God, through technology, or through the hand of providence reducing our numbers so that a regenerative population remains and breeds. Such misplaced faith underpins our inaction and our inability to see 'the time of crisis' as a protracted moment beyond our sense of duration. Our future is not ensured. The crisis, then, is not that there are critical factors in the world around us but that we neither see ourselves as the problem nor seek the solution. We simply do not see. Thus, whatever we name as crisis is never what is most critical.

So informed, we say that if humanity is going have a 'future with a future', it will do so only if it embraces a project of *palingensia* (a project of its own re-creation). To say this implies that the problems that humanity faces cannot be solved just by science and technology, although re-creation will obviously occur in a world in which science and technology are deeply implicated. Our auto-transformation requires that we, in all our difference, find ways to ontologically re-create ourselves.

How to understand what this actually means and how it can be undertaken is central to the task before us. In contemplating this task, as the necessity of futuring, there are two naked facts that unavoidably confront us: we have no choice, and we have no agency to call upon other than ourselves. Should this prospect sound unrealistic or even mad, it has to be remembered that we, as a species, have already experienced a self-transformation of equal magnitude (when we moved from being nomadic to being settled).

Our notions about 'the nature' of our species and our species being needs to be seriously questioned. Certainly, we will need to go beyond the thinking of Darwin and Spencer—that is, we will need to go beyond biological and social characterizations of what we are. Likewise, our questioning also has to contemplate the demise of *Homo sapiens* and the rise of another kind of being.

As a book about the nature and future of the human species—where the species came from, what 'it' became and where it is going—this volume cuts into a very particular moment of human worldly existence, a moment in which it is quite possible that 'we' humans will find ourselves actually hovering on the edge of the third epoch of our planetary existence (the first epoch, as touched on, being the vast expanse of time of nomadic existence, the second being the past ten millennia of human settlement). This prospect suggests that biological and social destabilizations, stemming not least from climate change and the imminence of autonomic technocentrism (the ability of machines to reproduce themselves with an embedded directionality) will combine over the next century or more to dramatically alter the environment, nature and form of the human species.

Notwithstanding all the problems and challenges it faces, the project of *palingensia* demands to be confronted and conceptualized now. It cannot wait.

Thinking about how humanity needs to (re)orientate itself toward a future that will be very different from the present is indivisible from the development of Sustainment (the intellectual and practical project within which *palingensia* sits). As is being made clear, Sustainment is starkly different from all those activities that set out to sustain the status quo characterized by 'sustainability' and 'sustainable development'.

What will be put forward is an argument for revising the reading of human 'evolution'. While not contesting Darwin's account of the 'descent of man' and the fact that 'social selection' supplements his thesis, our case will demonstrate that these accounts are insufficient explanations of how 'we humans' came to be what we are. The correction to the form and process of the emergence of the human will come from a back-reading of the agency of 'ontological design'. This reading will be framed by engaging the debate on the relation among animality, the human, inanimate things and technics. It will concur with the view that nonhuman animate and inanimate beings have played a major role in our becoming what we are.[3]

We will argue that ontological design is the third naturalized, unnatural 'evolutionary' agency. So positioned, it will provide the underpinning of the book's narrative, which is essentially the indivisible relation between the formation of the world of human fabrication and the making of mankind itself. Implicit in this narrative is the necessity of thinking about the transformation of *Homo sapiens* in the face of deepening unsustainability and the failure of our species to recognize the dialectical character of Sustainment (which is to say that creation is always accompanied by destruction). That humanity has continually failed to comprehend what it destroys, and at what price, is integral to unsustainability as (an) ontology which anthropocentrism names. This ontology is the sovereign state of our being—individually and collectively, anthropocentrism rules with imperial oblivion, setting out to command 'the world'. Likewise, it can also be shown that 'our' ability to 'think in time', as Nietzsche recognized, has been a condition of extreme perceptual limitation. Unless we rectify these two flaws in our being, as they endowed us with an autodestructive destiny, our future will be bleak.

Within the remit of postevolutionary theory to be presented, the book actually contends that the fate of the species turns on a fundamental Darwinian truism: adapt or perish. Embracing adaptation will take 'us' (the adaptors) beyond what we currently are (*Homo sapiens*). Unless this happens, there are clear signs and emergent conditions suggesting that, as a species (as we are or as we might be), we will not survive. The problem is not so much what we do but what we are. Survival hereafter implies becoming Other than we are so that we may be able to continue dwell in a world that has been changed *by how we have been.* To reassert: adaptation is crucial to our futural being.

Orientations

On asking questions like 'Where did we come from? How did we come into being? What have we done? Where are we going?,' one cannot presume a linear narrative, a common history or a singular direction. While genetic evidence does indicate that *Homo sapiens* has had a specific place of origin (Africa, some 160,000 years ago), a proliferation of difference followed—this from the consequences of large-scale population movement linked to climatic variation, food availability, plural dietary patterns and associated biophysical change. At some point, determinate cultural differences also proliferated. What these differences evidence is that, while 'we' mostly share a common biology, we are not one. Contrary to humanist rhetoric, the human is not one and is not interchangeable with our species classification. Rather, the human has become the generalization of the category 'man' that was constituted and universality projected by the Enlightenment as an ideality (the knowing 'rational subject' directively acting upon the world in word and deed).

It should be remembered that 'the human' so viewed was defined against the produced underside of the Enlightenment—the 'inhumanity' of five hundred years of global colonization in which an Other, designated as 'animal, primitive, savage, soulless and irrational' was either annihilated by genocidal violence and introduced disease or 'civilized' (ethnocide). The 'dialectic of Sustainment' thus not only is realized by the indivisibility of creation and destruction that marks our mode of worldly engagement but also folds back into our own making: we made and make ourselves what we are by unthinkingly destroying what we were (individually and collectively).

A critique of the Enlightenment is not new. Anti-imperialists, such as Diderot and Kant, reflected a certain struggle between the need to accommodate universalistic concepts such as human rights and the realities of the cultural pluralism of the colonized. But what these thinkers did not grasp was that the Enlightenment's elevation of 'Man' as a universal rational subject, when projected onto cultures of difference, created an absolute Other that affirmed a position of cultural superiority over difference. Such 'enlightened' views did not command the day. Rather, it was the rule of 'natural law' that held sway. This allowed the cultural practices of indigenous peoples to be interpreted as a violation of natural law—a view used to justify their destruction and exploitation.

Yet, notwithstanding the discourse of humanism and its accompanying rhetoric, we have never become fully human, rational or without the presence of our animality. The trace of what we were and what brought us into being lives within us and still retains directive agency in how we are.

It follows that the account to be presented will be genealogical (relational). However, while many elements will be considered and connected, there will be no presumption of an available total narrative or of a position from which to speak it. Neither that to be observed nor observation itself can be contained—the relationality of 'our' becoming and being in the world cannot be contained by 'system'.

We shall ask where humanity is situated in time (as change, as a critical moment and as terminus and commencement) and in proximity to much else. More than just exploring the relation between the animal and human, we will consider connections to 'world' and 'things' as key factors in the becoming and destiny of the 'human' as a hegemonic condition of being. It is out of these relations that the adequacy of existing 'evolutionary' explanations will be tested.

As we leap from the prehistoric to the modern (and therefore into the domain of history), we will identify the links among 'world', imagination, reason and 'the subject'. This will help provide us with a more appropriate view of the current moment and our relation to our distant past and the imminent future. The historicity of unsustainability will be woven into this, as it impacts upon what we are and the world within which we dwell.

Many of the issues to be rehearsed are not new—many thinkers have engaged them. In particular, we will encounter the views of Charles Darwin, Herbert Spencer, Friedrich Nietzsche, Martin Heidegger, André Leroi-Gourhan, Bernard Stiegler, Giorgio Agamben, William McNeill, Cary Wolfe and Iain Thomson. Two perspectives will be brought into play to reconfigure existing debate: the agency of ontological design and the meta-narrative of Sustainment.

In contrast to competing claims within current debate over the developmental primacy of language, technics and visual symbolism, the argument to be put forward will show the equal and overarching significance of ontological design—as it, world and self-formation indivisibly implicate one another. While the primordial agency of ontological design is explicated in detail, the book also will project this agency into the complexity and challenges of the present, showing that it continues to act upon our being as a determinate force of our continual becoming.

Nietzsche: The Man in the Middle

Friedrich Nietzsche reportedly had scant direct familiarity with Darwin's writing, but he did develop a view on evolution and the theory of natural selection. He did this via the influence of Social Darwinists, most notably Herbert Spencer. Notwithstanding his disparaging remarks on Darwin's ideas, Nietzsche was also certainly influenced by them. This seeming contradiction was in keeping with his disposition to confront the thinking of almost everyone he took seriously. He read almost everything sceptically.

In many respects, what Darwin argued actually lent weight to Nietzsche's positing of the directional forces of human development resting with the inherent agency of nature. His problematic perspective centred on the transformative power of natural drives, which provided a basis for his critics to designate his thinking as vitalist. Nietzsche's main heterodoxical polemic was posed against the claimed agency of transcendentalism and metaphysics—that is, that the power of God and 'man's' mentalism provided the means by which humanity advanced. Here was the fundamental commonality with Darwin wherein an inherent process, rather than 'the designing hand of God' or a transcendent intelligence inscribed in nature, was the motor force driving life forward.

Nietzsche also took up and radically modified the Social Darwinists' argument that the social character of human beings was equally an evolutionary factor in the development of the species. Nietzsche's notion of 'social selection' was neither as crude nor as brutal as Spencer's. So said, he did accept 'the social' as a natural phenomenon displayed by many animals, rather than a consequence of a human construct of mind.

As said, what will be unfolded is the case for another fundamental 'evolutionary' agent, a third factor—ontological design as it is implicit in human artifice, created object-things and the world we and they formed. Two observations now follow.

First, in the account to be given, Nietzsche occupies a middle position, upon which the natural and the artificial turn. This position facilitates movement between the past and the future. Second, the triadic forces of the biological, the social and the artefactual acting together bring received notions of evolution into question. If evolution, certainly from a Darwinian point of view, is taken to be a telos of progressive development of the species, the three forces that have directed the changes in human beings look to have brought an ambiguity to (our) 'being' where it could be said that, although there have been biological advances, in some ways our being has remained the same; then, in other ways, especially in our attunement to 'the natural world', we have regressed.

Our primary concern is not to revisit the volumes written on Darwin, whose thesis has been substantiated and remarkably further extended by the discoveries of geneticists. But, besides contesting the sufficiency of the bio-environmental narrative of human development, there is one issue that needs to be contested—one that vexed Darwin and that has proliferated across more recent Darwinian discourse. It turns on the unqualified use of the term 'design'. Our concern here goes well beyond the lunacy of 'intelligent design' versus Darwinism. As we shall see, the whole question of how design and 'evolution' have been discussed historically is fraught. The still-common reference to 'design in nature' makes the point, for it is counter to Darwin's characterization of 'process' to back-project the idea of design onto nature.

The development of our species has been dominantly viewed from a perspective that reifies what we are. The very notion of 'human evolution' captures this disposition. As an object of study, we became centred and then disassociated from animals and inanimate objects. As we came to be considered as a 'thing in itself', our essential worldly connectedness became covered over. This has led to a failure to sufficiently comprehend our being-in-the world. In turn, this has meant that the very notion of 'world' has lacked consideration and understanding in its difference. Placing the historicity and history of human emergence in this wider context of connectedness and world allows us to explore our ontological designing as implicated in the very acts of 'self and world formation' and the 'nature' of our being-in-the-world.

The already recognized ambiguity of humanness equally demands examination, not just in the context of the crucially connected human/animality relation but also in terms of the degree to which the species has actually 'evolved'. Here the question of what has and has not been overcome has to be asked. To what do our propensity to violence and our sexual conduct truly belong? Do we regress as 'we' continually technologically amplify the ability to destroy and kill in ways that distance us from the consequences of our actions? What has been lost in the rise of the hegemonic category 'the human'? In the contemporary condition of life, is not 'evolution' (in its purely general and biological formulation) stranded—surely it simply cannot deal with the rate of human-induced change (climate change being a case in point). Is it not the case that adaptation has to move from the natural to the artificial?

Our narrative journey will follow many directions. It will span huge expanses of time. There will be gaps and leaps, but it will have six identifiable objects of focus posited with, clustered around and intersecting with the human: (*a*) the agency of the inanimate; (*b*) animals/animality; (*c*) world; (*d*) technics; (*e*) design and (*f*) reason. More than this, the perspective to be taken is posed against the continual erosion of 'the serious' within globalizing popular culture (wherein 'entertainment' becomes hegemonic). A concern with 'entertainment' as it has become negation is not new—it is implicit in Nietzsche, expressed overtly by Carl Schmitt more than seventy years ago, evident in the demise of the 'public intellectual' in the past three decades and demonstrated by the marginalization of critical thought in universities together with the centring of instrumentalism.

Part I, 'First Pass', is a deliberate deferral. It holds our story at bay. It does this on the conviction that to look back requires that we establish where 'we' currently are. More specifically, it sets out to provide a broadened context in which it is possible to discuss the relation between the human, design and experiential time. It does this in three ways. Chapter 1 considers the location of the human condition after the Enlightenment, in the face of omnipresent nihilism and with loss of historical directionality. Chapter 2 places us ahead of ourselves, presenting our emergent condition as 'unsettlement' and our imperative as a move toward Sustainment. So that we may gain an appropriate placement of our being in the being of our circumstances, chapter 3 examines the issue of proximity as it is understood beyond just spatial distance, time and physical engagement.

Part II, 'Emergence over Origin—A Relational Account', looks at the various ways human emergence can be understood and the kinds of narratives that do this. Starting with the arrival of 'the human' via natural selection, chapter 4 registers the progression from animal/hominid to animal/human in relation to time. It exposes the limitation of a purely biological explanation carried by 'natural selection'. Chapter 5 moves on to discuss un-natural selection, characterized by social selection, as a significant contribution to the evolutionary theory of human development. The problem of how social selection, especially via the influence of Social Darwinism, was taken up to legitimize eugenics is also discussed. Chapter 6, is where the significance of design, tools, technology and things is put forward.

Part III, 'The Leap', leaps forward to the contemporary. It reinforces one of the major messages of the book: the need to understand past, present and future as they constitute 'now'. To give substance to this inquiry, chapter 7 questions the nature of time by going beyond time as measurement to a more fundamental understanding of time as change. It then considers human beings' existential problem with time (named 'chronophobia' by Bernd Magnus). Looking at change in more detail, chapter 8 discusses time in the context of futuring and defuturing.

Part IV, 'From "Where We Were" to "Where We Are"', shifts the focus to what we are and where we are going. It makes clear that human beings cannot be delivered just via an evolutionary and postevolutionary account. Chapter 9 explores three key relations. First is the fact that, as animals (albeit human animals), we share a world with other beings that are elemental to that world. Second is that 'the world' and the idea of the world are not the same thing. Here we argue for the importance of understanding this distinction. Third, it is argued that one cannot understand the nature of human beings without it being understood as a 'being-in-the-world'. Chapter 10 presents a greater level of detail by looking at the relation among animality, making, the development of imagination and the human mind. It moves from life in a condition of the pre-imagined to the emergence of imagination and, later, reason, including its power and limits. The question of how the human subject needs to be understood is broached in chapter 11. Specifically, this chapter questions the 'nature' of the subject, its connection to the human, the rise of a debate over the 'end of the subject' and the breakdown of the subject/object binary. Questions about the subject, humanism and 'posthumanism' are also posed.

Finally, part V, 'Now-ings', brings all concerns rehearsed to contemporary concerns and futures—initially through chapter 12, which looks at climate change via the notion of a 'new dark age'—an age of ignorance, a time of prospective darkness created without intent by geoengineering, and a time wherein human psychology changes. In the context of 'unsettlement', the fate and future of cities are revisited, expanding on the signalling of the issue in chapter 8. Chapter 13 is concerned with the political, in particular the post-political, prospect in which the consequences of climate change are placed in the wider frame of unsustainability and defuturing, including consideration of the relation between climate change and conflict, leading to the end of politics as it is currently understood. Our penultimate chapter, chapter 14, asks maybe the most difficult question, which is this: 'what do we have to become in order to be?' The last chapter, chapter 15, simply provides concluding comments that rearticulate the narrative the reader has travelled and negotiated.

Part I

First Pass

Photography: Peter Wanny / Illustration: Tony Fry

I say the question of man must be revolutionized.

—Martin Heidegger

We are not one; we never have been. We come from others and have, in truth, constituted our selves from and as difference. Notwithstanding genetic commonality, 'man' is not the consensual naming of a species but a culturally specific imposition upon other designations of 'our' being created at other places and times by others. Thus, 'man' is an expression of the power of she or he who names. Yet, now, with its Enlightenment endowed universalized status, this naming folds into the language of generally accepted usage rather than predilection. But we still do well to remember that, in contrast to how in the past and in cultural difference 'we' have named our selves, what is erased by our collective name 'human' is the possibility of seeing ourselves, be it in various ways, as a being among the company of animals. Questions of what we were and are and what we are becoming are central to the task before us. But, first, we need to establish the context for posing these questions and why they need to be posed. To do this, we will follow two narrative paths.

Story One tells of the voice that speaks where and how 'the human' has been conceptually configured in the modern world. Story Two goes to the issue of where 'the human' is conjuncturally placed in this world (the condition of 'the human condition'). Linking both stories is a meditation on questions of proximity that helps make sense of why there is a setting out to think 'what we are' in relation to where conditionally we now are in the plural 'state of our being'. At this point, it should be acknowledged that, to date, *Homo sapiens* has occupied the given world in two ways.

The first and longest way was to dwell in the world with the world as home. Life so dwelt was to wander over large and small distances as the vagaries of climate and availability of food dictated, yet never to be homeless. For all the environmentally determined different types of nomadic hunter-gatherers, the world was often a harsh place. Notwithstanding the harsh times that often depleted populations, the species survived. The viability of nomadic existence is evidenced by the fact that it was the way of life for around 150,000 of the 160,000 years of *Homo sapiens*' earthly habitation—this with mostly a stable population of forty million-plus humans. Of course, for many hundreds of thousands of years, nomadism was the form of existence of the hominid forbearers of *Homo sapiens.*

While there are still a few nomadic peoples, this mode of 'being-in-the-world' was fated to end. The narrative of this transformation centres on events ten thousand years ago in the Fertile Crescent of the Middle East.[1] As the climate changed in the West, where it became colder, and in the East, where it became drier, people converged on the Fertile Crescent, where food remained plentiful. In good seasons, people roamed, hunted and gathered. In bad seasons they harvested crops like wild einkorn (an early form of wheat). Slowly, small rural settlements were created and very basic forms of farming started to emerge, ushering in the practices upon which urban life would come to depend. Thus began the transformative process of making 'a world within the world' rather than the world being the home of human being; this opened the second mode of earthly habitation—human urban settlement. Unknowingly, this instigated those processes that were eventually to lead to contemporary conditions of material unsustainability, with the emergent prospect of mass homelessness.[2]

As we shall explore later, 'we' have now come full circle. Climate change (the very condition that first prompted human settlement to be established) now threatens the continuity of human settlement, as it currently constitutes our dominant mode of habitation.

In summary, 'nomadic life' can be claimed as the first epoch of human world occupation, while 'settlement' can be named as the second. However, as will be shown, it is now becoming likely that this latter epoch will also come to an end. By human measure it will not happen quickly—yet the process has already started and is likely to run for at least a few centuries. As in the past, this change will be driven by climate and environmental events arriving from the future (as they have been thrown into the future).

I

End of the Story

I walk among men as among fragments of the future.

—Friedrich Nietzsche

This is 'now'—the locus of where we currently are and will look back from.

Over the past few decades, announcements of 'ends' have proliferated within contemporary theory. In the West, one can cite the end of many discourses, including the Enlightenment, modernity, history, man, metaphysics, philosophy, narrative, the subject, art and the novel. Each of these ends was situated by its proclaimers within an *aporia,* judging the particular discourse terminal. Our concern here is not with assessing the validity of each of these claims. Rather, it is with shifting how the notion of 'end' is thought and then placing it in the same register of determinate circumstances that defines the slow termination of the present epoch of humanity (the epoch of settlement). However, in so doing, we will recast some of the discourses deemed to be at 'the end', not least as they impinge on how the future is viewed and potentially engaged. Triggering this situation is an emergent condition of 'unsettlement' as the opening of a third mode of habitation (after nomadism and settlement), which is now unfolding slowly, unevenly and universally. It is linked to both a changing climate and, as we shall see, a destabilization of the conceptual foundations of modern existence.

The Enlightenment

Specifically, as a starting point to engage modern existence, we need to understand the inextricable relation among the Enlightenment, human agency (and the loss thereof), singular truth and history. Over the past four decades, via poststructural theory, each one of these categories has been made problematic.

As Ernst Cassirer told us in 1932 in *The Philosophy of the Enlightenment* (a text regarded as an 'incomparable guide' that 'occupies a unique position' in writing on the period),[1] the Enlightenment project created a sphere of reality of law and reason that generated the modern state and social order. Thereafter, 'Man' was 'born into this world; he neither creates nor shapes it, but finds it ready made about him'.[2] Yet, in his being-in-the-world adaptively and productively, 'Man' is world-transformative. Henceforth, the notion of all power being ultimately vested in God and his creation (nature) was supplemented by the power claimed by an individuated 'rational man'.

Prefigured by the Renaissance and the recovery of the Greek classics, the Enlightenment sought, from the seventeenth century onward, to go beyond the idea of system to become the 'intellectual atmosphere' in which all other knowledge existed.[3] It initiated a series of discourses that were to form a culture that centred on the ascent of reason (and, by implication, science) over God and unrestrained nature, together with a universalized utopia based on the rule of 'natural law' bonded to the notions of progress, 'civil society' and a liberal political order. The intellectual ambition was to contain the sum of all knowledge and, in its actuality, constitute its own reality and truth. Above all, the Enlightenment provided the intellectual foundation and authority for the global imposition of modernity. No matter what is said about when, how or if the Enlightenment has ended, it laid foundations of thought and action that live on. Besides establishing the natural world as a primary object of scientific study, it placed absolute faith in the power of reason and presented 'the world' as a 'standing reserve of resources' for 'man' to exploit. But, more than this, Enlightenment thinking underpinned a model of development executed by the policies and practices of modernity that extended the inhumanity of sixteenth-century European colonial expansionism, accelerated productivism and, in so doing, tipped the dialectic of Sustainment toward destruction.[4] Notwithstanding attainments in the arts and sciences, the Enlightenment and its interlocutor, modernity, created a quantum leap toward the unsustainable. This came not only from the destructive consequences of the 'means of production' facilitated by Enlightenment knowledge and practices but also from the underside of its universalization—its dark side.

Notwithstanding an exception that recognizes the fact,[5] the dark side of the Enlightenment rests with an anthropology that designated the world of the Other. The classificatory system of 'natural law' was used to distinguish between the human and the nonhuman, placing an Other outside 'the human'. This law, initially defined by the Church, designated the human by what it regarded as civilized conduct (wearing clothes, not painting the body, not practicing wild rituals, and the like); people who were deemed not to conform to natural law were not regarded as human and could be treated as subhuman, as animal. Such behaviour toward indigenous people was especially common where colonists were out of sight of the institutions of civil society.[6]

Natural law was used to absolve the colonizer from moral judgement for enacting violence against the colonized by making such action a matter of compliance to the law. 'Natural law' effectively legitimized genocide and exploitation, a universal 'war on savagery', and 'civilizing missions' (like those in Latin America, as well as the Crusades in the Middle East). 'Natural law' rested on a set of principles drawn from reason, taken as universal and mobilized to underpin 'the law of nations'. A body of thinkers, not least St. Thomas Aquinas, advanced its theoretical foundations.

Simply being a member of a culture designated as outside the natural law and the Law of Nations (as it was derived from natural law) was sufficient to warrant the punishment of extinction or complete subjection to the rule and will of 'the master'. Eurocentric theory from the birth of the Enlightenment to postmodernism has never adequately acknowledged the complexity and contradictions of its relation to colonialism. Early and late exceptions are few and mild, and, while Kant made critical comments, perhaps the most vocal and critical was Denis Diderot (1713–84).[7]

Unquestionably, the Enlightenment became deeply implicated in the formation of the modern mind, the hegemony of reason, the authority of scientific enquiry and the philosophical dominance of metaphysics. Likewise, it constituted what was to become a dominant aesthetic disposition. But, even more than this and overarching all its other facets, the Enlightenment established and enhanced anthropocentrism bonded to an economy based on the attempt to dominate nature. This perspective is encapsulated by Francis Bacon in his *New Atlantis* of 1626, where he expressed his ambition as to 'endow the life of man with infinite commodities'. Bacon's *Novum Organum* (1620) was one of the foundational texts in the elevation of science and proto-systems thinking.

Cassirer pointed out how the Enlightenment created what retrospectively looks like an iron cage of metaphysics—a cage from which a good deal of modern philosophy has relentlessly striven to break free. It constructed a view of knowledge based almost totally on the products of its own activity. While it is now obvious to us that the Enlightenment was a thoroughly Eurocentric undertaking, the nuances of this are not always seen. Across several centuries, European thinkers drew a veil over the value of the domains of knowledge of Others that they themselves had appropriated (as they extensively drew, directly or indirectly, for instance, on the mathematical and scientific knowledge of the Middle East and Asia). Moreover in their proto-humanism, Enlightenment thinkers, especially anthropologists, designated mankind as a dominant object of study with significant ongoing consequences. Likewise, the Enlightenment asserted that 'reason' should become the unifying and central intellectual reference point of the century.[8] Reason should therefore be acknowledged not merely as the ability to think rationally but as a particular discourse that created a mode of thought 'according to its own rules'.[9]

What even a brief critical review of the Enlightenment makes clear is that it was not sufficiently rational; even more important, it was insufficiently relational. While forming specialist disciplines and divisions of knowledge claiming to produce universal knowledge, it failed to make vital 'horizonal connections'. In so doing, it was blind not only to its own and wider causality but also to the inhumanity that accompanied its humanism and against which modern 'civilization' was defined.[10]

Nietzsche and Nihilism

One of the Enlightenment's transformations was the establishment of a general condition of compliance enacted by a normative individuated subject who increasingly acted to displace social agency by the powerlessness of legitimized self-interest. This characteristic of the modern individualistic subject became linked to what Friedrich Nietzsche was to name 'nihilism'—a concept he redefined in his own terms.[11] Such a secularized individual lost a religious foundation of value without gaining anything to replace it, while also feeling helpless in the face of the scale and nature of worldly problems. Notwithstanding a century of resistance by class collectivism, this subject has now gained hegemonic and normative status in the late-modern and postmodern world. Helplessness lives with boredom and takes solace in entertainment.

For Nietzsche, nihilism was the diagnosis of an unrecognized and very specific crisis within Western culture. He viewed this crisis as stemming from the loss of three things: human agency, the foundations of truth and a ground of moral judgement. Nihilism created a culture cast adrift, existing with a strong but unexamined sense of loss—experienced as a loss of a world that rested upon fundamental meaning, whether vested in God, the absolute, truth or community. Living this loss created overt or repressed feelings of sickness, malaise and dislocation. He held two specific discourses to blame for this situation: Platonism and Christian morality (neither of which he believed provided an objective ground for moral judgement).[12]

The dissolution of meaning resulted in the inability of individuals to mobilize their interpretive capability in ways that could appropriately inform or direct their actions. In contradiction, conformity increased at the same time as the rhetoric of individualism proliferated. Whatever perception Nietzsche had of this situation at the end of the nineteenth century, it would now be massively magnified in our age of electronic media and the rule of information, wherein the ability and the space for critical reflection have almost totally disappeared. The feeling of loss of agency continues unabated and is summed up in oft-heard phrases such as, 'I know what the situation is, but I am powerless to do anything about it' or 'there is nothing I can do that will make any difference'. Nihilism understood in this way now appears not only as a feature of public social, economic and political life but is also manifested in the private sphere wherein huge numbers of parents feel they have no agency over the conduct of their teenage children.

Nietzsche argued that what results from this loss of agency—that implied loss that nihilism named—was not just a sense of powerlessness but also a feeling of alienation from the individual's creative capacity (this loss is now manifest in the rise and 'power' of 'the consumer'—effectively a displaced cultural producer). Compliance unconfronted masks this existential loss.[13] Mark Warren has pointed to a gap between nihilism and modern experience as a feature of modern culture that metaphysics failed to fill. The gap is that between the world in which we would wish to live (and that was once believed to be possible) and the actual world in which we now live and work.[14] In other words, modern Western individuals have lacked the knowledge to identify, make sense of and gain the power to act transformatively on the structural situations in which they find themselves. In recoil, 'making the best of it' meant living unaware in a life without depth, where superficially held values substituted for firm ethical reference points. Such values, notwithstanding the fact that people were 'informed and sustained' by them, were deemed by Nietzsche to be embedded in the bankruptcy of European culture.[15] Unsurprisingly, his views generated violent recoil among many of his contemporaries.

While individuals might voice a rhetoric of 'free will' and claim to be exercising it, their actual utterances often simply mirror clichés authored by the media as it puts the language and appearances of 'its' world before them. Thereafter, it does not require a huge amount of insight to discern both the emptiness out of which such utterances emerge and the feeling of nothingness that underscores this. By implication, a subject so framed has no moral ground and nowhere to take a stand. All that seems available is a position of conformity to a media-authored position of speech.

The defuturing face of unsustainability has been nurtured by a culture steeped in nihilism so characterized. Unquestionably, a large segment of humanity knows the problem is serious but does nothing about it (*akrasia*), or a sense of helplessness rules.[16] Additionally, the dominance of a biocentric understanding of unsustainability and sustainability and its projection into the public sphere actually compound the situation. The fact that 'the problem' is human-centred (is us) goes unrecognized. In many ways, this problem actually implicates Charles Darwin.

What Darwin exposed, albeit in his reluctance, fear and quietism at the prospect of the wrath of society, was that neither knowledge, design nor God underpins any intrinsic meaning to life. He established that 'life' was actually a pure process depending on no agency other than itself—thus totally undercutting the very ground of life having a source of foundational meaning. It followed that whatever meaning we discern is no more than human construction and projection. But, while the very notion that meaning rests on some kind of higher agency (God or reason) imploded, dogma still ruled. The message Darwin whispered and that subsequent biologists have amplified has still yet to be fully heard.

Without knowing it, Darwin sowed the seed of Nietzsche's nihilism. It is thus no mere coincidence that Nietzsche, with his mostly mediated knowledge of Darwin's ideas, pronounced 'God is dead'. Nihilism was effectively let loose in the world of Darwin's shadow. These remarks beg to be seen in the company of those on the Enlightenment as it empowered the rise of secular society with its overblown sense of the foundational power of reason.

There were three ways that Nietzsche proposed to overcome nihilism. First was to expose it for what it is (the form of life that 'we' have become). Second

was the imperative for us to act to overthrow that which we have become—
including how we view 'the world', our selves and all that we understand. Both
these actions were based, problematically, upon consciousness as the means
to deliver his proposed changes. Yet he was calling upon one of the elemental
losses that nihilism names.[17] Nietzsche's third point of advocacy in response
to the ascent of nihilism was the acquisition of historical experience, but
historical experience not validated by metaphysics or religion.[18] In the light
of this perspective, it is appropriate that we now turn our attention to history.

History and Genealogy

While theories and philosophies of history proliferate, it is safe to say history
is marked by three essential characteristics: telos (temporal and directional
drive), narrative (an ordering and interpretation of historical events), and
power (that which mobilizes and directs the narrative).

The historicity of events does not become history until an act of narrativization is undertaken, no matter whether the narrative is an oral account
from memory or a fully documented, researched, written and published account. As Nietzsche recognized and as is increasingly acknowledged, all history is perspectival—there is no mode of description that is not grounded
in a position of observation. Likewise, history is not underpinned by reason
(as post-Hegelians would have it). Rather than being a repository of meaning, history actually posits it. Equally, history is exclusive, always arriving via
processes of exclusion and inclusion. Three conclusions can be drawn from
these conditions of limitation. First, all history rests upon a constructivist
practice; second, it is always perspectivally framed and determined by the
forces that direct such framing—which means it can never deliver a definitive
truth (truth here cannot be divided from power); and third, the perception
of events is transformed by events in the present (take for example how the
fall of communism in the USSR has revised the history of its creation and
creators). History is in fact always a back-casting from present knowledge and
concerns. It is of the 'now'.

Just as truth cannot be divided from power, neither can it be separated from a particular perspective; notwithstanding the hegemonic status of certain discourses, there is no totally overarching neutral and true historical narrative. The unfashionable but unshakable observation of poststructuralism that 'indeterminacy rules' directly aligns with meaning having no foundation other than of human invention. Meaning is likewise inherently anthropocentric—it can be but a product of the human domain.

Confronting a crisis of truth, as Nietzsche made clear, is indivisible from that crisis of the loss of agency that is nihilism. To lose agency is equally to lose the ability to exercise critical judgement and to distinguish between the true and the false. This is evident not in aberrant social conduct but in the reverse—in social hyperconformity.

Once narrativized, historical experience becomes history, and predominantly history is employed ontologically. It constitutes a sensibility able to inform action. Conversely, to lack historical experience is to exist with a restricted reflective capability that, at its most general, diminishes the ability to adequately see and understand the world around you. We also need to fully grasp the impossibility of human beings being ahistorical. We simply cannot escape our historicity as it constitutes memory and experience. The past is given determinacy by our family, environment, culture and subjectivity, arriving in our lives as a directive force of our future. In so many ways, we are its victims and its beneficiaries. We may break free of what we were to a degree, but often what we still are seals our fate.

It is against this backdrop that the case for turning to genealogy is made. Genealogy is a political historical practice deployed as a cultural politics. It is counter to history as a totalized discourse. Again taking its lead from Nietzsche, as Mark Warren makes clear, genealogy is the sum of actions in situated local contexts with their own relations among logics, imperatives and practices.[19] However, to get to this reality requires stripping away a superstructure, be it based on economic and 'political ideologies' or on cultural (including religious) beliefs. So realized, genealogy is able to connect processes generated by socially connected actors and groups with those material events and actions that brought these social entities into being.

Genealogy comes to the present via a particular mode of diagnostic history that critically explores the multiplicity of relational factors that intersect with and constitute events. In its concreteness, it needs to be seen as supplementing ontology. It does not accept history as received. Its efficacy centres on a deep and symptomatic reading of power as dispersed across plural situated practices which are not reducible to dialectical dynamics. Genealogical accounts act to disrupt the notion of 'reason in history' while affirming history as a source of meaning. The Nietzschean method, as constituted by his trenchant and specific forms of criticism, combined with a modest, slow investigative process of empirically detailed analysis, strives to build an overall picture in the present that does not conceal gaps and omissions. The genealogical method was brought into contemporary critical theory largely via Gilles Deleuze's rigorous engagement, in the early1960s, with Nietzsche's philosophy and then, later, by Michel Foucault under the influence of Deleuze (as he indicated in his seminal essay on Nietzsche, genealogy and history in 1975).[20] The vast bulk of Foucault's later work adopted and extended the genealogical method.

The specificity of genealogical criticism outlined by Nietzsche centred on three forms: the logical (with a focus on cultural formations and their ideas); the genetic (a way to name pathways, traces and relations); and the functional (the contextually specific agency of meaning).[21]

The past, as a reflection in the present, is constituted by memory and by history unified as narrative. So often events—especially large, life-changing and world-transformative events—make no sense at the level of individual experience, existing only as impressions and disjointed incidents amid chaos. In contrast, historical accounts often arrive as either a violent ordering or in contradiction to what was experienced.

A need to refuse, rupture or condemn the grip of the past by subjecting its injustices and concealments to caustic criticism and judgement was well voiced by Nietzsche—'man must have and from time to time apply the power to break up and dissolve the past in order to live'.[22] Nietzsche recognized that history can cover over the past and that one has to find the force to disclose it. Here is the connection to nihilism, for part of the loss of human agency is evidenced by an inability (increasing, it seems, with each generation) to critically confront history. In turn, this inability extends the loss of agency.

It is impossible for us not to be historical subjects. We are both our history and a registration of the historicity of the continual passage of our species at that moment which is now. In this setting, we are the result of the confluence between 'world' (our world), history and historical process as they ontologically design the nature of our being (a relational determinate process without a single telos). Events direct not only our fate but also our form. But, at the same time, we need to understand that to acquire agency is to be actively engaged in making history and, in so doing, creating that which ontologically designs the designing of a socio-materially fabricated world that in significant part designs what we are and can do. While such *praxis* is always against the grain of history, it comes equally from historically and culturally created resources and possibilities.

Against this backdrop, a loss of agency is a specific loss of capability to be *an active, located and future-directive* world-formative historical subject. The subject position of loss here can perhaps be defined as the condition of the 'consumer'.

Cutting across the historical cast of Nietzsche's notion of nihilism is the massive impact, over the twentieth century and continuing into the twenty-first, of the instrumentalization of reason and modern technology. These two 'developments' have dramatically changed the circumstances to which Nietzsche was reacting. This is to say that the loss of agency that nihilism announced has in significant part been taken up in the inanimate domain by technology (as mind and matter). Technology is becoming an ever-heightened means of the ontological designing of 'being now'. As such, it is a material instrument, 'a tool of knowledge' and a medium of communication. In its continued acquisition of power, there can no longer be any appeal to consciousness overcoming the power of technology any more than there can be an appeal to consciousness overcoming nature. Just as life can be lived or not with a critical and responsive/responsible relation to nature, so does this now extend to technology. Contestation thus centres on the designed and designing subject.

Yet design, critically transformed and mobilized, can provide a redirective mode of engagement with defuturing technology (here seen as the ongoing nihilist impetus of the technological world of and within the world of human construction). Design so transformed can become a means for reclaiming agency. As we shall see later, reclaiming such agency is also a way of recovering a fundamental relation to time—the loss of time is also a loss of a sense of bodily and species finitude (and thus it also folds into contemporary nihilism). Reclaiming such a relation to time directly connects to how we experience ourselves, our historical experience as a potentiality, and design 'as an agent of and for our own future'.[23] Seeing ourselves in time (the process of change) can be linked to understanding design as that which (ontologically) changes us through its changing of the world. This circling is at the centre of that 'history in process' that needs to be created.

To lose the ability to design is to lose everything. Here is the distinction between, for instance, the homeless who make a world for themselves from whatever they find on the street and those who totally abandon their very being to its fate and reach their historical end.

2

Start of a Story

We are no longer in a state of growth. We are in a state of excess.

—Jean Baudrillard

Earlier, the claim was made that we are 'hovering on the edge of the third epoch of our planetary existence', with the first epoch being nomadic existence and the second, sedentary existence (settlement). To tell the story of the opening of the third epoch requires that we grasp what is actually happening globally now as the past and the future arrive in this moment. This will be done here briefly, as a prelude to the entire and substantial second part of the book, which is devoted this investigation, asking: where do we humans find and characterize the directional trends within the present moment?

In passing, it was indicated that biological and social destabilizations, stemming from climate change, were major factors in shaping human culture and destiny, turning 'us' away from a nomadic life toward settlement. As indicated, for a vast expanse of time (some 150,000 years), *Homo sapiens* existed with meagre resources, often in conditions that were climatically extreme. Trying to comprehend what this was like taxes our imagination considerably. Consider, for example, as recent research has discovered, that for more than 100,000 years (between 180,000 and 70,000 years ago), Britain was so cold that it was totally uninhabitable for hominids—there was simply no hominoid life there at all.[1] More generally, that human life endured such an ice age as it enveloped the planet is extraordinary. But 'we' only just did—the paleontological evidence suggests that the species dwindled to just a few thousand.

Our species' survival depended on the biological and social ability to adapt to environmental change. At the immediate and pragmatic level, it required dietary change and geographic movement in search of more congenial conditions. Such action, as it was reactive to both slow and rapid climate change, directly influenced global population distribution. But, as *Homo sapiens* moved, resettled and remained in a particular environment for an extensive period of time, biological processes of adaptation occurred. Physiology altered to create what was eventually to be misread as racial difference. Here we need to acknowledge that biological adaptation was as important for Charles Darwin as natural selection. He spent a good deal of time thinking about the selection of those adaptive traits that were able to change over generations (and in relation to nonadaptive traits). The wide spectrum of capacities of different peoples in different parts of the world to tolerate vastly different climates, from the arctic to the tropical, is the most overt example of this.

The situation we humans now find ourselves in is that climate change is and will be happening at a rate to which we cannot adapt biologically. Figures presented at the international climate change negotiations in Durban, South Africa, in December 2011 indicate that, on current trends (where the level of warming is almost twice that for the years 2000–2010), the Earth will warm by three and a half degrees Celsius by 2100, and there will be a one-metre rise in sea levels.[2] At the same time, the majority of the world's population is now sedentary and city dwelling. This means that immediate mobility in the face of change is not easy. The reverse is true, at least initially. The most likely tendency will be to seek technical supports to enable people to stay where they are. Thus, the crude response to increased temperatures will be more air conditioning. The reverse will also be the case: more cold equals more heating. In both instances, more energy will be used, and, thus, unless there is a huge expansion of renewable energy technologies, emissions will rise. The time frame and the prospect of increasing climate change will override initial reactive responses to the problem—the issue of time has, in fact, been massively underreported.

We are told by a vast body of science that there is a delay of around thirty years before emission impacts arrive, that the atmospheric life of carbon dioxide can be more than a thousand years, and that current research suggests that even if there were to be a massive reduction in emissions, the situation created would be irreversible for 1,000 years.[3] Likewise, no matter what we do, sea levels are set to go on rising for 400 years, and deep ocean temperatures (the planet's thermostat) take around 250 years to change. To add to this picture, we are informed that if current trends continue, a 'tipping point' will be reached where climate instability will flip into a condition of instability beyond any human ability to model, understand or in any way deal with.[4] Even if there were to be an instant and comprehensive adoption of measures to reduce greenhouse gas emissions, major problems will endure. The point to be made here is general: no matter whether the periods of time are less or greater than those indicated, what is very clear is that the contemporary rhetoric of climate change hardly speaks the time frame of the problem.[5]

Facing this situation requires hyperadaptation. However, other factors may come into play to make the situation even more complex and dangerous. One such factor is the potential introduction of geoengineering interventions into the climate (about which more will be said much later), which could potentially amplify any disaster. More than this, as again we will register, climate change also has the ability to generate major global conflict.

Over the next century and a half, the biophysical and the immaterial environments of technology and of human beings will significantly change each other.[6] We are no more able to see our distant future than were our prehistorical ancestors. The third epoch of our being may not be—but just may be—the last, but one can say with some confidence that its arrival is certain. Obviously, we can no longer be the nomads of old—not least because geopolitics and our numbers make this impossible. But, likewise, we can no longer be and remain totally sedentary (which the majority of us now are). The kinds of changes we will have to contemplate will be considered later. The key point being made at this moment is that we are unavoidably on the edge of a fundamental change of how we occupy and then exist upon the planet we claim as 'ours'.

There are a series of linked events that are increasingly starting to look predetermined or, as Nietzsche would have it, 'fated'. They are inscribed in the directional drift of historicity.

The carbon economy, at least as it currently exists, will end; the climate will continue to change for at least several centuries; and, as suggested, new dangers and challenges will arrive. Food supply will certainly become a more critical global issue (even if ways are found to produce enough food to feed the global population, it is very unlikely that a significant percentage of people world-wide will be able to afford it). Strategic planners are viewing the prospect of hundreds of millions of hungry people moving uninvited across national borders, triggering massive conflicts.[7] As a result of rises in sea levels, it is projected that over the next seventy-five to two hundred years some seven hundred million of the planet's coastal dwellers will be displaced.[8] This displacement will add to a likely more general fragmentation of the human global population and may prompt both conflict and new postnation formations. The technosphere will continue to grow, with ever-greater transformative consequences upon both human and nonhuman life. The combined consequences of all these factors will be vast, and one wonders whether the species itself will fracture.

This probable frightening picture and responses to it will be engaged at length in Part V of this book, but for the moment we just need to register that three scenarios can be expected to unfold: very large numbers of people will attempt new forms of earthly habitation; others will attempt to retain or remake past modes; and huge numbers of people will simply be abandoned to fend as best they can for themselves. Many structures—geopolitical, urban, economic and social—will fall! The notion of a single form of human being will erode as 'development(s)' take different directions.

Bluntly, Sustainment will not be an option—either people with the means, and out of necessity, will create ways to sustain themselves, or they will die. In this context, the third epoch will arrive with a percentage of us becoming other than we currently are.

Thinking against this backdrop requires that we start to embrace ontological futuring practices from a far more critical and strategic basis, this so as (*a*) to be able to adequately interpret the emergent experience of the fractured human condition as the status quo implodes under the pressure of an ever-growing defuturing human global population; and (*b*) to be able to make new modes of agency that are viable, intelligible and efficacious.

In essence, what is being suggested here is action toward the relational development of a new kind of 'human being' who can once again bring the hand, the central nervous system, the brain, reflective thought and imagination together with tools to make a 'world-within-the-world', this time out of a mode of synthetic adaptation predicated upon an ontologically inscribed disposition toward futuring and thus sustainment.

'We' are travelling toward a point at which we will have to learn how to redesign ourselves. This is not as extreme as it sounds, for we have always been a product of design—albeit unknowingly. Now, if we are to have a future that in any way resembles how we currently are, such a relation with design has to be made explicit and developed. The possibility of achieving such change is lodged, as we shall see, in the very nature of our becoming by design. So, rather than this change being read as an invitation to embrace biological engineering or any other technological determinism, what it actually means is changing, by design, our relation to one another (our sociopolitical ecology), to object-things (and those modes of exchange upon which our existing economy and techno-sphere stands), and our perceptual field (how we see, know and feel).

What this adds up to is an intellectual project beyond the scale of the Enlightenment, a breaking free of the drive to bring all appropriate-able earthly resources and forces under human control.[9] We remain the same at the cost of the negation of time (as this negation registers a failure to grasp 'our' finitude as of variable duration according to how we dwell).

Such thinking begins with a sober assessment of what we need 'to be' (in order to continue to be), this based upon understanding how ontologically we became what we currently and plurally are. Unevenly, mostly unconsciously, we are at a moment wherein we cannot stay as we were or are but as yet cannot see (at worst) the need or (at best), with any clarity, what it is we have to become and how to become it.

But, as culture's children, we have to become readable—this need is set alongside a failure of the Enlightenment, of humanism, to 'study man' in ways that actually delivered fundamental emancipatory knowledge grounded in an acceptance of taking responsibility for 'our' irredeemable anthropocentrism.

Restating, and as we will soon elaborate in some detail, there was no external agency—metaphysical or transcendental—that brought us into being. There are, however, a number of ontological contenders. It is being argued here that it is a matter of discerning not which one of them was the primary cause of our becoming but rather how they all functioned relationally. More than this, while human being has undergone many changes, in some respects 'we' have remained the same. This sameness is our animality, and it is what breaks the human/animal binary apart. The repressed animal and the anthropocentric refusal to name the self as it is bonded to its animal substrate, must not be excluded from our identity but must be embraced as the essential foundation of our relationality.

3

Proximity: A Question of Distances

And *who* are we?

—Hannah Arendt

Proximity will be addressed here as an important way to think relationality, specifically, some of those relations that have been covered over and now need to be brought to the fore. Proximity should be taken not as a spatial question, a measure of distance, but rather as a sensing directed toward what is existentially close or far from us and how we are relationally positioned to our self.

Thinking proximity places us before our nearness to the end of our own and other species, to our animality, to our body, to death, to nature, to others, to our identity, to the past and the future. It confronts the fact of our 'ek-sistence' as it is always lodged in a condition of being that is always becoming. Ek-sistence is not life as such. It is the actuality of our mode of being here as a socially constituted being (an individuated and collective social subject being among beings) who is ever exposed to change.

Many of us find ourselves in the same moment both here and in an insecure 'there', and so constantly between the time of now and its delay, the sign and its object, the real and the unreal, 'what is' and what appears. Then again, we can find ourselves alienated from that which we are seemingly close to, yet within the blink of an eye find that alienation is banished and a feeling of certainty descends. Yet a doubt endures. Is certainty an illusion? Do we know the answer to this question? In truth, asking questions of proximity unsettles, for it is an opening that puts our self before its self.

What Am 'I' Near?

Becoming human is an appropriative event. It is an activity that takes from the world and others in order to be (including being in the world amid humans). But, in our making of our self ('me'), we equally make a world around us (my world) that collectively ends up making us. What is actually being made here is the objectification of the human being itself through its proximity to and its interaction with the human, nonhuman beings and 'things' of the world. Such making transcends basic needs and creates its potential for freedom (a drive beyond need). Yet the converse is true: the world of human creation can and does extinguish freedom and the essence of humanity. Ambiguously, our ekistence is always poised between creation and destruction.

What we know intuitively always prefigures, inflects and deflects cognition. Martin Heidegger understood this situation and explored it through the foregrounding of fore-structures of meaning (fore-having, fore-sight, fore-conception)—appropriation is driven by re-cognition, interpretation by the projection of knowledge (as *phrönesis*—that knowing that belongs to and is recognized by the self that acts in an advanced proximity to its self).[1] Hans-Georg Gadamer also took up these notions in his consideration of prejudice as an eternal prefiguration of knowledge.[2] So did Emmanuel Levinas, who moved it forward by thinking proximity more rigorously in relation to intuition, the sensible and cognition.[3] It is worth looking at what Levinas has to say in some detail.

Levinas observes that intuition always travels ahead of the sensible, as 'sensible intuition' and, as such, it is 'the sensible conceptualised'.[4] In this context, proximity does not belong to 'the movement of cognition' and is manifestly a disposition opposed to any claim of the 'impartiality' of the intellect. What is already known is formative of intuition, and, as such, it continually constitutes the horizon of what is possible to know/not know. Proximity here is a thinking otherwise of objectivity; it is also a means to explore the division that metaphysics created among sensation, sense and the sensible. Proximity defies reduction and is certainly not, as Levinas makes very clear, 'a certain measure of the interval narrowing between two points or two sectors of space'.[5] Rather, it is 'a restlessness, null site, outside the place of rest. It overwhelms the calm of non-ubiquity of being which becomes rest in a site.'[6] Proximity, so thought, references the oscillation between our humanness and our inhumanity, our knowing and our unknowing, and it shows itself in what we say, the stories we tell and the histories we create. It keeps us ever unresolved (including to our selves).

Most problematic is what the Enlightenment projected as (the) human and humanism. As we saw earlier, the application of 'natural law' constituted an Other outside the designated fully human and, in so doing, legitimized inhuman action against such fellow beings. Thus, while humanism was and is universally projected as an inclusive address to the whole of humanity, it is not. Rather, it was, and is, predicated upon exclusion of Others. By implication, the question of 'our' proximity (to the Other and animality), is therefore repressed.

Humanism, in its metaphysical essence, can never be what it presents itself as being—fully humane (hence the call of posthumanism to go beyond humanism). It has not delivered the dignity of human being.[7] Humanism has never transcended that animality that dominated the conquest of resources above all other species; humanism is but 'the other within' that makes 'man' the 'most dangerous of animals'. Here the question of difference arrives, difference not between the human and the animal but between the animal and the inhuman. Jean François Lyotard asked 'what if what is "proper" to humankind were to be inhabited by the inhuman?'[8] Put directly: what if we are not human at all but the inhuman in a masquerade?

Irrespective of our fundamental nature, we have a fundamental character-istic that enables us to prefigure the outcome of an action prior to undertak-ing it. We thus have a unique relation to artifice—a proximity to 'the thing' before it materially comes into being as objectified. It is this that distinguishes us from animals that use tools. It is thus neither the use of the tool itself nor technics which makes us unique. This is to say that, at an ontological level, we are all 'designers'. Design (as prefiguring) is our key and defining attribute: as such, it articulated the transition from pure animal to the human/animal. Yet our primeval relation to designing and making—as it enabled the formation of a world-within-the-world—opened a passage toward our own end. The most direct marker of the start of this process was our rupture from the natural: the more we became denaturalized, the more a sense of alienation enveloped us. Eventually, the compromised human gives way to that autonomic being: the inhuman. In this context, the 'end of man' equates to man being overtaken by that of a creature or thing of his or her own creation from which the redemp-tive power of 'creative alienation' has been erased.

Not only would man then have created a complete synthesis of biology and technology; he or she would be the un-natural product of this fusion. What begs to be understood is that such a 'product' would at this point be the real-ization of the very process that brought 'man' into being. The question that hovers around this prospect is: will a memory (embodied and/or industrial) of the transcended being endure and have agency?

At the moment we are not in a position to answer this question. But even to voice it constitutes a proximity to the task of 'thinking being' that no amount of forgetting can ever fully displace. We are already living with the unsettling prospect of what we might become.

Being Here: The Self, the Social and the Physical Body

How near is our self to what we are? What is the proximity of our socially constructed self (our formed human way of being—understood by Martin Hei-degger as our *dasein*) to our biological animality as it constitutes more of what we are than mere bodily functions of our 'bare life'? This question confronts us with what Nietzsche observed as the 'simplification and falsification mankind lives in' as it folds into our 'retained ignorance'.[9] So much that is taken as firm and fact transpires to rest on an illusion. The form of that self, its subjectivity, stands upon its *ontic* foundation (its animality). This relation breaks any simplistic division between the self and its environment of dependence. However we name this dependence, the act of naming and the name itself vanishes. No matter what we do or do not know, we are elementally within 'it' (*phusis*) in common with all else that lives but as that specific being that lives.

The human is born as and made out of the trace of a substrate (the particular animal from which we 'evolved'). Unlike all other animals, we are not born as the undeveloped form of what we shall eventually become—we are not as dogs, horses, lions, kangaroos and so on. Rather, as John Dewey and, later, François Lyotard told us, we are educated into humanity.[10] The ancient Greek creation of 'scholarship and training in good conduct', named *paideia* and translated by the Roman as *humanitas,* indicated a closer proximity to the 'true' nature of education. It recognized that 'our very "being-in-the-world" is shaped by the knowledge we pursue, uncover and embody'.[11] Whatever lip service contemporary 'outcome-based education' pays to learning, it is a long way removed from what education was and could be.

Temporally, our animality has been named as 'barbarous', brute, savage. As such, it was that to tame, erase, expel, repress. Yet this human/animal distinction was dominantly Eurocentric, not universal, as evidenced by diverse indigenous animistic cultures that claimed a spiritual commonality with all natural phenomena. The humanist self's refusal of its animality is coexistent with a view of the body as encapsulated within its own mortality. Yet the body is not just an object delimited by the objective condition of its own mortality within its own finitude. For it is also an 'inscribed surface of events' brought into being by the historicity of all those events that modified its form. As such, it is also the prefigurative site for the becoming of other futural bodies of the species.[12] All this is to say that the body is a continuum in transmitting the effects of ontological design—it is always the link between the one and the other. So, while we can concur with Maurice Merleau-Ponty that we perceive with our bodies, the perceptive reach of our bodies has its locus beyond our knowledge of any real agency.[13] As again Merleau-Ponty pointed out, our being has two modes: an unknowing 'in itself' and a knowing 'for itself'.[14]

Biopolitics comes into this picture (crudely understood as a reduction of the human to a politics centring on the management of bodies) as it folds the body into the state.[15] The biocentric theory of the state expounded by Thomas Hobbes asserted that existence within the civic state is indivisible from existence as a natural state into which the body dissolves. This was based on the proposition that, while subjects were constrained by and within the body politic, in the last instance the laws of nature always ruled. It followed that the human falls back into its animality, characterized by Hobbes as a perpetual regression to violence ('war of all against all'). Obviously, there is a biological substrate to our being, but the ecology of our dependence is equally indivisible from the social (the social ecology). We cannot come into or remain in being without others. Our proximity now can be seen to be relational, spatial and a-spatial. The animal, the self and the other effectively coexist, placed in the world in a distance that is no distance within a single point that is an 'us'. Yet this complexity is masked by the drive to identity that claims to tell us who and what we are.

Across the entire world/self relation, there is a constant proximity to our alienation from that upon which we fundamentally depend. Our preoccupation with our individuation masks our dependence upon a social ecology; our investment in the world of our fabrication diminishes our perception of our absolute dependence on the biophysical ecology; our focus upon 'the moment' manifests an almost total inability to comprehend time; and the dominant power of the image continually obscures what is most essential to see. As we shall explore, unless we can actually view what we are, we will remain unable to adaptively remake ourselves, and, unless we can do this, we will have only a very limited future.

Here we need to recall Hannah Arendt's distinction between 'being in the world' and 'being of the world'. The former is a given condition, but her use of 'being of the world' suggests an ontological materialism whereby 'we' are a product of the world. 'We' are made by the world and are world-makers: for us, the one cannot be without the other. This is a fundamental condition to our being—it always has been so—near and yet distant from the consciousness of most. The evidence for this is nowhere more pronounced than in the dominance of instrumental action wherein an assumption is made that resources are simply there at our disposal to be used at will (Heidegger named resources in this context a 'standing reserve').

The Touch of the Hand and Instrumentalism

As we shall see, it was the hand in its making, especially in the company of the tool, that delivered the animal to its potential of humanness, for 'all the work of the hand is rooted in thinking'.[16]

The hand brings the issue of proximity close to us. It is a key sensory instrument of proximity. The hand reaches out, touches, is touched, guides, makes, communicates, caresses, gives and takes, grasps, strikes, welcomes or rejects, plants and harvests. It picks and peels, crushes and opens, lifts and carries and, in so doing, places us back among our ape-like ancestors. Yet, while the abilities of the human hand outstrip those of primates (because of biomechanical differences), it equally holds, joins and unites. It marks an affinity, a commonality, a potential for exchange, a touching of worlds.

In service to the mind, the hand prosthetically extends itself with language and gesture, with the tool, as with the machine, the weapon, the musical instrument, the artist's brush, the surgeon's scalpel, the spoon that feeds, the pen and so on. At the same time, the hand harbours knowledge and is quicker than the mind: the hand that catches a ball struck with the force of a bat, the hand that directs the actions of the potter, the hand that recoils from a heated surface, the chef's hand as it holds the knife that slices the carrot.

The hand is present at the act of creation and destruction. It conjoins being with Being, confirms presence or announces absence, asserts or denies the presence of an Other. It divides or unites, embraces or rejects its environment, separates life from death, the world from the self, and, as Aristotle would have it, acts so that 'the animal's survival cannot be prolonged'.[17] The historical reach on thinking the hand is extensive, as is evidenced by the literature. It also registers debates in which a good deal is at stake (see especially Jacques Derrida's 'Geschlecht II: Heidegger's Hand').[18] This literature extends to the issue of proximity at its most critical.

Martin Heidegger pointed out that 'Man does not "have" hands, but the hand holds the essence of man because the word as the essential realm of the hand is the essence of man. The word as inscribed and what appears to the regard is the written word, i.e., script.'[19] The rise of the typewriter was viewed by Heidegger as the destruction of the word, which in turn meant the destruction of the power of the hand (as the giver of identity via the script) and thus the diminishment of 'man' through the ascent of 'the same'.[20] Michael Heim, an early critical voice on information technology, transposed Heidegger's analysis of the typewriter into the world of word processing and took the issue toward the standardization of the appearance of ideas.[21] In contemporary circumstances, standardization proliferates in myriad forms that generalize instrumental functionality. In this setting, those arguments that claim that the singularity of the subject is rapidly diminishing cannot be ignored.[22] Neither can the displacement of the autonomous producer by the standardized consumer, where 'consumption' acts, with the support of the design industries, as a surrogate search for difference.

The conjuncture of the 'end of man'—here understood as the coming to the end of the species—links to assumptions about a moment in the past wherein our being was nontechnological. This has never been the case. As we shall soon see, 'we' have never been without the ontological designing of tools as this relation prefigured technology. Now, in an age when technology has become hegemonic, not least as the primary agent of inscription of thought and action, the relation between our technological being and our becoming fully technological hangs in the balance. The externalization of our central nervous system is one critical mark of this moment; the diminishing significance of the hand is another (the loss of the hand as an agent of craft and memory, wherein the hand of experience was passed into memory via both making and the inscribed word).

Hand and language were linked at the very birth of our being with language. The hand pointed, designated and described the feature of that which became familiar. It said: I know you or you are a stranger, come here or go away, you are friend or foe. It picked up things and, in touching them, enabled their qualities to be revealed beyond the distance of sight. The hand touched the face, the mouth, and in its knowledge and expressiveness informed speech—it opened the way to language. As human beings evolved, so the abilities of the hand increased. Central to this development was its function within a schema of ontological designing. Interacting with what it created advanced its capabilities—it learnt from what it itself made as well from the act of making. But, at some point, this process peaked, and the very things that the hand brought into being—machines (first mechanical and then electronic)—started not just to reduce and replace the efficacy of the hand but to continually erase the marks of its identity. In a certain sense, the loss of hand-focussed craft skills overlaps with the notion of 'the end of man' and our becoming other than what we currently are.

We should understand that, in making a world, we largely made it by hand and, in so doing (from the perspective of ontological design), made ourselves what we are. Certainly, the development of our brain was crucial, but, without the capabilities of the hand, the brain was an agent without an actor.

The hand that laboured took our being beyond the realm of necessity. It, as the agent of engagement between 'our being' and 'the being of the word', created that excess that opened the possibility of human freedoms and, in its production of surplus, established the conditions that enabled those modes of exchange that made economic life as it is generally understood possible.

As we view 'man's' history, refracted especially via Hobbes, Kant, Hegel, Darwin and Marx, an evolutionary schema appears in which signs of freedom were asserted and thereafter projected as the species' destiny—toward an 'end state' of fully realized humanity. From this perspective, all work that reduced labour to mere function and thereby negated its ability to establish a proximity to human formation was able to be regarded as a reduction of 'man' to a lesser being, obstructing the realization of freedom. In contrast to being an agent in the service of human emancipation, labour so viewed was simply a means to secure bodily survival. It was in this context that Marx designated political action as central to creating the conditions under which workers collectively gain their freedom. Of course, from a contemporary perspective, the political control of the means of production was shown to be insufficient in realizing 'man's' projected destiny toward full liberation.

Yet, what Marx also argued was that not only does 'estranged labour' estrange man from 'nature', 'man from man' and from herself or himself, but it also alienates 'man' from his 'species being'. The contradiction he identified still resonates: while the material transformations brought by the capitalist mode of production give the appearance of objectively serving material advancements, in fact they diminish the human condition. Many significant thinkers, who, like Marx, have faded in and out of fashion, have underscored his analysis, not least Hannah Arendt.[23] What we now see is the manifestation of this condition in the naked form of the time-blind 'universal unsustainable consumer'. Central to Marx's thought was the recognition that objects produced purely as a means to create surplus value lose a proximity to their producer and became 'lifeless'. In becoming anonymous commodities, they are divested of their aura and power. The act of production is negated in the very 'nature' of the fetishized product.

As the distance between what most human beings *make* and *their selves* increased, capitalism responded and, with the assistance of designers, sought to establish a heightened attachment to the commodity via the 'sign economy'. Objects thereafter became reinvested with symbolic power that transcended any extant exchange value and marginalized utility. Sign value also acts here to reduce the duration of residual use value (redundancy can thus be created by the expenditure of sign value by another sign long before utility is expended).[24]

The consequences of transforming the processes of capital's symbolic realm have been profound. Naturally endowed needs (coming out of bare life) have been effectively overwhelmed and replaced by manufactured desires wherein wanting a commodity has been made indistinguishable from needing it. This powerful transformation is at the very core of commodity culture and its dynamic relation to extending unsustainability. So understood, the designed sign economy is a major defuturing force. More than this, the very essence of labour as life-generative has been turned—the production of excess as it informs, exceeds and erases needs has become a negation of our very being, a negation of our finitude. So, in contrast to human labour forming a world and selves, it is now equally a force of unmaking of both 'the human' and 'the world'.

Marx's understanding of production moved toward grasping the ontological designing consequences of what was produced:

> Labour is, in the first place, a process in which both man and Nature participate, and in which man of his own accord starts, regulates, and controls the material reactions between himself and Nature. He opposes himself to Nature as one of her forces, setting in motion arms and legs, head and hand, the natural forces of his body, in order to appropriate nature's productions in a form adapted to his own wants. By this action on the external world and changing it, he at the same time changes his own nature.[25]

But he overlooked a key fact of proximity that continues to get overlooked— 'man' is not outside the biological realm of 'nature'. In fact our closest element—our animality—is constantly overlooked and cast as a residual problematic. 'We' never see that which is closest to us but only the next closest. It is this that drives the closest out of the domain of experience. In so doing, it follows 'the law of proximity'—wherein the closest is the most difficult 'thing' to see, and thereafter distance to the close regulates visibility.[26]

Marx did not foresee the environmental consequence of the unrestrained appropriation of natural resources. In both respects, the defuturing character of our anthropocentrism eluded him. However, to restate, in his observation that, in changing the world, 'man' also changes his own nature, he prefigured a central tenet of ontological design.

Part II

Emergence over Origin:
A Relational Account

Photography: Peter Wanny / Illustration: Tony Fry

The greatness of Darwinism, however, is that it provides a precise account of how the appearance of purposeful behaviour can emerge from a senseless mechanical process.

—Slavoj Žižek

Two narratives of how human beings came into being have dominated debate in the modern dominantly secular era: creationism (as a fundamentalist Christian position and as a belief held in various form across multiple faiths) and Darwinism.

Darwinism, as supported by subsequent scientific discoveries, not least genetics, totally undercuts any claim to truth mounted by creationism and its latter-day fiction 'intelligent design'. It therefore appears that there are but two options from which to choose: fact or faith. However, it will be argued that Darwinism is an insufficient explanation, even when supplemented with social evolutionary theory. It does not explain adequately how 'the human' came to be, for it does not acknowledge the part played by ontological design (the agency of the object world of things) in our becoming and subsequent transformations. Three intertwined arguments will be put forward to address questions of natural selection, un-natural selection and design. Together they will constitute a perspective by which to view: what we have been, are and will become. But before we can move forward there is a key question to confront which folds back into all three positions of argument. We need to ask, be it very provisionally, what exactly is a human being?

For Charles Darwin in 1871 (as he detailed in *The Descent of Man and Selection in Relation to Sex*), 'man', the human, was a biological species descended from apes, whose evolution could be accounted for in the same way as any other animal. His thesis was actually predated by Alfred Russel Wallace's paper 'The Origins of Human Races and the Antiquity of Man Deduced from a Theory of "Natural Selection" ', published in 1864.

Prior to and then accompanying this biological model of the human was the idea of man as a product of *social* evolution. Darwin's theory of natural selection became transmuted into a political ideology—Social Darwinism. The precursor could be found in the 1830s in the positivist sociology of Auguste Comte. Subsequently, it was fully enunciated as 'structural functionalism' by the reactionary and extreme liberalism of Herbert Spencer, who brought together in an overarching theory competition between individuals, the survival of the fittest and laissez-faire capitalism.[1] Spencer's thinking was used to support eugenic theory and the movement it spawned. As such, it became associated with scientific racism, imperialism and fascism. Essentially, society was viewed as an organism (as function and metaphor), and this particular idea became widely held. It was influential, for example, in the development of urban sociology and in the creation of cybernetics and systems theory (as indicated by Norbert Weiner's *Human Use of Human Beings*, published in 1950).

Conceptually, the notion of a biological foundation for social evolution and human development predated Darwin. It was one of the recurrent ideas of the Enlightenment. For instance, Immanuel Kant, in much the same vein as Thomas Hobbes, asserted a 'cunning of nature'; as he put it, 'the means employed by nature to bring about the development of all the capacities of men is their antagonism in society', with such 'capacities' being 'destined to evolve completely to their natural end'.[2]

Organic relations still at base underpin many current perspectives, ranging from ideas of social ecology to sociobiology and the organicist philosophy found in some of Ludwig Wittgenstein's writings.[3]

Clearly, the human is not simply the name of just another animal, but nonetheless 'it' partly remains animal—with an animality of and beyond a body that is brought to presence only in the company of its coexistent Other, the human. Yet what the human knows both of its self and of its animality is limited. There is no knowledge of the whole, and the available, fragmentary and partial forms of knowledge of mind, body and species-being somehow defy assemblage and any clear divisions (of the three things mentioned). As something more than a pure animal, the human is clearly not just a social construction, for sociality is not exclusively a human provenance. But, in difference, the human has been the unnatural result of formative processes that, as we shall see, were created out of our animality—as the animal that we were engaged and were engaged by, 'things of the world'. As will be seen, we were not self-created or merely an animal adapting to its environment, nor were we an autonomous entity divided from 'the world'.

The resolution of the human as known slides into the domain of the unspeakable—in thinking what we are we move between the obvious and mystery, as well as our refusal to confront what it is we are. The union of the animal and the human is not uniform or ever fully secured. The balance can be tipped and overwhelmed, not least by pain. The human is fragile, a hugely uneven gradation, open to regress and a product of perpetual illusion (not least when appealed to as if it were an existential totality). Given the cultural plurality of its forms of creation (the variations of culturally constructed worlds), the very notion of the human as a singularity can be dismissed.

Not all 'humans' have posed themselves as outside that realm of 'all living things' named 'animal'.[4] Certainly, different cultures, past and present, name and view what Eurocentric culture named a 'human being' in various ways. So, for the moment, all we have as 'the human' is a globally imposed and contingent complexity: a figure of change made the same in large part by conventions of recognition. Out of the nonhuman, in the presence of the dehumanized and the prospect of the posthuman, the question of the human and the humanized still remains open.[5] In the face of numerous forms of the unsustainable that threaten our very being, confronting this question of what exactly we are ever presses. The question travels with us and is always present when the word 'human' is uttered.

4

Coming into Being via Natural Selection

I cannot help thinking a good analogy might be traced between a relationship of all men now living and the classification of animals.

—Charles Darwin, 1839

Whatever is said, no matter how it is said and with what we humans think we align ourselves, what we say is expressed from an irrefutable position of human-centredness. On this position, Marx's view on the relation between 'man and Nature' stands for every possible statement: 'man' is 'a being for himself'.[1] 'We' are inescapably anthropocentric—no matter what we say or how we think and act, we do so from a perspective grounded in this state of being. We cannot be other than *anthropos*—identification with anything other than ourselves comes from and returns to what it is we are. Even when seemingly we are acting against the anthropocentric drive to humanize the world or to emphatically transpose ourself into or onto the concerns of nonhuman beings, the impositional will of being human is always enacted.[2] All action is but a (re)configuration of what the human decides is meaningful.[3]

The Picture from Being Centred

Essentially and unavoidably, whatever we say or do, anthropocentrism is the enacted locus of what we are. It cannot be abandoned; it is the foundation upon which all our values stand. Nothing has an intrinsic value, for nothing posits value but us: all meaning is so centred in us. Likewise, so is all need.

None of this is to say that we, in common with other sentient beings, do not have the needs of our 'bare life'. But it is to say that such needs are mediated and often overdetermined by our mode of being anthropocentric (at the extreme, we can be willing to sacrifice our 'bare life' for a value—here the power of humanness overwhelms biological force). There is no position of observation other than our own, for otherness comes from us; it is our projection. To attempt to 'go along with' an Other is to travel with the shadow of our idea of what we deem to be the otherness of the Other. The only prospect of understanding is in recognizing that our knowing is always anthropo*centric*. It is our *habitus*—the structuring of the structure of what we are. However, there is a profound existential difference between knowing one is anthropocentric and not knowing it.

While unable to transcend being anthropocentric, we have a vital need to acknowledge what we are and then to act in the light of what we have come to know. There can be no recognition of or responsibility for what the real consequences of our actions in the world are without this. Fundamentally, all ethics rest directly or indirectly upon this recognition. We have no other corrective.

It has been our inability to confront *what it is we are* and *what it is we have done over time* that has driven us toward the domination of and damage to the environments upon which we depend. It is this structurally inherent 'unsustainability' of what we are that is currently leaving us stranded as a species. We (in our plurality) are out of our depth in the complexity of the world-within-the-world of our creation and are mostly unknowingly collectively acting in ways that reduce our species being, our finitude. Here is a fundamental condition of limitation in which we live as body, species and techno-dependent beings. As we live toward death and, in so doing, strive for life, so much of what we reach out for in order to be is itself a negation of being.

The world into which we are born is both an *ontic* unknowable entity and a world of anthropocentric ontological fabrication. What there is to know (the meaninglessness of 'what is') and knowledge created by the production of meaning (no matter by what discourse) do not correspond, but we mostly think and act as if they do. It is metaphysics (knowledge) that makes this world present, yet it cheats us. The unknown is unbounded, and (our) knowledge is limited. The fact we are named *Homo sapiens* (a knowing being) is a conceit of our creation. We deceive ourselves that we know 'the world' by naming it. We underestimate the extent to which we impose—that is, stamp—our self on virtually everything. The trace of our presence, the scars of our actions, the heritage of our neglect can be seen in every extant environment on the planet (be it the ugly or the beautiful, the healthy or the harmed).

Of course, indivisible from how we think and see, the 'nature of our being' is how we define our difference from 'animals' (not least when we totalize the difference between animals and us).

Revisiting Natural Selection

Darwin's contribution to understanding the emergence and the process of life is immeasurable, if not unique (although, as seen, the insights of Alfred Russel Wallace were also very considerable). Remarkably, Darwin anticipated much of what genetics and biochemistry were later to discover, although, as we shall see, he did not fully embrace all the biological forces that made us what we are.

Before we get to the issue of our own creation (which, for the moment, we will call the human superstructure of the animal), there a few remarks on natural selection and adaptation that need to be made.

Evolutionary biology, informed by genetics, has made it clear that the characterization of natural selection as the 'survival of the fittest' is simplistic. Current notions, gathered now over several decades under the term 'modern synthesis', have exposed a far greater complexity of determinant factors.[4] These include random genetic drift, variations within a population (due to the presence of multiple alleles of a gene), and, more contentious, the fact that speciation is (usually) due to the gradual accumulation of small genetic changes. Darwin's focus on organic biological process, environment, species and individual change has thus been extended with knowledge gained from the study of genes, phenotypes and the dynamics of populations.

In time, all species are fated; they are finite. They have a moment of becoming and a time in which they will disappear—for some species, the time between their evolutionary arrival and departure is short, whereas for others, it's long. Some species, as Darwin well knew, have traits that improve their fitness and ability to persist and flourish over an extended period of time (others are highly specialist, dependent upon a very particular environment and diet and thus are extremely vulnerable). Yet, at the same time, notwithstanding our greater grasp of the complexity of the process, for every species, evolution is a selfish struggle for survival. This struggle for us is never just biological. For example, it is (and has been) possible to understand Nietzsche's notion of 'will to power' in the frame of survival as a struggle toward the future (as well as a value imminent in historical practice).[5] But directionality here exists without purpose or goal—it simply 'is'.[6] In the general sense, this drive to 'continue to be' can be taken as genetically inherent in all species, but it is more than this for us. For Nietzsche, it was a structural feature of a mentalism wherein the struggle for existence folds into a struggle for power over that which could threaten it. As such, it was seen as a condition of being, rather than as an overtly mobilized directional force of mind.

As many have noted, Nietzsche was significantly influenced by Darwin's ideas, while at the same time making many disparaging remarks about him. He seemingly displayed the not altogether unique characteristic of wanting to take issue with the thoughts of those very thinkers whose ideas he found most significant. What Nietzsche actually did was to extend Darwin's thinking, rather than dismiss it.[7] He did this partly by drawing on the ideas of Spencer by pointing out that 'man' creates a reality which partly removes him from natural evolutionary processes—specifically by coming out of a material and social world constructed and occupied by immediate forebears and distant ancestors. At the same time, Nietzsche was unaware of the degree to which his argument would have had more substance had he extended the second most important element of Darwinian theory—adaptation.

Moving to the present, what we see is that human-made environments (structures, artefacts and the sum of the technosphere) have negated the temporal conditions of our biophysical environmental dependence. Because of this, the gap between biological and sociomaterial adaptation has ever widened. Living, as once we mostly did, amid slow environmental transformations to which biological adaptive processes could respond has become displaced by human-induced, rapid terrestrial and atmospheric transformations.[8] As this rate of change has come to override evolutionary time, the need for humans to adapt has become ever more urgent. But now the only available option is to adapt by artificial means. Survival will thus now increasingly become a biosocial ontological design project. What this implies is still not fully clear and is the cause of a great deal of trepidation. It could possibly arrive as genetic modification combined with ontological changes that significantly alter how we act and what we are. So, rather than pose the issue of adaptation in the human/animal frame, we must place it in the context of the relation between the human and the artificial.

What is being identified here is a design process wherein techno-environments of structures and 'things' (as well as changes within socio-structures) act together materially and socially to facilitate our adaptive capabilities. This does not presume utopian visions or a simple social/technocentric task. Nor does it imply the attempt to impose uniformity in terms of 'what we are'. More than this, there is no presumption that currently available approaches to design are adequate to the task. Certainly, systems-based models of environmental design (including bio-mimicry) and technocentric sustainable design are not what is being advocated here.

It is interesting that Darwin confronted the issue of design as problematic and that his contemporary acolytes have embraced the concept with a great deal more enthusiasm and generated a far larger problem.

In 'The Life and Letters of Charles Darwin', we read:

> I cannot see as plainly as others do, and as I should wish to do, evidence of design and beneficence on all sides of us. There seems to me too much misery in the world. I cannot persuade myself that a beneficent and omnipotent God would have designedly created the *Ichneumonidae* [wasps] with the express intention of their [larva] feeding within the living bodies of Caterpillars, or that a cat should play with mice. Not believing this, I see no necessity in the belief that the eye was expressly designed. On the other, I cannot anyhow be contented to view this wonderful universe, and especially the nature of man, and to conclude that everything is the result of brute force. I am inclined to look at everything as resulting from designed laws, with the details, whether good or bad, left to the working out of what we may call chance. (Extract of letter to Asa Gray, a minister, May 22, 1860)

And then,

> One word more on 'designed laws' and 'undesigned results.' I see a bird which I want for food, take my gun and kill it, I do this designedly. An innocent and good man stands under a tree and is killed by a flash of lightning. Do you believe (and I really should like to hear) that God designedly killed this man? Many or most persons do believe this; I can't and don't. (Extract of letter to Asa Gray, July 1860)

Finally,

> With respect to Design, I feel more inclined to show a white flag than to fire my usual long-range shot. I like to try and ask you a puzzling question, but when you return the compliment I have great doubts whether it is a fair way of arguing. If anything is designed, certainly man must be: one's 'inner consciousness' (though a false guide) tells one so; yet I cannot admit that man's rudimentary mammae [nipples]...were designed. If I was to say I believed this, I should believe it in the same incredible manner as the orthodox believe the Trinity in Unity. (Extract of letter to Asa Gray, 11 December 1861)[9]

We find none of this angst about design in the writing of, for instance, Daniel Dennett, for example in *Darwin's Dangerous Idea*, a book setting out to test Darwinian thought in the frame of contemporary science and social imperatives wherein design is liberally peppered over Darwin's entire project.[10] Despite its many merits, not only does Dennett's book fail to understand the nature of design, but it ignores Darwin's disposition toward it. With his unwitting totalizations, Dennett undoes the very thesis of causality he mobilizes.

He does this by asserting that the system of life was neither the product of the 'grand designer' (God) nor the force of reason. Thereafter, Dennett employs a modern notion of 'biological design' and maps it onto Darwin's understanding. Any notion of 'design in nature' is yet another anthropocentric back-loading.

Design is grounded in human agency—as a prefigurative capability, it causally goes together with imagination, which, as Immanuel Kant demonstrated through his exposition of 'transcendental imagination', was prior to and generative of reason. The capability to design (to prefigure action toward an imagined end), at its most basic, will be shown to be one of the distinguishing characteristics of being human. The actual agency of design is vested in both the designer and the designed (whatever is designed goes on designing). This distinction needs to be made quite clear in relation to Darwin.

What Darwin identified was determinism vested in mindless and, therefore, meaningless biological processes that were self-generative. There was no primary design agent. As Iain Thomson makes clear in addressing Heidegger's ontotheology, in the end, all meaning stands upon metaphysics, which itself grounds meaning in belief (theology).[11] In contrast, design presumes intent embodied in a prefigurative act. That something can appear as designed is no evidence that it was designed: the spots on the leopard's back, the beauty of the rose, the elegance of ebony can all be used within the act of design, but they are not its product. To mobilize design metaphorically is to confuse. There is no design in the process of the creation of life, because, if there were, it would be a force outside this process, and this is exactly what Darwin refuted and the view that Dennett's argument claims to be supporting.

Out of the Animal: Human Emergence and Time

From Darwin, Nietzsche learnt to put man 'back among the animals', but with the qualification that 'he' is the most cunning and sickest (by which he meant that 'man' reaches depths of violence and depravity beyond all other animals).[12]

That great zoologist of the twentieth century, Jakob von Uexküll, with his understanding of relationality, radically undercut the notion of the independence of the actions of any animal. Rather than placing them in any hierarchical order, he characterized their relation metaphorically, as a 'gigantic musical score'.[13]

Both Nietzsche's and von Uexküll's perspectives are united by the same condition of limitation—the impossibility of transcending a constructed view from the anthropocentric position of observation. We observe animal life not from the outside but from the inside. We are other only for ourselves. Thus, it is fair to assume that for all other animals we are just another animal, albeit an extremely dangerous one. Of course, observation generally lacks self-reflection on the act of seeing. Observation is never mere observation, for it is always configured by the observer's point of view and operational discourse—to start with, the observer designates what will be observed. It is thus always a projection of metaphysically framed knowledge (as seen most overtly in scientific practices).

Grasping our relation and proximity to animality/animals escapes us.

The assertion of difference overwhelms the vast amount we have in common, from bodily functions to reproductive drives, fear and anger. Likewise, our relational connections, be it for food (raising and slaughtering livestock), the extension of our senses (the use of dogs), pleasure (the use of fish, birds, dogs, horses), emotional comfort (pets), or aesthetics (bird-watching, wildlife photography, animal paintings) do not get assembled into a relational picture of human appropriation. More than this, the totalizing category of animal flattens the huge differences between them and between them and us. In reality, we see animals in varied ways and proximities to ourselves. Some we are well disposed toward, some are drawn into our world and lives; others are viewed just instrumentally, as food sources, and then there are those from whom we recoil and that we fear. Likewise, animals dispose themselves toward us in different ways. They seek what appears to us as affection and establish an instrumental relation based on being supplied with food; they are fearful or hostile. To assert our humanity, we exclude our animality, and, in so doing, we keep ourselves open to this exclusion.[14] At the same time, we can interact with those animals that become close to us only on the basis of a shared animality (which we name as (mutual) affection).

In the Beginning

There was no 'first man'. We did not arrive by virtue of originary *ur-time*, out of 'Adam and Eve' or from a noble or divine birth. Rather, we arrived out of a now-lost species over a vast expanse of time. The idea of a 'missing link' to apes and chimpanzees has now been abandoned by informed sources—it no longer serves any useful purpose.[15] What is known is that there were partially bipedal hominids walking the planet six million years ago, and around two and a half million years ago there were hominids walking fully upright.[16] The earliest hominids, classified mainly as *Australopithecus*, were African, displaying what have been named as the three criteria of humanity: erect posture while walking; a free hand during this locomotion; and a 'short' face (identified by the size and position of teeth). The development of the brain came along with these characteristics and had a direct relation to them.[17] Development was dependent on processes of material evolution whereby the body and the mind increasingly, if slowly, embraced higher levels of complexity. Paleo-archaeological information indicates that the more the hand was employed, the greater the demand made on the brain. As a result of this demand, the more the cerebral structure improved (improvement being indicated by the increased size of the brain, as evidenced by an increase in the size of the skull's brain cavity),[18] the more the brain developed a capacity to advance social interactions, which in turn stimulated the brain.

The interactivity between the hand and the material world, together with the strengthening of social contact and structure, established the key relations between the construction of a social world and those actions that started to form a world of proto-human existence within the world at large. But the slowness of the rate of change is hard for us to comprehend—incredibly small changes took hundreds of thousands of years.

World formation (of a world-within-the-world) was an ontological condition. There was no vision, just a deposit of change via process. The formation of an unnamed world that evolved alongside its maker was central to the coming into being of the human and was indivisible from the partial rupture of the human from its retained but repressed animality. Obviously, the more this activity became intrinsic, the more 'the world' that was being formed was prefigured by intent (by design at its most basic level) and the greater the gap and difference between other animals and hominids became.

In Heideggerian terms, being-in-the-world of human creation (a world of constructed perceptions, material actions and symbolic exchanges) became the condition of being for 'world-forming subjects' that, in turn, was 'formed-by-the world'. In addition to defining the essence of ontological design, this point is also a key indication that there is no clear division between subject and object. Thus, being located in this place of mental and material habitation unified the relation between a world being transformed and human formation (in which animality remained and remains ever present). This ambiguity goes to the way Heidegger was to understand *Dasein* as being both 'there' and/or 'here'. We would want to say that *Dasein* is not reducible to being the locus of the one (the human) or the other (the animal).

Contemporary debates on the human/animal relation have paid considerable attention to Heidegger's ideas, particularly from Part II of his *The Fundamental Concepts of Metaphysics* (a book based on lectures of 1929–30, published first in German among his collected works in 1983 and, later, in English in 1995).[19] The main focus of attention has been on his explicated comment on the stone being worldless, the animal being poor of world and the human having a world.[20] So, while there is a good deal to say on the implications of Heidegger's argument, the focus here will be on the animal. A more nuanced engagement with the relation among the stone, the animal and the human will come a little later and will seek to add to existing accounts.[21]

In essence, the stone was viewed by Heidegger as independent and inanimate; as such, it lacks sentient quality and, in its unfeeling, has no sense of its existence—hence, it is deemed to be without a world. The issue of the animal 'being poor of world' is clearly more complex. The animal does have a limited world, but, for Heidegger, the animal is constricted in a world as a condition of environmental confinement that for it is 'a fixed sphere that is incapable of further expansion or contraction'.[22] All animals are claimed to be captive to their conditions of existence, and, while 'open' to other things, they are (by degree) in a state of captivation within the 'nature' of their ecology—it is their *habitus*. Here again, difference begs acknowledgement—a bird in a forest or an ape in a jungle 'experiences' the open in some form or another, while a steer in a feedlot or a chicken in a battery cage lives in an environment of absolute ecological deprivation. At the same time, all animals are captive to what it is they are—they all have the individual or collective character of *'being absorbed'* within what it is they are (which means they cannot simply be individuated into that which has no existential selfhood).[23]

The captivation of animals within environments of our creation so that they are 'present-at-hand' is of concern. How, ontologically, we are with animals in the world of our formation, how we have denaturalized them again disrupts any notion of the delimited world of animals as a continuum. We render them almost worldless (as with battery chickens) or place them in a world that is just an appendage to our world. Thus, animals become captured by (us) at the most fundamental level (as with genetic manipulation and management). Increasingly, the future of many animals will be via this induction into the world of human creation (a crisis of biodiversity and a demand for increased food productivity will both prompt greater denaturalization). Like us, if trailing, animals are en route toward the artificial.

Georgio Agamben notes that 'the animal behaves within an environment but never within a world.'[24] In contrast, the human behaves in a world and, in that regression which is their animality, also in an environment. The binary does not hold. One can add that it is not just animals that can be 'claimed to be captive to their conditions of existence', for there are millions of dispossessed humans who are equally entrapped and are the 'poor of (the) world'. Their world is a world of not having. Transposing oneself into such conditions does not, however, provide any insight into the condition of 'the animal'. As Heidegger discusses at length, such 'going along with' is an act of imagination, an act of fiction, which has no proximity to the experience of not having.[25] At best, all it can deliver is empathy, which, while not without value, does not equal understanding.

There is no nonanthropocentric point of view to see the world of the animal. A poverty of world is of no concern to animals; they have no need for it. The very term 'poor of world' used by Heidegger was brought into critical focus by Jacques Derrida, who deemed it 'strange'. More generally, Derrida drew attention to the other pronouncements on the qualities and nonqualities of animals by Heidegger and his lack of knowledge of zoology and most of its literature.[26]

A need to know is purely a human need. One could argue that what an animal lacks of world, we lack of environment. Both they and we are in our own ways held captive. Our openness, our freedom, is inappropriately generalized—our reality is relative. In many ways, 'we' remain captive to our animality and, as such, share some of the environmental circumscription of animals. More than this: is not our condition of becoming open to becoming closed (e.g. job security, the domestic, urban life) the very essence of our being captured in a transmuting environment (once 'the world itself' now dominantly a condition mostly within the insecure settlement of the world-within-the-world)? While in the context of the everyday, our animality remains mostly concealed. Yet it can instantly arrive in the open as lust, fear or violence. Moreover, 'the irresolvable struggle between unconcealedness and concealedness, which defines the human world, is an internal/eternal struggle between "man" and/as animality.'[27]

Again, against the binary of human/animal, one can also ask of the placement of pleasure and pain—do they not gradate from the human to the animal? Cannot pain itself consume the totality of one's being? Is not suffering, as Jeremy Bentham would have it, the most fundamental ethical issue?

Coming out of animality, becoming proto-human and human is always an appropriative event. This has been said by many thinkers in many ways—Marx, Dewey and Heidegger are but three examples. The nature of the appropriation is multidirectional. There is the making of the maker *as they* make and the making of makers *by the* made—this as ontological designing enacted in making and through the made. At the same time, there is the power of inductive education as 'we' were/are induced into human conduct by the pressures of social conformity. Then, to a lesser degree, there is the reflexive experience of the exploitation of matter as 'the environment' is 'taken' as a standing reserve for our use—but with a failure to recognize that, as 'we' change/changed the environment, it changed us. Prefiguratively, all of this was in place well before *Homo sapiens* came on the scene 160,000 years ago.

Making (as change) is for us the active construction of experiential life and implicated in ideas, meaning, symbolic forms, objects, structures and thus material and immaterial relations. It is always temporal—as making is always of and in the medium of time. Everything (made) is an event, some thing in place and time. Making is the agency of human and world formation, and, as such, it is the objectification of human being in a world. In its objectified form, making became industrialized, and, as it did so, time itself increasingly became a product of industrial process. Making became programmed, time-managed, rationally sequenced, measured, time-costed and itself time-directive. Here is a history from Taylor's study of time and motion, to programmed automated robotic production, informatics and the 'real-time' transmission of high-speed information. As pointed out by Bernard Stiegler, industrial time is now 'real time'.[28]

'Real time' is the time without delay, time without the possibility of a moment of reflection. It is the time of a posthuman future, and this future 'can only be anticipated in the form of an absolute danger. It is that which breaks absolutely with constituted normality and can only be proclaimed, presented, as a sort of monstrosity.'[29]

In our postindustrial technological intervention in time, time is again being changed (by the speed of change being taken beyond the globalized transformation of the time of industrialization). Yet this is being done without any 'real' grasp of consequences.

The made is never therefore an end in itself but always remains a means. To experience the made—to see it, to hear it, to touch it, to smell it—is always hermeneutical, and what becomes known can only but be drawn from a constructed memory. The made equally holds a narrative—the story of its coming into being and its use in being. The story is time. Yet memory is likewise posited in things made. They come from an appropriation of 'the before' as carried by a convergence of language, image, objects and technics.

Emergence: Out of the Phylum

We *Homo sapiens* emerged out of a phylum—the collectivity of all those hominoid beings before us as *they* accrued and developed intelligence, all gathered in a bequest of knowledge, materials, techniques and tools. All that 'we' achieved came from appropriation that was oblivious to any correlation between development and destruction (readable as a 'will to power'). 'We' have, in our coming into being (as it ruptured our relation to our zoological heritage), always, inherently and mostly unknowingly, been disposed toward the unsustainable. Of course, this condition did not become critical until we (*a*) became of sufficient numbers and with a volume of 'productive output' to dramatically amplify our negative planetary impacts and (*b*) created a way of life removed from directly observing the impacts of our actions upon the natural environment and thereby adjusting our actions accordingly (which is what hunter/gatherers did). These impacts, while having planetary consequences, most fundamentally diminish our finitude.

As we shall consider in some detail, the crucial factor in our species' emergence as creators and destroyers was the use of tools. Initially, something like 2.5 million years ago, a stone was picked up by a proto-hominoid animal and used to smash an object containing food (for instance, a coconut, other nuts or a marrow bone). The stone was simply a bodily extension 'much like an animal uses it claws'. But it was this use of the stone that emplaced the means to prefigure the arrival of stones as tools. We have now arrived at a point where the nature of the stone, the animal, the human and the world evoked by Heidegger can be revisited.

The animal picks up the stone and slowly discovers, in its use, new capability. Slowly, oh so slowly (the paleontological consensus is that it took well over one and a half million years), two flint stones are picked up and smashed together to reveal something new. No doubt a huge number of stones would have been smashed together before this moment, but this time and in a flash—an *augenblick*, the instant or moment when reflective thought arrives—a potentiality is seen. The stone is perceived as something else (retrospectively named as what we would now call a tool, a chopper), and the experiment of use begins—who knows for how long? But, nonetheless, this is the birth of a new skill. Now technics and ontological designing move from the prefigured (the object and idea with potential) to continually enacted innovation. But, again, the process is slow—very slow. Yet, what has begun now will never stop.

Without the stone, the animal that is about to become hominid would not have started on the path toward humanity. The inanimate was animated in a process that was to eventuate in the formation of the animal/human nexus and the world-within-the-world of 'its' creation. The determinate factor to emphasize was the arrival of a relational potential of becoming in which chance could not be discerned from destiny. So, while the stone could never materially become more than stone, it could become appropriated in use to become a material thing able to be directed toward 'thinging' in particular ways—thereby becoming an employed agent of change with symbolic value. As such, it could and did acquire functionality as a designing object of use, innovation and causal change of its user. It was, as said, a crucial agent in the animal becoming other and more than itself. Appropriating the stone was the appropriative event par excellence!

Complexity of thought started to increase as a result of the continuing and dynamic interaction of mind, hand, tool, environment and the made. Over millennia, this developmental dynamic (which cannot be reduced to mere technics) established, along with the rise of the power of language and the symbolic, a brain that increased in size by a third. Our cognitive capacity could be said to have arrived out of the prelinguistic encounter of the animal with the stone. The ontological designing journey that began in this moment has not ended. But what is now evident is that the complexity of the agency of what designs (us) is beyond our comprehension. What remains open is the question of our fate—is it actually sealed by this agency? The proposition that underpins almost everything said here is that, in large part, it is. What this means is that our destiny and design conflate. As all that has gone before tells us, the human is a product of the world of its own creation, and, while this world impinges on the animal that we are, it remains much of what it always has been in the given world of biophysical natural and unnatural change.

What has been passed over in summary begs visiting in more detail.

The picture of the biological evolution of our species constantly changes as research continues to reveal new information. So said, it seems that, around five hundred thousand years ago, the *Palaeoanthropians* had displaced *Australanthropians* and *Archanthropians* and established themselves in Europe, Africa, the Middle East and Java. Over perhaps the next three hundred thousand years, prior to the arrival of *Homo sapiens* from Africa (and while they gained more genetic complexity),[30] their antecedents were exposed to climatic conditions beyond our grasp as the planet experienced an extreme ice age. What is evident here is the relation between climatic change and the global distribution of a proto-human population. For instance, as glaciers retreated, people followed in their path—this was how the Neanderthals arrived in Europe.[31] Much of the differences displayed by the peoples of the world can be attributed to this process of moving directed by climate (and the search for food) combined with biological adaptation as it was understood within Darwin's schema. Large numbers of our early ancestors perished in this period, but equally there were vast tracts of time when adaptation was possible.

As noted, *Homo sapiens* first appeared in Africa 160,000 years ago (or earlier). The evidence here is quite specific. A comparative analysis of a sample group of mitochondrial DNA confirmed that 147 of the people in the sample had inherited genes from an African woman who lived two hundred thousand years ago and who was an ancestor of *Homo sapiens* (subsequent research on the male 'Y' chromosome confirmed these findings); this research, which still stands, has been both reviewed and updated.[32] However, like most research in the area, it creates as well as solves problems.

These first *Homo sapiens* were named Herto people after the village in Ethiopia where their remains were discovered. These people were extraordinary survivors—as said, their evolutionary precursors had endured the harshest conditions over the preceding three hundred thousand years. These geographically specific conditions, which veered between very wet and extremely dry, drove people to the coast and changed the way they lived and their diet. Environmental challenges reduced the population to just a few thousand. This kind of population crash is called, in evolutionary biology, a 'bottleneck'. What it produces is rapid biological evolution via genes spread across a small population.

For tens of thousands of years, *Homo sapiens* coexisted with two other hominid species: *Homo erectus* and Neanderthals. All walked upright; all had a free hand and a large brain and were intelligent. How two of the three species became extinct remains unclear, although there is a view that *Homo sapiens* was the most aggressive.

The vital fact to grasp about *Homo sapiens* is that 'we' were/are the last products of zoological evolution. Our creation of a social ecology and our commencement of making a world-within-the-world (a complexity of 'co-evolution' in tools/technics, design/matter and language/culture)[33] broke the absolute determinism of the biological chain of being.[34] The question that now stands before us is: 'what of what we are will remain the same?' Certainly there are many indications of the ability to fall back into a precivilized condition. If so, it is not inconceivable that, as a species, we could divide, one-half undergoing quasi-reversion to a form of barbarism, the other half becoming biotechnical mutants. The speed at which technology has become implicated in life (measured against the time frame of human development) affirms it as an ontological condition of our existence and becoming. Living as a being increasingly technologically immersed evokes a futural vision of human becoming, looked at from the present, where the line between science fiction and science fact is almost indistinguishable.

The preoccupation with the question of the transformative nature of 'human nature' is clearly not new. It was certainly widespread during the Enlightenment: René Descartes, Jean-Jacques Rousseau, David Hume and Kant were all especially attracted to this question, but it was Marx who materially grounded it. He considered 'the nature of the "species being" of man' and 'the making of the human being'. His thinking clearly echoed his age, which drove his engagement with Hegel, produced a very critical reading of Ludwig Feuerbach and later showed the influence of Darwin. What is being made evident here is that 'human nature' was not given to the human but was a project of self-construction, but without design, a guiding hand or mind. It did not erase the animal, but animality was suppressed. The result has been the arrival of a complexity between humanness and animality that is still not fully grasped.

5

Coming into Being via Un-Natural Selection

We are unknown to ourselves, we men of knowledge.

—Friedrich Nietzsche

The human and the animal, both within our being and within being in general, are usually presented as a binary, but in reality they coexist as a biocultural continuum. We came from the animal, and animality still remains elemental to our being. Many of the problems of human conduct in the natural world stem from a repression of this fact—out of our illusion of difference, 'the animal' is treated as absolutely other (not just within our own being but within being in general). Animals do not have rights, but likewise we do not have any intrinsic rights over animals. In our invention of rights there is a fundamental need to question those that human beings have given themselves—not least those that reduce all of life to a standing reserve.

Human Emergence and Un-Natural Selection

Under that veneer of mannered appearance which we call 'being civilized', animality is that which we are at most pains to conceal, yet it drives so many of the desires and actions that we are never able to fully control. Our proximity to our own animality is not a fixed relation. Within our everydayness, it fades in and out, demanding that we visit our biological needs and deal with uninvited emotions. One can agree with Agamben: 'man…can be human only to the degree he transcends and transforms the anthropophorous animal which support him' but part company when he says 'and only because, through the action of negation, he is capable of mastering and, eventually, destroying his own animality'.[1] Animality is never fully mastered: we cannot be what we are without our animality, and humanism belies the fact we can never be fully human.

Jacques Derrida wrote tellingly of the (omni)presence of the animal in our thinking, writing, reading, interpretation—as this 'it' is always arriving and asserting itself as a figure of interest or concern, as metaphor, or that which stands alongside our attachments (to food, image, friend, foe and more).[2] We clearly dwell with animals and, in so doing, identify with them, ignore them, love them, hate them, abuse them and use them. In so many ways, in our anthropocentric blindness, we violate them and, in general, understand very little about them.

Our variable relation to our animality has been an ongoing process in our emergence into humanness. We can appropriately consider this passage of becoming from environmental captivation to a world in which 'the human' strives to subordinate both 'the animal within' and an external 'world of animals'. Our own animality can perhaps now be seen as both a defence against and equally an object of erasure by 'our' technological colonization. However, it may be that we cease to be one (species), for technology may well divide us as it becomes for some more embodied (perhaps by culture, class, wealth or even coercion), for others (the abject and politically hostile) an object of absolute recoil.

Now, of course, at almost every level (from medicine and industrialized farming to the indirect reduction of biodiversity as a result of technologically induced environmental impacts), domesticated animals are no longer completely outside the technosphere.

Our knowledge of our own finitude makes us unique among animals (expressed in the cliché 'we are the only animal that knows it is born to die'). But so many animals instinctively react to us with fear. Uncannily, our historicity has marked us as the master predator. This is seen in many ways, from most animals fleeing from us to the animal being taken to slaughter—it seems as if they have a knowledge of their death travelling ahead of itself.

We cannot speak for animals, but we do. The animal that we find the hardest to speak of is the animal that we are. But there is another perspective: that of those animistic cultures that mimetically take animality—often the animality of specific animals—as the basis for constructing their identities and worldviews. Such cultures view animals not as science does—as Other—but as experiential and mythological co-habitants of a material and immaterial world. In varied proximity, these cultures live with the animate and the inanimate as the locus of their spirituality, establishing particular kinds bonds, enacted practically and symbolically, with animals, biota and objects. It follows that asking the degree to which animals do or do not have worlds is again an issue of cultural proximity, rather than fixed geometry.

As we saw earlier, Enlightenment thinking, underpinned by natural law taken to 'the world', was extremely problematic in relation to those Others it deemed as subhuman/nonhuman. Besides not giving recognition or value to indigenous people and their knowledge, it designated such Others as primitive, animistic savages and treated them as such. While the forces of modernity at times waged 'war' on what were deemed savage Others (and did so in Africa, certainly, well into the twentieth century), they mostly acted with neglect, while almost completely failing to recognize the plural forms of 'human' being. It was in this condition of ignorance that the colonizing forces of destruction, prior to and during the Enlightenment, so often had no idea of what it was they destroyed. Against this backdrop, Sigmund Freud gave us a more timid and Eurocentrically illuminating characterization of civilization—'the word "civilisation" describes the whole sum of the achievements and regulations which distinguish our lives from those of our animal ancestors and which serve two purposes—namely to protect men against nature and to adjust their mutual relations.'[3]

To reemphasize: one cannot universally ask and answer the question 'what is the essence of animality or the human?' As has been said, the 'human', notwithstanding the rhetoric of humanism, is not a unified whole. We are not what humanism has led us to believe we are. How our species being is understood still remains plural, although there are continual attempts to homogenize it (via globalization's cultural totalization). It follows that 'we' do not 'have' one world, one socially constructed reality. But, likewise, we do have commonalities, including those between us and other animals.[4] In such a setting, both difference and similarity go unseen.

The human/animal relation is complex, both between the human and animals and within the human as animal. However, there is one very clear distinction. Every animal, other than the human/animal, is a 'being-as-itself' (that is, it is nothing other than its animal being). In contrast, the human/animal is a 'being-in-difference' (that is, it is 'the given' and 'the made'). The question here becomes: what can be changed, and what will remain the same? The 'nature of the human' (as opposed to 'human nature') has the capacity to be changed in certain respects (as adaptive capabilities evidence). But, because the animality of the human slides between concealment and disclosure, is still only partially acknowledged and lacks an independent discourse, the question of the same remains open (notwithstanding the continuity of savagery). Key here is a still-partial retrospective ability to recognize our animality when it manifests itself and the more problematic inability of the anthropocentric subject to access its animality or humanity as an object of inquiry beyond a reductive representation. As William McNeill points out when discussing the necessity of distinguishing among humans, animals and inanimate objects as fundamentally different: 'However obscure their grounds, these distinctions initially appear self-evident for us. Yet in terms of what criteria do we make such distinctions?'[5]

At an absolutely fundamental level, we do not ontically see ourselves. What we do see is what we have been inducted into seeing—a human being, a human face. Animality remains hidden and understood reductively in terms of bodily functions and the instinctual. Animals see us in our animality, but what do they see? To say 'merely another animal' (not that they would assume an anthropocentrically created category or any category at all) is doubtful. For, in almost all cases, if we take their reaction as an indicator, we are seen as an object of fear. As Heidegger points out, the animal does not apprehend something 'as something'.[6] But what is certain is that many animals observe us according to the difference in their manner of seeing but, even so, with a commonality vested in danger.

But how do we see ourselves, and how does technology inflect our perceptions?

We (the privileged) can be brought to see ourselves as an observed self—that is, as a play between a constructed identity and an image observed; reflection here is both a mirror image and the adoption of a projected image as they overlap as a mental picture. Besides being talked into our identity, being told what we are (affirmatively or negatively), we are that bricolage of adopted archetypes taken from the technologies of reflection, projection and body enhancement that capital and commodified culture seductively place in our path. Effectively, we see ourselves as a self-made production, whereas we are more of an ontologically created product of the world of our formation (of course, at the extreme, for some, drugs and cosmetic surgery and implants also get into the picture). Beyond these observations, technology already has the capability of bridging and linking medical science, behaviour management and surveillance.

Such developments can be placed within the underside of an ontologically designing continuation of the ill-understood domination of 'our' animality. No matter how we appear or view our selves, the animal that we are lives on—and is subject to a domination that still travels under the aegis of the applied veneer of cultivation and 'civilization'. What is so troubling here is how instrumentalism erases a questioning of causality (of anything) and so provides just another layer of concealment. Additionally, the history of the limits of metaphysics needs to be placed within the very ambiguous frame of the overcoming of the animal.[7] For what becomes increasingly clear is the lack of understanding of our (plural) continuous becoming as it came out of our base animality and what knowledge of our first becoming actually exposes. Largely, we do not grasp that we are the result of ontological design. But to grasp this is to understand the nature and consequences of those attempts made to overpower our animality.

Lest there is any doubt, the point being made about our animality is not that it should be elevated or celebrated but that it should be appropriately acknowledged and better understood as materiality beyond the discourses of humanism as it has been moulded and repressed. While this has started to be recognized theoretically and historically,[8] unless this knowledge is acquired and used projectively, we will not be able to create a vital future for ourselves (as a developed form of what we already are) and for those interdependencies that are vital to sustain us and our Others.

Ontological Designing and Technics

The human/technology relation folds into the living/nonliving, organic/nonorganic relation that has been characterized as 'anthropogenesis'. The philosopher Bernard Stiegler has presented anthropogenesis (specifically, the relation between the human life and technicity) as a new addition to evolutionary thought. This proposition is not uncritically supported here: rather, as has been intimated and will be argued, technics was present in its basic tool-being as an active agency in the very coming into being of the human, but this view is partial. In addition, the attempt to claim primacy for the determinism of this specific agency is flawed. For instance, for Stiegler, the agency of technicity and then epiphylogenetic memory (memory as inscribed in being within the environment) and of epigenetic memory (memory posited in genetics) or, for Agamben, the agency of the coming into being and use of language was viewed as the primary factor; for Leroi-Gourhan, with his particular interests in the visual, the arrival of symbolism (the making of marks) was decisive.[9] But, in contrast to these positions, we assert the relationality of each in the company of ontological design over any singular claim of causality. It follows that ontological designing of technicity is not being put into opposition with these agencies.

Clearly, with a relational assemblage it is not a matter of giving any particular form of agency a position of primacy, for the actuality of agency *is* relational at multiple levels. To take just one example, the relational complexity of memory can be denoted as:

- biologically inscribed memory (coming from the animal as the interaction between body and mind)
- memory located in place (as the interaction of being and/in place)
- memory inscribed in technics (memory posited in technics whereby whatever is present is both a mark denoting all the incremental progressions that preceded it and the designing basis of what will come after it)[10]
- language as memory (as it contains and proclaims a world and its past)
- image as memory (as a deposit for recall)

Memory infuses things, language, image and making, as they together constitute an 'ecology of mind' dissolving any clear perceptual distinction among subject, object and world. So understood, mind is a connectedness beyond cognition, a continuum in which ideas and actions are born and travel. Technics was present and active at the commencement hominoid memory and ever increased in presence and power. In this respect, its accumulation has reached a point, as Stiegler recognizes and examines in detail, wherein memory has become industrialized and mind externalized. Human beings are now in a triadic and expanding regime of enframed determinations. What we are and become is increasingly the consequence of a designing environment of cultural manufacture, material and immaterial technologies and, increasingly, biogenetics wherein the demarcation between mind and encoded matter cannot be clearly discerned. The generality of past modes of analysis—calling up, for example, the agency of technology or of the culture industries—is now patently inadequate.

At some point in human development, acting on the world turned and started to act back on the actor as a memory of the action event. Reflection upon this moment, its ramifications and the ability to express what happened to others all came together in specific conjunctures in which knowledge could be generalized and replicated. This knowledge was not just able to be transferred intersubjectively; also, and inseparably, it was able to be transferred by things (material and immaterial) as they were interrogated as memory (as memory is embedded in object-things themselves—such object-things arrive out of what they were as well as what they are). The ontological designing of memory grounded in such things was able to prompt not only the act of its reproduction but also incremental transformations of knowing and the object-thing. This is to say that things were seen not simply as they were but also as they could be. Any notion that object-things can be placed in the frame of evolutionary process is broken by imagination going ahead of material change. To note that transformations occurred is not to suggest that they happened quickly (as the eons it took to get from one stone tool to sixty by the time of the arrival of *Homo sapiens* illustrates). But it is to recognize a trait central to the articulated relation between humans and object-things, our becoming, and the world of our creation in which we become. It must be emphasized that, while this process is legible in a prehistoric context, viewing it in a late-modern world of advanced technologies, the naturalization of the artificial and the industrialization of mind and memory creates an extraordinary complexity well beyond any current ability to comprehend. While our proximity to this world appears to be close, its actual agency resides largely in the domain of the unknown. Let's take just one example of this concealment.

Information now travels at a speed for which a measure can be and is assigned, but there is not a single human being able to create an imaginary that in any way corresponds with the visualization of such a speed. It is not of our world. Yet whole industries are created in, for and by this world of industrialized memory and its related externalization of our central nervous system.[11] Not only are the actual and ongoing ontological designing impacts of this industry and its products unknown *but* also almost nobody is even asking the question—Stiegler being significant among the exceptions.

Of course, memory has been a key objects of politics—the past, history, is always a product of selection and editing (as George Orwell astutely wrote in the late 1940s in *Nineteen Eighty Four,* 'who controls the past controls the future: who controls the present controls the past'). In ambiguity, we now have the technology that seriously advances this capability. The industrialization of memory and the accelerating speed of the management of information increasingly intervene in such a process via its modes of documentation, storage, representation, reconfiguration and erasure. Yet the memory and its instrumentalization remain firmly anchored in what Bernd Magnus called 'chronophobia'—it has little sense of time and is obviously dislocated from any perception of the future.[12]

Rather than having any logical sequence, what is being described here is a transhistorical event of convergence, at an imprecise moment, in which that 'blink of the eye' (the *augenblick*) becomes possible. It was in this flash, in this instant that arrived and just as quickly was lost to recall, in this hyperrapid passing moment, that imagination was born and continually replays. Out of this fleeting moment, the journey of the hominid began. Stone tool in hand, he began this journey toward human being that is still and ever remains incomplete. This is to say that human being as an auto-initiated project started to arrive at the same moment as the ability to prefigure, to have intent, to act on the basis of accumulative knowledge and to remember the before and after of 'the object-thing' that was realized. This moment was the coming of design. What it did and still does is to open a world of its own wherein 'being-in-the-world' comes into being in a world-within-the-world. This journey had no destiny, no end point marked by the arrival, the attainment, of a being who is able to be recognized as fully human—a being from whom all traces of animality are totally erased (the actual prospect of the total technological erasure of our animality is now being viewed not as the completion of the human but its end, with the arrival of the 'zombie').

There is one more qualification to add to this sketch. As Kant knew well, man was never an animal endowed with reason, for, as was to become recognized and widely accepted, imagination came before reason; it was the crucial factor that spawned it. Reason came out of the hand of the hominid holding the stone.

Soon the place of technics will be further explored, but for the moment we need to return to Darwin's ideas and his influence.

Social Selection and Its Underpinnings

As said, there are two modes of Darwinism: biological and social. While Social Darwinism was triggered by the concept of evolution and while Darwin recognized the significance of sociality across many animal species, as will be remembered, the actual idea of Social Darwinism, explicated as an ideology, was given most of its impetus by Herbert Spencer.

Writing in the shadow of Comte and Darwin, Spencer aimed to fuse biology with sociology into a telos extending the idea of social evolution. His methodology, 'structural functionalism', centred on the notion that society is a living organism and grows in a way akin to the cellular construction of a biological entity. All the elements of the parts of the organism were deemed to have interrelated functions. He elaborated this in his earliest book, *The Principles of Sociology* of 1876. As we saw, his dangerous ideas (as they nurtured eugenics) were extremely influential (not least upon Friedrich Nietzsche). Spencer was regarded as one of the major thinkers of his age. At the same time, his ideas were politically reactionary. Besides the incipient racism that was backloaded onto and perhaps by degree flowed from his unrestrained laissez-faire liberalism, he popularized the idea of mapping natural selection onto social selection.

Three linked observations follow from this summary: (*a*) Spencer's political ideas needed dividing from his sociology—but they attracted followers who did the reverse (most notably in the rise of sociobiology in the 1970s); (*b*) his positivistic sociology begged critique—and received it over time; and (*c*) sociocultural 'evolutionary' development did play an important role in the advance of human social life. Thus, while Spencer's framing of social structure and life within a biological metaphor (the organic) was problematic, as was his model of social interaction, importantly it did support the proposition that the development of *Homo sapiens* was not merely a result of biological process. Although, as has already been shown, this notion was not exclusively Spencer's, it again begs to be revisited.

André Leroi-Gourhan made it very clear that the rise of social structures was totally independent from the zoological roots of human beings.[13] However, there were, again as we have seen, other key evolutionary factors, including design and language.

Writing a decade after Spencer's *The Principles of Sociology,* Nietzsche pointed out that language arrived as a means to strengthen social commonality, bonds and exchange.[14] The passage from an animal having the ability to make sounds to a human with the ability to speak paralleled the organization of animals in social groups and the emergence of evolving social structures in which forms of communication move beyond the purely functional toward the symbolic.

Prefiguring Agamben's thesis on the social development of the species and Stiegler's concern with memory, Nietzsche ascribed considerable agency to the symbolic form of social customs that could be copied and remembered.[15] Customs so viewed could become habits totally located in the sociocultural domain, while he saw instinctual 'drives' as lodged in the biology of the 'the animal' that we are.

Memory of customs can now be understood as the harbinger of the social rules of conduct. Likewise, also as a locus from which to project beyond the present, memory is a condition that enables thinking in the medium of time; from such thinking, acts of futuring become possible. While Nietzsche, under the influence of Spencer, wished to create a convergence between natural and social selection, what actually converged was biological advancement and an expanding, efficacious social sphere. It is this sociality that started to keep the animal in check. Yet, as again Nietzsche was to argue, the drives emanating from animality provided the powering forces that sociality, in part, managed to hone and direct. Thus, the human species was taken beyond 'bare life' and the imperative of pure survival. Thereafter, self-overcoming and overcoming 'the animal within' became common features of our coming into social being.

While Nietzsche made a massive appeal to the power of 'drives'—for him the biological motor of evolution and of life itself—the power that brought us into being and propelled us futurally forward had to be far more than this. It had to be, as indicated, the combined conjunctural assemblage of the biological, the collective willing of the sociocultural and the ontological designing force of technics and object-things, all layered in memory, language and the symbolic. The significance and power of ontological design (technics in this schema) displaces any claim (including Nietzsche's claim) to consciousness as a self-transformative agency. Moreover, besides the more fundamental force of ontological design, there can be no appeal to 'the self' at the moment of the human coming into being. Selfhood was not a feature of primordial humanity.

In contrast to the evocation of consciousness, what Nietzsche more usefully outlined was the notion of structurally posited values—these coming from drives and inculcated practices transferred over time within the customs and habits of a society's past.[16]

Our aim here is not to attempt yet another comprehensive reading of Nietzsche's 'will to power' and its relation to what has been more coherently understood in his idea of 'drives'. Rather, it is to show the ontic nature of those conditions that underpin our ontological designing as they include, for instance:

- our embeddedness in the process of natural (biological) *and* unnatural (biomedical) selection
- cultural determinism as illustrated by our 'need' for food always being mediated by culturally constructed diets
- exposure to those instrumental practices of the technosphere as they are constitutive of modes of technocentric being

To comprehend the force of ontological designing indicated briefly by these three examples is to understand that power, competition (in the Darwinian sense) and survival all need to be totally reconfigured outside and beyond any biological model of evolution.

Effectively, 'will' and drives presume a sentient being and mind, whereas the telos of human transformation now and, to a great degree, in the future rests with inanimate material agents that have been given agency by human action. Put in simple terms, we gained power above that given by nature by that power coming to be posited in 'things' of our own creation. Belatedly, we are discovering that these 'things' acted back upon us in ways that ontologically transformed the 'nature' of what and where we are. Thus, while, for Nietzsche, drives were an inherent feature of all life, 'we' placed ourselves in a situation whereby we were subject to them in our animality but also were directed by powerful artificial versions of the unnaturalness of our human becoming.[17] In the forming of a world-within-the-world, a partial transference was therefore made from determinism by natural forces to a created ontologically designing of object and nonobject things. The enormous power of such things will be considered in detail a little later. For the moment, another construction of auto-human formation needs acknowledgement: culture.

Social Selection and Culture

The emergence and development of culture, in the creation of the material form and significance of world-within-the-world, under particular climatic conditions, was a major factor in the formation and ontologically designing interaction of the differences of that being that gets called human (a designation that de facto covers over difference). Culture was deemed by both Marx and Nietzsche to be elemental to the creation of a 'second nature' that was itself 'evolutionary' and folded into 'life' itself.

Fundamentally, culture is practice and as such it became a locus of being. We live in and by (a) culture. It forms what we are as much as our genes do. Culture designates the very essence of our humanity and sense (or not) of our animality. The intent of Nietzsche's problematic vitalism and nihilistic critique of culture was to try to unify our first and second natures—our animality and humanity.

What is clear is not only that this aim became ever more unrealistic to realize but also that, in Nietzsche's schema, there was no agency to attain it (he talked of interpretation and materiality which were on the inside of that which they had to be external to in order to have agency).[18] At its primordial, culture was an extension of and gave form to social practice. As such, it was a strengthening of the collective in the face of the challenges of survival, not least from nature, and the means by which anthropocentrism was structurally inscribed. This view in effect rewrites Nietzsche's will to power in the context of the human as a will without a subject.

The place of culture as a means of overcoming nature was clearly not uniform across cultures. However, those cultures that were the most aggressive in this respect are those that have become most dominant (and indivisibly structurally disposed to the destruction of the cultures of Others by striving for global cultural hegemony). Moreover, this trajectory has been unceasing. The initial overcoming of 'nature' by our distant ancestors in order to survive transmuted, over time, into a mode of survival *grounded upon* the destruction of nature.

The world of human creation fused the artefactual and the symbolic. The making of artefacts and, later, their symbolic deployment (in ritual) came out of a pragmatic situation (survival). Such action as it continued, along with the development of language, constituted another dimension of reality (culture) through which everything external to it, as well as the plurality gathered under the aegis of humanity itself, became refracted. Eventually, within the Western mode of this reality, the idea of the unified social subject was born—a singular human being subjugated to the rule of power. This being was posited by the Enlightenment (as one of its key projects) with a sense of self, within a regime of power, with a *claim* to independent life enacted via capabilities, desires, beliefs and moral values informed and managed by reason and the institutions it created. While notional aspects of this mode of being had existed in the West in varied forms since Classical Greece, it was during the Enlightenment that the idea of the subject became elevated and epistemologically designated as the 'consciousness' and counterpart to the objectified sociopolitical, legal, economic and cultural forms of the age. At its most basic, this enduring idealization was based on the notion of and the dialectical relation between 'the world' and the self—as both are experienced via 'subjectivism' but engaged and understood through 'objectification' (of Others and phenomenal forms).

Notwithstanding the layering and exposure of a great deal of complexity, contestation and a considerable critical enterprise by progressive philosophy—from phenomenology to poststructuralism, and over an extended period of time—the sovereignty of the concept of the subject functionally persists but is seriously compromised.

Making sense of worldly experience is indivisible from being-in-the world in a particular worldly location—a location containing all those practices, forces and semiotic elements that shape modes of cognition, perceptions and interpretative capabilities. But, more than this, we live in a particular kind of ecology and culture that equally lives in us. The most overt example of this is language. Language is more than just a practical medium of communication, for it is also a historically embodied and socially formative environment of becoming.

In common with Nietzsche, Heidegger made sense of experience as an active complex practice (in and) of being. But, unlike Nietzsche, who viewed culture as an unstable medium of intersubjective and sensuous activity, Heidegger mostly held a direct address to culture at bay. The exception, of course, was his infamous and disastrous venture into political culture.

In the modern era, the commodification of culture by the intervention of capital has massively transformed it. Culture arrives out of the relation between all that constitutes the symbolic domain, individual and collective experience, but all of this itself has become ever more entangled within what emanates from the marketplace, including products from the media and entertainment industries. Culture is increasingly constituted as a manufactured commodity that people buy. As such, it occupies a space of nihilism and completely loses, in the words of Walter Benjamin, 'its aura' and thus its ability to bind a community to common values and beliefs.

Un-Natural Selection Reconfronted

The relation among human artifice, cultural ecologies and biological evolutionary forces has delivered forms of unnatural selection. As we have seen, the human itself has never been simply a biological consequence.

Artifice is indivisible from design—it is both its product and its agency. As soon as hominids picked up a stone, made a tool and started to use it to alter their environment, they started to transform themselves, as well as initiating the process of forming a world-within-the-world. They also ushered in the process of 'evolution' beyond natural selection and adaptation. Maybe Darwin could have deduced this situation, but he did not. Certainly, present circumstances make it far more evident. What, however, is identifiable is that the future of humans ever rests beyond any kind of natural evolutionary dynamic. Rather, our future is directly in our hands as a species. Our collective actions in the coming decades and centuries will determine whether our species, as a finite being, is going to be reduced or extended, whether we will survive or die.

6

Coming into Being via Design

O men, in the stone an image is sleeping, the image of images.

—Friedrich Nietzsche, 1885

Design cannot be equated with how it is usually projected as a category, discourse, or professional instrumental practice: as structures, objects, images and so on. Rather, all such projections can be subsumed by seeing design being as an elemental facet of the prefigurative character of our being. This is to say that all we create is prefigured (and in some way registered or expressed) as 'the idea of the-to-be created'. Over the totality of all that brought us into being (and our being itself), this prefigurative disposition has resulted in the creation of the world-within-the-world of 'human' fabrication.

Design is more. It is an enormous complexity that is negated by almost every way that it is addressed. There is a turning away from the complexity and a turning toward trivialization, narrowing and containment by divisions of knowledge and specialisms. The argument made is 'if design is deemed to be everything, then nothing can be said of it'. This is not true—as this book strives to show. To understand what we are, have done and need to do demands that the complexity of design be engaged. The inability to do this, the inability to bring thinking about design to other thinking (not least in the arts and sciences), as it has directed other world transforming forces, has had and continues to have serious negative consequences for humanity. It marks a lack of comprehension of the directionality of artifice, form and the temporality of what is brought into being upon Being itself.

Tools

Animals, as well as humans, use tools. But it is only the human that uses tools to make tools and employs them prefiguratively to make object-things. Animals do not create technologies.

Crucially, the passage from animal to human tool-use was unbroken. More than this, tools actually played a vital role in the transition from the animal (that is, not human) to the human (that is, animal).

The notion that tools, technics, played a central part in the 'invention' of the human is not new. It was voiced, for instance, by André Leroi-Gourhan in the 1940s and rearticulated by Bernard Stiegler in 1994.[1] As Stiegler pointed out, invention here implies a movement that forms the inside and the outside of that space in which the human arrived. While we need to work over the actual process that Leroi-Gourhan detailed, the causal perspective of ontological design needs acknowledgement. Bringing ontological design and tools together will take us toward registering the importance of unnatural evolution.

The hand reached out, touched the world, and the world replied. Human action has always been predicated upon feedback. Tools, from the most basic to the most sophisticated, have merely extended the capability of this interaction.

The hand and tools, deployed in the world, do not just exteriorize the body and the intent of mind but, as indicated, constitute a prosthetic conduit between the inside and the outside, being and world. Stiegler, among others, says that 'we' are prosthetic beings.[2] As such, not only do we extend ourselves via prosthetics but, as seen by tools, they also ontologically design us as they act back upon what we are and do.[3] No matter their form, their agency is thus always a double movement—in one direction toward the world, in the other toward us.

In our self- and world-making, we touch and are touched by 'the world', and developmentally the prosthetic character of technics has been a key determinate force in this process of continuous exchange. What we are and where we exist are constituted within a naturalized artificial ecology that we, via design and technics, have created. We draw everything into this ecology by making the whole of 'nature' a material and semiotic 'standing reserve' to appropriate in this ecology's formation and deformation. In so doing, we, in our difference, have significantly but for the most part unknowingly made the world of our creation a negation of the biophysical world of our absolute dependence. In this context, tools harbour a memory of creation and instrumental use. They provide a link to the past and the future that rests upon actions of the hand in the present. In this respect, they are a product of thought that both prefigured and prefigures forms of thinking that cue actual or potential modes of use.[4]

Tools are means of amplifying the now innate and still largely undiscerned human ability to destroy in the process of material creation (making). So framed, the whole of human creation—celebrated as the rise of civilization, its materiality and culture—underscores ecological and ethnosocial devastation.[5] In their ambiguity, tools/technics can be employed to eliminate or save, build or demolish. They travel toward us with an ethical imperative that their very instrumental configuration conceals and negates.

The vector force that passes through tools, via the human agent, travels out into 'the world', as said, to transform both it and us. Our own transformation by tools has been skeletal and cortical. From the spear-thrower to the miner, from the tanner of hides to the layer of railway tracks, over time and in difference, tools have always had biomechanical, bodily designing consequences. But, equally, the demands tools made on the body were matched by those they made on the mind. For, as now, many palaeontological anthropologists tell us, tools also played a major role in our cortical development.[6] Tools obviously made the interactions between hominids and 'the world' far more complex. Dealing with this complexity and the demands it made on the development of modes of communication has been indicated as a significant factor in increasing hominoid brain size.

Tools disrupt the common perception of the brain as a fixed command centre. In company with the hand, they act as an outreach of the brain. More than this, they also extend the hand's ability to act with mind and memory, sometimes much faster than thought-directed action is able to do. Together the brain, hand and tool changed the given world to make a world of hominoid fabrication within it. This transformative capability is the essence of not only ontological design but also its unnatural 'evolutionary force'—a force that Stiegler applied to technicity and, as indictated, named *epiphylogenesis* (as remembered as evolution by other than just biological means). Design as prefigurative cognition and practice as the designed and its feedback are prior to, after and beyond technics.[7]

The prehistorical story of the hominid, the tool and our coming into being is indivisible from the passage of the animal/animal to the human/animal. This story returns us to consider in more detail the agency of the stone as it mediated the relation between the animal and the human.

The stone as tool, as already outlined, was prefigured by the hominid genus *Australopithecines,* from which the genus *Homo* diverged/emerged about two and a half million years ago. The stone used was not just any stone near to hand but a carefully selected pebble that could be used to extend the impact of the force of the hand: to smash nuts, shellfish or bones (to remove marrow), and so on. There is, in fact speculation and contested evidence that *Australopithecus Afarensis* was doing this more than a million years earlier.[8]

What is uncontested is that stone tools became more sophisticated and specialized over many hundreds of thousands of years.[9] They developed from crude tools used to bludgeon and hammer, to flaked pebbles able to scrape flesh from bone and, eventually, to fine stone blades and axe heads. During this process, such tools were used to make others of wood and bone (obviously, the biodegradable nature of these materials is the reasons why almost no evidence of their existence has survived).[10] There are, however, a few late examples of multimaterial tools that indicate that an extraordinary level of sophistication was reached (like the Natufian bone sickle with embedded flint teeth).[11]

By the time *Homo sapiens* arrived, around 160,000 years ago, there were about sixty different types of stone tools in use. In his seminal text, Leroi-Gourhan presented a detailed account and analysis of these tools; he equally gave recognition to just how significant they were in taking the genus *Homo* beyond its zoological roots.[12] The conceptual mix of tools in use forty thousand to thirty-five thousand years ago more or less matches that now found in the remote indigenous communities of the present: this mix includes spears, harpoons, hooks, knives and needles.

Six observations now follow directly from remarks made:

1. The process of tool development has both been unbroken and has continually speeded up since it commenced.
2. The break with animal tool-use was final once tools were used to make tools.
3. The very first tools become the 'core tools' from which others were made—tool-making to make tools and ever more sophisticated tools has remained a norm extending from the distant past to the present.
4. The rate of world transformation has been in direct ratio to the increased volume and power of tools,
5. The ontological designing of human beings by their use of tools has again been continuous, but growing ever more complex.
6. World-formation and the formation of the human were both elements of the same ontological designing process. This simple statement belies a contemporary condition of inordinate complexity evident in the world of artifice, material exchange, sociopolitical difference and cultural existence.

It is also worth reemphasizing that, from the very commencement of ontological designing, tools not only changed the body-muscle distribution, hand physiology, hand/eye coordination, and similar functions but, to restate, were also among the most important agents in human brain development. As Leroi-Gourhan put it, tool makers gained technical intelligence, which 'presupposes a pyramidal brain area and areas of association identical with ours'.[13]

While this process of body/brain/world ontological change has been unceasing, from the rise of modernity onward it has been accompanied by an externalization and reification of human qualities. Just prior to this moment, but most significantly during the development of machine tools, our skills, knowledge and memory were expropriated and made into a functional feature of specific machine tool technologies that had the ability to repeat the same task to produce a standardized 'interchangeable part'. But, just as the use of tools was transformative of our being, so equally were those skills taken from us and externalized via appropriative immaterial technology we ourselves created. The instrumental rationale of this movement was to enhance technology's embodied labour capabilities (and thus its productive capacity).[14] The instrumental impetus here comes from 'capital logic' (technology + volume output = reduced cost of labour and lower product unit price). What remains unclear is how the ontological designing power of such technology can be grasped and checked once recognized as an unbroken historical impetus that is increasingly taken as a given.

Unlike Leroi-Gourhan, we do not see any break between *Homo faber* and *Homo sapiens*—making tools drove cortical/cognitive development, which it-self created the conditions of reflection in the temporal gap that divides the identification of a need, the fabrication of the means to address that need and what was made. As Stiegler pointed out, Leroi-Gourhan's argument was based on a determinate function of the brain.[15] However, and in contrast, the onto-logically designing agency of making and the made placed increasing demands upon our cortical, muscular and skeletal development. Here the development process is integral and circular; the repetition of the fabricative action made demands upon the brain that increased the brain's efficacy in directing the eye and the hand, which in turn generated feedback from sensory-informed action and performative assessment. Such a process does not rest with any conscious awareness of agency in the first instance then or now (although, in very different circumstances, we, in our difference, are still a product of ontological designing of our actions and interactions).[16] 'We' remain still in the process of becoming, which is equally a drift toward our ending—'what begins must finish'.[17]

Making as a potentiality arrived via an *'augenblick'* as it harboured and lib-erated the seed of imagination—technological intelligence was therefore not just pragmatically instrumental but prefiguratively creative (albeit initially at the most modest level). This moment of human emergence out of the ability to make a world-within-the-world was indivisible from the creation of the conditions for a culture of the proto-human. The divisions among made object-things, their perception as symbolic objects, a specifically constituted way of life, and the making of symbolic forms existed as a telos.

The palaeontological focus on the tool and its application lacks recognition of tools' ontological design agency as it generated a crucial supplement to the object-thing created by the use of the tool itself—which was never merely a product of artifice. Thus, the making of object-things was equally a making of meaning that was to become attached to matter, making, the made and its use. The very basic attainments of directed labour constituted the initial building blocks of cultures of symbolic difference. Here, then, was the production of a world made meaningful that, while irretrievable for us, is embedded in what we are. The moment of the coming of meaning was the moment when the human/animal division became deeply and eternally inscribed. More specifically, world-making was never just a matter of the material fabrication of environments but was equally a making of the *habitus* that structured our becoming and of meaning able to articulate the transition from the animal/ animal to the proto-human/animal to the humanness of *communitas*.

Of course, making so understood preceded any polarization of art and technics—one cannot (yet a profusion of examples exists that speak to the contrary) backload contemporary divisions of knowledge, categories and values onto a prehistorical world of artifice and thereby tell a story of the development of the human being as a unified entity. While one may be moved by prehistoric imagery and encounter it presented by modern aesthetics as 'art' and the product of creative subjects (including geniuses), such characterizations are totally misplaced.

The earliest evidence of likely material-symbolic activity comes from excavations at the 'Twin Rivers Cave' in Zambia by Lawrence Barham of the University of Bristol in the 1990s. His work revealed a large number of pieces of pigment. They suggested that early humans engaged in body painting rituals as early as four hundred thousand years ago.[18] What is clear is that bodies were decorated a long time before images were made on the walls of caves.

The nature and purpose of such decoration is unknown. While claims are made that it was ritualistic, this cannot be confirmed, and anyway how would one understand what ritual meaning was for a hominid of this period? One could claim that such decoration was for marking tribal or family differences and thus implicated in the creation of identity of and within the species. One could also just as easily consider that the application of colour to the body was practical—perhaps camouflage for the hunter. A sociobiological thesis that associates body decoration with the loss of body hair has also been voiced. So, although such speculation may be interesting, it has nowhere to go.

Anthropology tells us that marking the self implies belonging (including as a branding of ownership), difference and recognition. No other animal did this, and one can wonder whether the production of a sign of difference did not itself prefigure an identity symbolizing nonanimality, or at least difference from the animal.

In comparative terms, the oldest symbolic object to date was found in the Blombos Cave (a cave in a cliff calcarenite limestone) on the Southern Cape coast in South Africa. The Blombos Cave people engraved pieces of ochre. These simple symbolically inscribed objects are around seventy-five thousand years old and are claimed as the oldest known 'artworks' in the world. They are thus around twice as old as the cave paintings of Europe (the forty-thousand-year-old images of Lascaux, in France, being the most famous—the fame here is not indivisible from the art institution that elevated their importance and neglected imagery in caves in many other parts of the world).

While prehistoric object-things get designated as symbolic, what their actual symbolic function was escapes us, and the very designation itself is a back-projected idea that may well be problematic. 'We' are simply in no position to ascribe symbolic or utility function to object-things that for us appear to have an indeterminate functional nature.

Clearly, the thinging of these (ontologically designing) things would have been elemental to a particular milieu of self and world-making. Part of that milieu may have been the development of skills—tactile and cognitive. Technics and technique would have gone hand in hand, as the remaining traces of these symbolic practices evidence.

The question of who or what invented the human presumes an agency external to that animal that became human. As Darwin knew but found disturbing, there was no external intent, no outside causal force, no design, no creator or creative act that brought (human) life into being. Rather, there was a process, there was a stone and there was the ontological designing of stone as it became tool and as it came to be employed by the animal in its (rich) impoverished but to-be-expanded (and later bio-environmentally impoverished) world. Here, then, with the ontologically designing ensemble of body/tool/mind, is a reiteration of the nonbiological 'naturalized artificial' dimension of human 'evolution' as it established the relational foundation of the biophysical and cultural structures that constituted what we have become.

The power and massive influence of this designing extended over an enormous expanse of time, as we saw earlier, prefiguring and, in significant part, realizing *Homo sapiens.* Such a condition of relationality is more dynamic and directive than that provided by any cybernetic model of feedback or second-order systems theory (Niklas Luhmann's reduction of complexity to system to understand complexity acts to conceal the unbroken interrelationality of *phusis* and the unreachability of the ontic).[19] There was no single causal agency driving cognitive-cortical development (as with Stiegler and *techne,* Leroi-Gourhan and the symbolic, and Agamben and language); there was just a set of conjuncturally located self-intersecting relations. In no way does this observation negate the subsequent developmental significance of *techne,* the symbolic and language. It does, however, position design as a key factor, without claiming for it any meta-designing presence.

Passing Figures of Technology

Etymologically, the word 'technology' is grounded in '*technikon*' (that which belongs to *techne*—a kind of knowing that gets reduced to 'know-how' from its original Greek, where it meant a bringing forth out of *poiesis*—which in turn meant bringing something into being by natural, instrumental (making) or aesthetic (artistic in any medium) means). By implication, *poiesis* bridges the natural and the artificial. In this relation, technology took *techne* from knowledge to practice and, in so doing, created an environment that we have called 'the world-within-the-world'.

While this world, as the naturalized artificial, is more than just technology, it is technologically infused—things spring forth (*ursprung*) technologically. This world has gone beyond the knowledge and means 'to make' and now has to be viewed as a becoming, a source of origination in its own right. In this respect, 'we' now exist in two kinds of intertwining 'natures': the biological and the technological. Both 'natures' are governed by specific but inherently internal processes (over which 'we' have very limited and diminishing control). In this context, two illusions persist.

The first illusion is the persistent proposition that the 'manipulation' of 'nature' equates to controlling it. Yet, in spite of the efforts and attainments of the natural sciences, many of the fundamental forces of 'nature' and their (re)actions are still steeped in mystery (this is true, for instance, of climate, gravity and life itself). In this respect, and so often, instrumental accounts of function frequently stand in for a real understanding.

The second illusion is that there remains, as is being pointed out, an absolute failure to realize that technology has taken on a life of its own, that it is an environment, an ecology, a 'will-to-will' that increasingly exists as a fabricated nature. For example, as forces of mind and matter, neither the Internet, nor the medium of the televisual is within the control of any individual, corporation or nation. Likewise, so many tools are no longer under the command of a specific human maker. For example, robotics production can now be directed by data culled and delivered from supply-chain feedback. Likewise, image recognition and guidance systems directed by artificial intelligence are turning aircraft pilots into systems servants, while at the same time pilotless aircraft are picking targets and launching missiles at them. Now, remembering that human beings have never merely been users of tools but were ever also their product, we see clearly that the mutual transformation of humans and technology increases at an ever more rapid pace. As Heidegger remarked nearly sixty years ago, 'the essence of technology pervades our existence in a way which we have barely noticed so far'.[20] His fear that 'technology threatens to slip from human control' is now effectively being realized.[21]

It is becoming increasingly difficult to recognize the actual 'nature' and agency of technology because it is being rendered invisible at two levels: operationally, it is out of sight (unlike the mechanical age) when based on technologies like microelectronics, nanotechnology and solid-state physics; in association, its ontological designing is shifting from physical to mental labour and into the domain of entertainment. Overtly and quietly, technology has deeply invaded everyday life at a profound level and has effectively become an occupied temporal environment. It follows that it can now no longer be simply viewed and employed as a means, not least because so much of it hides behind an interface. Added to this is the ontological designing of contemporary technologies: while often viewed as support (e.g. within education and administration), these technologies are part of an induction into instrumentally biased education and perception (a condition of being technological).

In summary, the extent to which modern technology has transformed our being-in-the-world is still underrecognized. Certainly, there is a general awareness of its material presence in the fabric of the world around us and how we engage it, but what is not grasped is how it has changed (and is changing) time and memory.

Time is not the same thing as the means employed to measure it. Time is change. It is a medium in which events occur (Aristotle); it is specific to a 'thing' itself, for 'everything has its own time' (Heidegger). So characterized, technology has accelerated change and so speeded the passage of time, with events now occurring in compressed time. Insofar as we live in an age of accelerated change, the time that everything has (the being of things) in the world around us diminishes. But, more than this, as technology has speeded the progress of the unsustainable, so 'we', as a finitudinal species, live a reduction of time.

What can be learnt from Stiegler's foregrounding of the industrialization of memory is that memory and time are being stolen from us.[22] This is not new: the externalization of memory began with the invention of writing and the diminishment of time, with accelerated productivism. What is new relates to the speed at which memory is taken from mind and installed in time-shrinking technology, objectified and valorized by very specific technologies (like informatics and many artificial intelligence-based systems).

Of Object-Thing(s)

The term 'thing' is deceptive and etymologically complex. It can seem simple, self-evident and interchangeable with 'object'. But in any considered usage, and specifically in how it will be employed here, it is no such *thing*.

The *Oxford English Dictionary* tells us the word has many origins in Old Saxon, Old English, Middle English, Old Frisian, Old High German and Old Norse. From these languages, a multiplicity meanings for 'thing(s)' endures. It has meant a political, legal or social assembly or gathering (such as a public meeting, council, parliament or court of law); that with which one is concerned; an entity of any kind that exists; substance or object; the other of the symbolic; a person in contempt; an item of property; articles of apparel and more. Heidegger tells us the Greeks term for 'things' (πραγματα) resonates with an array of meanings.[23] The ancient Greeks used it to denote 'that which one has to deal with in one's concernful dealings'. More pragmatically and immediately, the term was reduced to usage characterized by what Heidegger names 'equipment'. The modern Greek usage defines it as affairs of interest (practically and politically).

Recently the 'thing' has attracted philosophical and philological inquiry, as well as the recovery of its more arcane political meaning.[24] Our engagement with the notion of thing(s) touches on and extends a view of things from a perspective grounded in the object relation of tools, techn(e)ology and making a world. As such, object-thing(s) enable us to name much that existed prelinguistically in the sense of the made that was not prefigured by its name, be it a social article (an event) or a substance (a made object).

We have seen the object-thing 'stone' implicated in an event of being as becoming. World-less, it was world-shaping.

Maurice Merleau-Ponty considers the relation between the stone and the world, as it presumes a synthesis in which the one is of the other, while recognizing that they exist with totally different horizontal limits.[25] He resolves this seeming contradiction by evoking experience as the means to realize the synthesis.[26] All things, no matter their material or immaterial form, once perceived, exist relationally as a singularity equally elemental to the whole (world). They are bound up with one another rather than being independently given to perception. All things thus exist in a horizonal structure whereby their identity is derived from what they are not and what they are within an experiential typology. As Merleau-Ponty puts it: 'The thing and the world only exist only in so far as they are experienced by me, or by subjects like me.'[27]

But we have seen beyond the subject of experience. We have a sense that there is, was and will be a world of object-things beyond my immediate perception that are indivisible from me and human becoming. Such recognition requires what John Sallis calls a *hermeneutical shift* between thing, world and memory.[28] In this context, world was formed via remembered relations between environments and things, rather than by an act of fundamental disclosure. Moreover, because the identity of an object-thing is contextually located, it has a particular but provisional presence. What is being marked here is the move from an essentialist phenomenology, based on the notion of a thing showing itself from itself, to a hermeneutical phenomenology where things show themselves from within the world ('world' here is not the geophysical object but the experiential locus of a being-in-the-world), to the ontological designing of a 'world-in-being' wherein object-beings and beings-in-the-world prefigure a form of being, perception and experience.[29]

Making things (with tools) can now be seen as not just an act of ontological design producing the 'nature' of a being in the world, world-forming actions and a world-within-the-world *but* equally a basis to fabricate a way of seeing formative relations between the made object-thing as it constitutes the possibility of an identity of the maker and the thing-in-the-world. What things impart to us is a consequence of what Merleau-Ponty calls their 'sensible aspects'. To explain this relational perspective, he uses the example of the colour of a carpet, which to be totally communicated to another requires address to its material, texture and so on.[30] His thinking here was equally applied to how we view our bodily selves. Our bodily 'thingness' arrives as an assemblage of parts: head, eyes, arms, hands, torso, legs, feet and so on as it moves toward and exists within a world of other things as a whole, rather than as a mere collection of parts, both similar and different. In this setting and without overt objectification, the thing that we are is indivisible from the person we become.[31] We are effectively placed within a pattern of linked things that give the status and character of (a) life in and for itself. Within this pattern, we become present for each other only from a particular and worldly point of view.

Phenomenology of the Thing

Object-things, no matter their form, can never be simply taken as empirically given and thus deemed knowable descriptively. Obviously, a thing is not its name; not so obviously, it is an entity with indeterminate agency in immi-nence. Hermeneutical phenomenology brings the identity of things into ques-tion. It sees the thing in a relational field of existence as objectified, image, the experienced and the remembered. Yet it stands on the fundamental proposi-tion of phenomenology enunciated by Edmund Husserl in 1911 that 'research must not proceed from philosophies but from things and problems'.[32] But, as we have seen, there are no things, no objects, without subjects.

Object-things present themselves, in contrast to how their being is pre-sented by a perceived image. They thus have a presence that is defined against that which is other than the thing and an identity that references other things. Phenomenology sets out to disclose what is actually present, the very being of the thing. In so doing, it recognizes that the experience of the thing is always the result of a partial perception and thereafter con-fronts the identity of the thing as it exists between its being (what it is) and its mode of being made present (de facto a distinction between appearance and being).[33] Presence, however, cannot presume singularity or passivity of an object-thing (especially when it is an object-thing-making thing—a tool).

In having a time of their own, object-things change—an overt agent of change for much of what we bring into being is, of course, use. In use, object-things not only acquire their agency (what Heidegger called thinging) but also disclose their essence. In acting upon the world, they always transform it in some way. In their animated condition, object-things are never alone; they are with us and in company with us. Object-things become simultaneously objects of inner and outer transformation and experience. Again, as John Sallis comments:

> the radicalness of phenomenology requires that one avoid simply identifying the things themselves with empirically given things; and so to construe phenomenology as empiricism is precisely to miss its radicalness, its directedness to the originary.[34]

Our world—the world of human fabrication within the world—is a world of active object-things. From our very beginning, their ontological designing contributed to bringing our being into being. The artist, writer, musician, cabinet-maker, politician, surgeon, chef, welder and so on would not be what they are without the object-things that have enabled them to become what they are. Not only is the lineage of ontological designing of the human unbroken from the age of stone tools to the present, but to understand this is to realize that human being, nonhuman being and the being of inanimate things are all relationally bound in (our) Being. We are of the stone, the animal and the human.

Lest we forget: the memory of things is vested in things themselves—they are iterations of remembered and forgotten forms. Memories are short and long, exposed and concealed, held in tradition or erased by 'progress'. With the industrialization of memory, memory itself is being made a thing.

Part III

The Leap

Photography: Peter Wanny / Illustration: Tony Fry

The inability of the human being as the 'subject of history' *to comprehend the world is a painful thing.*

—Christoph Wulf, 1989

From our preoccupation with the prehistorical, we will now take a leap to the modern, its formation, and beyond. We will be leaping out of where we have been and leaping ahead to where we are going. In truth, all that we deem to be the narrative of our worldly existence is an interval between two points of the unknowable. We know almost nothing of our distant past and even less of our immediate and distant future, except to say that the problems we have thrown into it are speeding toward us with constantly increasing velocity. The narrative claims that fill that space we call 'history' are but clustered fragments. Any account of our being as Being defies narrativization, and there can be no position of observation from which to write a meta-history of the human. The very notion of 'world history' (in a global sense) is an ethnocentric conceit. Thus, there is no history without a leap, and the leap we make here is filled with a multiplicity of historical fragments that all who care to look can find with ease under the heading 'the history of civilization'.

All the concerns that have so far been raised in earlier chapters will remain in play; some of them will be revisited in greater detail.

We understand, at least to some extent, how human beings came to be what they now are; what is far less clear is how we can continue to be out into the future as measured against the time taken to arrive at 'now'. One can ask questions. What, in difference, are 'we' becoming? What exactly delimits the time we have? Most important, is our species fated? If we have a future, how do we find the will and the means to get to it? Clearly, one cannot expect definitive answers to such questions, yet they demand to be thought. For the alternative, like it or not, is simply to drift blindly toward ever-deepening defuturing.

7

Why Make the Leap?

The disaster takes care of everything.

—Maurice Blanchot

In making a leap from a distant past to now, the issue of time returns to confound us—this as much due to time's misplaced characterization as measurement at the hand of physics. More than this, we also have to discover how to make the leap from where we are developmentally now to where we need to be futurally.

Time Wise

Time cannot be contained as a discourse: the gap between *chronos* (time as a medium) and *kairos* (time as the right and opportune moment) is unbridgeable. So, too, is the gap between the characterization of time by physics (a dimension) and a philosophy of time (multiple levels of temporality wherein everything has its own time). Notwithstanding a commonality of word, there is no shared object of reference. Time objectified is always time negated by change (*aeternitas*, a continuum of the pure present of a passing away and a passing to—a moment while futural has no past or future). In an essential sense, as Heidegger, Einstein and Aristotle all pointed out, 'time is nothing' and exists 'merely as a result of events taking place within it'.[1] All events are change.

Physics has taken the measurement of time beyond normal 'human' comprehension. Who is able to grasp that 'a second is the duration of 9,192,631,770 periods of the radiation corresponding to the transition between the two hyperfine levels of the ground state of the cesium-133 atom'?[2] As measurement, as an anthropocentric invention (as is all measurement), time is merely an operative mechanism of regulation. Instrumentally, it works and makes many things possible. Yet it adds nothing to how the phenomenon of time needs to be understood phenomenologically.

As we have already pointed out, everything has its own time (even a clock);[3] time is endless change and is not uniform. Nothing is exempt from change; nothing in and of 'the world' is eternal.

Our perception of time in the everyday is delimited by several factors:

- The event of our own being-in-time (which we 'take' as our foundational reference of time, wherein the sense of our own mortality directs the intensity of life—thus we live toward death, with a diminishing sense of permanence)
- The notion of the passage of 'natural time' (day/night, the seasons and so on)
- Our being put before abstracted time (historical, pre-historical and cosmic)

As Heidegger pointed out, 'the fundamental phenomenon of time is the future—everything changes toward the future and constitutes it'.[4] *Dasein*, as that event of being-in-the-world, is change and a futural negation of 'now'. To be human is to seek to be directive of change. The essence of this action is prefiguration; it is design. By implication, all design(ing) is design in time.[5]

Leaping Forward

We human beings in all our differences, as the defuturing core of the unsustainable, have an absolute need to leap from what we have become to what we essentially need to be: futural. But, currently, our mode of change is a negation: it is a dissipation of our species time. To have a need does not mean to know it. Even when it is recognized, need is responded to in difference. The futural project that is needed is 'the Sustainment'—a commonality able to be worked toward only as a making of time in the face of that negation which is defuturing.

Conceptually, we can say (at the very least to ourselves) that to become other than we are requires two linked moves: the recovery of imagination (which means acknowledging that it has been lost) and the establishment of the sovereignty of Sustainment (that which demands to be imagined).

To do this is very hard. It involves a great deal of destruction—including of the existent dynamic of production (which has never ceased to accelerate over the totality of our being as makers); and overcoming productivism's blindness to what it destroys as it creates. Likewise, 'need' has to be turned on its head to become a condition of limitation. Which is to say that what one might want can be viewed as uncontainable, but what one actually materially needs is finite. This is not to reduce need to a utilitarian formula or to suggest needs are uniform. Rather, it is to acknowledge that one can place 'a self in need' before an ethical diagnostic that asks 'is what is needed futural?' The imperative to do this does not centre on any kind of moralism. Rather, the ratio between our accelerated entropic mode of being (our unsustainability) and our finitude provides the basis of measuring need as futural (or not). Wants can proliferate, but only without transgressing the condition of limitation of need. Obviously, the ease with which such statements can be made in no way reflects the complexity of bringing them into any kind of reality (not least across the politicocultural divides of difference).

Development, as embedded in the rise and fall of reason, has never been development defined as that, which directionally, is fundamentally futural. It has always stood upon practices of erasure: practices that were incapable of discerning the value of what was being destroyed in relation to that which was being created. Globally, industrially, economically, development has never been ethical. Writ large, the map of the world, the dispersal of people and global inequity all supports this claim.

In the light of remarks made, what does the leap really mean?

First, it means leaping to reconceptualize 'the world' and reforming ourselves within this new understanding. This is nothing to do with redrawing the geopolitical map and everything to do with repositioning ourselves within our mode of being-in-the-world. It is about how we see ourselves as conduits connected to object-things, animals and human Others, dwelling in every respect in mind and matter. This leap effectively folds into a continual act of a self-world re-creation and remaking (a generalized and unending project of ontological design that learns from how we came into being as an indivisible self/world-formative construction).

The leap also means bringing unsettlement 'to light' and confronting the actual instability of that which appears to be a stable foundation of modern life—urban existence. As with the initial event of our becoming 'human', urban existence did not occur at a preselected moment and in chosen circumstances. In the same way, whatever affirmative change can be created, 'we' can be sure it will not emanate from an abstract system, no matter of what order or how formulated. Change here can be but an overcoming of nihilism— a designing out of a created wasteland.

As indicated, the ability to move and adapt is what enabled *Homo sapiens* to survive massive climatic changes for more than 150,000 years. Increasingly, over the past ten thousand years, 'we' human populations have become more sedentary, concentrated and encased in thermal mass (mostly steel and concrete). In the unfolding climatic circumstances of this planet, this makes us extremely vulnerable. At the most basic and biophysically, this condition exposes us to, for instance, greater risk from 'natural disasters' (as our cities grow larger and denser), pandemic vector-carried diseases, the impacts of heat (islanding), extreme weather events of every kind, fires and loss of fresh water supply. In the face of this situation, we need to change how we dwell in the most simple of ways. Our manner of earthly habitation has to be deformed and transformed.

Notwithstanding a growing, if still very marginal cluster of material practices that claim to be promoting and enabling such actions, change cannot be attained purely via instrumental means. The only path to Sustainment (the project and product of transformation) has to be led by *praxis*. Thus, before action is taken, it has to be placed before a comprehensive, theorized and conjuncturally located understanding of the problem to be surmounted, as well as a very clear sense of capability and limitations.

A prerequisite for this hugely daunting task, besides the courage to begin it and the recognition that it is an event beyond the familiar register of time (and history/historicity), is to move, as we will, to reconsider the very notion of 'world' (and, thus, self).

8

The Passage from 'Here and Now' to 'Then'

The loss of material space leads to the government of nothing but time

—Paul Virilio

One cannot stop that which is powerfully predestined.

No matter whether or not we know it, you and I, together with the remaining population of this planet, are all living in a condition of increasing unsettlement—a condition that the agenda of sustainability has not begun to recognize. Having said this, and before moving to outline some specific features of our present moment and thereafter to a futural perspective to inform a *praxis*, we need to clarify the term 'defuturing'.

Unsustainability defines a condition trapped in the grip of relativism. It is regarded either as a correctable tendency of the status quo or as an absolutely irredeemable condition. In contrast, defuturing is explicit. As already said, it indicates a historically embedded process that has taken and is taking the future away. The history of this process centred on a failure to grasp and engage what was being destroyed in the making of the modern world. As such, unsustainability travelled with and was speeded by modernity in multiple ways. In particular, it was structural to the rise of capitalism and the production of wealth by exploitation of natural resources without account. Associated with this was the relentless increase in the capacity to produce goods that was enabled by rapid development of industrial technologies and processes and the eventual globalization of mass production and world markets. Within this economic Leviathan and supporting it was modern warfare, with its weapons of 'mass destruction', the creation of an extensive urban fabric accommodating a huge international labour force and the vast cultural and technological infrastructure of mass communication and entertainment that became deeply embedded in the 'everyday' everywhere. Design was implicated in the rise of every one of these developments, as was the hand of defuturing.

In the passage of defuturing, what has been negated gets objectified and named in various ways, like climate change (de facto the name of a damaged atmospheric system); the loss of biodiversity (de facto the name of the destruction of animal and plant species); and pollution (de facto the poisoning of air, earth, rivers, lakes and oceans).[1] While these 'impacts' are serious, what remains largely ignored is how an ontological designing resulting from those defuturing practices that negate a world of fundamental dependence has naturalized a state of being-in-the-world that acts against the future.

To suggest, as we have, that 'we' have been predisposed toward unsustainability from our inception (thus prefigured as agents of defuturing) is in fact to suggest that anthropocentrism and defuturing are indivisible. It has been our human-centredness that made us unaware of the extent and consequences of what we have destroyed (and continue to destroy). This 'trait' was not much of a problem until it became technologically amplified by the combination of our growing numbers and the ever-increasing power of technology.

Once more we assert, 'we' are the problem. Defuturing has been made elemental to the essence of human being, and it cannot be separated from our failure to recognize our animality.

But Exactly Where Are We?

We know we are a finite species on a finite planet (as are all species living on this finite planet; as are all planets). The common assumption that this issue exists at such a distance and at such an unimaginable moment means that it is disregarded. Our finitude may be distant, but equally it could be very near. Our fear of time, our 'chronophobia', draws a veil over what futuring demands we face.

Currently, in the face of significant environmental change, we confront the imperative to adapt. Our animality feels this need (animals get unsettled), but the human seeks 'solution technologies' so that this feeling can be ignored. Our future, its quality and possibility, depends on adaptation. Yet the need to adapt still gets scant public exposure. Most concerning of all is that the speed and extent of change (not least climatically) has taken us outside 'biological time'—because we can now adapt only artificially, adaptation is wholly in the domain of the human.

It is worth reminding ourselves that how we are now and how we live are a product of adaptation to a changing climate. Culture, climate and change have always been closely connected. Thus, our cultural differences (for instance, our dwellings, what we farm and eat, our dress, our rituals and traditions, even our cosmologies) are all inflected by the climates of particular geographies. Human settlement, which started in the Fertile Crescent in Southern Mesopotamia some ten thousand years ago, was (like later developments in the Near East and China) a product of a changing climate and its effect on the availability of food.[2]

The rise of human settlement was closely connected to the climatic conditions at the end of the Ice Age, around 15,000 BP (before present). The milder climate that followed the Ice Age stimulated an enormous increase in food resources over the next two thousand years.[3] Then the situation reversed during the 'Younger Dryas' (11,000–10,300 BP). During this period, the availability of food was drastically reduced. The Fertile Crescent of the Levant was one region not so adversely affected. Food sources like wild wheat and barley remained available. The Neolithic people of the region (the Natufians) were mobile harvesters of these crops. However, between 10,000 and 9,500 BP, conditions in this region had greatly improved, while climatic conditions to the East and West deteriorated. As a result, the Natufians became semisedentary. They took advantage of areas that were actually lush, with more than a hundred types of cereals, fruits, nuts and edible plants. They started to develop harvesting techniques—techniques that prefigured methods of agricultural cultivation. These favourable conditions, in turn, increased population densities. While people remained seminomadic, by 9,300 BP small settlements began to be created, and, by 7,800 BP, large, established villages were common–with the first city of the region (Urak) built about five hundred years later.

In our unfolding 'age of unsettlement', significant displacements of populations can be expected. Certainly, we cannot return to being nomads, but equally we cannot survive as sedentary in ever larger and denser cities that simply amplify our vulnerability to both extreme weather events and conflict. These circumstances, combined with what will be a growing need for climate adaptation, means there will be an increasing need to learn lessons of nomadic and seminomadic life from the past. Thus, presettlement climate and associated ways of life now starts to look like something we need to understand far better.

Futuring against Defuturing

Placing our selves before the challenge of defuturing, we are, for the most part, ignoring three fundamental factors.

First, unsustainability is relational. The actual complexities of causal relations get displaced by the ways they are rationalized and represented (which is to imply the limits of reason). This situation is serious: without an understanding of relational causality, there can be no way toward effective long-term solutions. This is evident when one looks at many of those actions that define themselves as advancing sustainability. Thus, building 'sustainable buildings' for unsustainable organizations making unsustainable products doesn't get us very far; neither do niche market 'green products' in expanding mass markets or low-emissions energy-generation systems in situations where there is an unchecked, expanding demand for energy or organic produce which is air-freighted from one side of the globe to another. Obviously, there are some worthwhile things being done, but, put alongside the scale and the pace of 'the problem', these actions are at best token, at worst totally irrelevant. The actual challenge is to deliver those ontological conditions that overdetermine market forces to reconstruct and redirect consumer desires.

The second point follows on directly from the first. The capitalist economy, which is hegemonic in nature and is a structure that structures, is predicated upon the proposition of continual economic growth. Because we are a finite species on a finite planet, our continual growth is as impossible as perpetual motion. More than this, the mode of exchange of the capitalist economy is disengaged from those fundamental relations of exchange of animal, vegetable and mineral matter (the general economy that life itself depends upon). Yet the nonrelationality of capitalism's 'restrictive economy' is barely acknowledged. Put simply, 'we' (and much else) cannot live postecologically. An inability to recognize this situation—effectively a failure of reason and techno-romanticism—has consequences that overdetermine 'our' ability to identify and deliver 'solutions'. Crucially, it obstructs the necessity of finding ways to move from a quantity- to a quality-based economic paradigm.

Unlike the failure of understanding that underscores factor one and the structural nature of factor two, factor three is now travelling toward us. It is the likely conflicts and geopolitical changes (including to the form of nation) that will arrive in coming decades from climate-change impacts.

According to research from many strategic think tanks and from nongovernmental organizations like the International Red Cross, huge numbers of people are likely to be displaced by climate change (maybe even 10 per cent of the global population by the middle of the twenty-second century). This situation is going to create not only a refugee problem of an unprecedented scale but, as many military strategic planners around the world are recognizing, also dangerous situations as threat as much as fact. Displaced people are likely to cross borders uninvited in huge numbers, states will fail and human populations will redistribute. There are other reasons why concern over conflict is high and why a number of researchers, notably Gwynne Dyer and James Lees, and lead research organizations, like the US Strategic Studies Institute, tell us that climate change equals conflict.[4]

The potential causes for conflict are many, and any ability to name and locate them over time is very limited. Here, briefly, are three already identified hot spots: the Northwest Passage through the Arctic, which is already opening up to shipping, where melting ice will also expose mineral resources upon which power bloc nations will stake claims (in fact, Russia has already created two brigades to protect its potential interests); Equatorial Africa, where agriculture and hydrological systems will fail because of heat, which will prompt hungry populations to move en masse and uninvited to other nations; and Bangladesh, where tens of millions of people displaced by sea-level rises who have nowhere to go will go somewhere. All of these prospects are imminent (that is to say, they can be expected in the next twenty to one hundred years). But this gives little sense of what will unfold over the next millennium and beyond (the temporal reality of anthropogenic climate change as it swings toward the longer 'natural' cycle of radical climate transformation that is elemental to the planet).

It is very likely that many nations will not be able to withstand the combination of the impacts of climate change, a massive influx of unwelcomed people and conflict. There are two informed perspectives on the nature of conflict: once it commences, it will continually increase, and it will be asymmetrical (which means it will have no clear beginning or end, no defined battlefield, and no identifiable distinction between combatants and civilians). Some states will simply implode. In some parts of the world, there may be a reversion to forms of tribalism. Without doubt, whatever is said here, the situation that humanity will face will actually be far more complex than the complexity mooted.

These kinds of changes, as they unfold over coming decades, will not only change the world we inhabit but also change us (in all our differences). As we have already made clear, no matter where we are, no matter our age, our economic status, our culture or beliefs, we will become profoundly unsettled. More than this, our actual psychology will change. Exactly how is hard to say, but what is clear is that so much that is taken for granted as the normal functioning of everyday life will no longer be so. Insecurity will dramatically deepen. It is almost certain that consumer-driven desires will be transformed and displaced, at worst by extreme nihilism, at best by recognition of the need for and action toward redefining the relations among humans, animals, things and environments. Critically, the way we understand time will have to change significantly and our propensity toward chronophobia be transcended. More concretely, our perceptions of urbanization and cities will alter profoundly.

It may well be the case, as will be explored in chapter 12, that cities as we know them do not have a future. Sea-level rises, heat islanding, extreme weather events and conflict could cause havoc on a scale that has not been seen since human settlement commenced. But such havoc was known in the long-distant past—when the Ice Age reduced the population of *Homo sapiens* to just a few thousand (of whom we are the descendants).

It would be erroneous to suggest that cities have only a single fate. To make this clear, a few prospects beg a brief review. The qualification here is that the perspective is of the order of around two hundred years. Measured from how we currently think, this seems a long time; viewed against our species' time, it is but a brief moment and, in geological time, but a nanosecond.

In a few decades, it is likely that cities, in whole or part, may start to be abandoned, that informal cities will dramatically grow, while other cities may well become fortified[5] (in some respects, this process has already started).[6] Another process that has already started is the movement of cities.[7] Yet another prospect, as the technology already exists, is the construction of underground cities. Most radical of all is the development of nomadic urbanism (at the most schematic futuring level, this suggests that urbanism and nomadism will be brought together through the notion of the 'urmadic' city—a city that can be moved, a city to create, a city of the not-too-distant future).[8]

What will all these changes add up to? Certainly, one can expect major disruptions to existing modes of earthly habitation (as suggested, there are signs that this has already started). What will eventually replace these modes, and how long will this take? Is it possible to answer such questions? Certainly, unsettlement, in shattering a sense of planetary stability, will prompt us to confront and answer them. Yet the still very limited view of time as event has to be transcended.

Futuring depends on learning to create a long view. Rather than constructing 'visions of the future', the aim is to create a way of thinking predicated on the future as world-making in the present and in conditions of uncertainty. At present, we dominantly still think and make in space, not time.

If we presume that a great deal of the existing material and immaterial made world around us will fall, we need to ask questions upon which to tell stories of change. For example, can nations survive as viable sociopolitical structures? What will come after democracy fails to be able to advance conditions of Sustainment? Will new geopolitical structures arrive, and what will they look like? Can we expect 'tribal cultural economies' to form out of conflict? What level of technological penetration of our bodies will occur? Will the integrity of the species *Homo sapiens* hold? How will existing communication technologies, national security structures, social structures, and food-production systems cope with global hypertrauma? The point of these questions, which are not exactly in the domain of the unthought or unthinkable, is that they are directive (and so futural) and beg ethical engagement. This is to say that we need to create those questions that inform the action of designing toward or away from their answers.

Whatever eventuates, it is almost certain that there will be considerable forms of economic, political and cultural breakdown. Rather than being negative or 'doomsaying', saying this is realistically facing the likely truth of human futures. What is absolutely clear is that, in order to deal with the future, there is an urgent need to confront all possible prospects and possibilities, both good and bad. For this to happen, there has to be a leap in critical thought, imagination and prefigurative action. To do this, we in our difference have to go beyond what we are at present. By implication, and acknowledging that progressions of the species are always uneven, there is a need to leap to and into another form of being. Insofar as this being has to be in advance of what we currently are, it would be a 'super-being', but of course the kind of usage to which the word 'super' has been put casts it into a pit of debased language. So, while such acts of naming are always problematic, let's coin a term that perhaps has a slightly more acceptable and less gendered connotation—for this 'super-being' now read 'humax'. We also note that the rhetoric of posthumanism gets nowhere near the challenge of this act of *palingensia*.

But what are we? Heidegger told us we are not like the animal—poor of world and captured within the 'ring' of its encircling environment. Rather, we are rich of world—yet our wealth comes via the gift of the stone and the animal (as our animality is transcended—or is it?).

Yet we have recognized that another kind of captivity delimits us: the limitation of anthropocentrism. It encircles us and restricts our ability to relationally comprehend and ontologically grasp what we are and do and to what we are connected. It is our absolute source of unfreedom. Once, all that had to be understood was the indivisible relation among the stone, the animal and the human. Now we confront all that this relation has brought into being as it ontologically constitutes what we are and will become.

Rather than the idea of 'sustainability' providing a route to salvation and the future, sustainability is actually unable to comprehend both what threatens and what has to be saved—not least because it just does not confront the root cause of the unsustainable: anthropocentrism. More than this, it does not realize that any future form of freedom stands on a new order of delimitation (unfreedom).[9]

Part IV

From 'Where We Were' to 'Where We Are'

Photography: Peter Wanny / Illustration: Tony Fry

> I believe that the only real significance of pre-history, whether resting on religious metaphysics or materialist dialectics, is that it situates the people of the future in their present as well as in their most distant past.

> —Andre Leroi-Gourhan, 1964

Who are we? We answer: '(wo)man'.

Notwithstanding the gendered problem of the term 'man' in English, its usage endures.[1] Heidegger puts the question of man into question when he suggests we ask not 'what man is' but 'who man is.'[2] His answer: 'man is a self...not indifferent to its own mode and possibility of Being.'[3] For Heidegger, then, it is Being that is the issue of focus. Most critically, he asserts that 'Man is a self, and not a living thing with some spiritual endowments, but a being that in advance *decides about its own Being,* in this or that way. This is quite a different fundamental position, based on man's possibility and necessity of Being.'[4] Crucially, Heidegger points out that 'only because man is a *self* can he be an I and a you and a we. Being a self is not a consequence of being an I'.[5] More than this, he framed his thinking here by earlier stating that asking about *man* is: 'the guiding question we must pose in all our reflections, the question of *historical* man. In asking this question, we must ask in the correct way. This—asking in the correct way—is the task of the philosophy of the future'.[6]

Heidegger designates the distinctive characteristic of man as 'care'. He speaks of care 'not as an anxious fussing of some neurotic, but this fundamentally human way of Being, on the basis of which there are such things as resoluteness, readiness for service, struggle, mastery, action as an essential possibility'.[7]

In Part IV we will be moving from looking at issues of our species origin, and the forces that directed our becoming to another frame of reference—the relation between our dwelling in a world (as world itself is brought into question) and the significance of imagination. This is engaged in terms of the place of imagination in the formation of 'the modern mind' and then 'the modern mind's' ability to deal with the challenges of a world it helped bring into existence, specifically as this world acts to defuture 'the world' upon which all else depends. In doing this, the limits of the agency reason will be exposed.

The final chapter of Part IV returns to the problematic question of the social subject to review how it has been understood and how this understanding is implicated in the unfolding of current circumstances

9

World-in-Being

The fact that we are incapable of learning anything from history any more says only that we ourselves have become ahistorical. No period has known such an influx of tradition, and none has been so poor in genuine tradition. λσγοζ, ratio, reason, spirit—all these titles are disguises for the problem of world.

—Martin Heidegger, 1929/30

Seemingly the most concrete of all things, 'world' is knowable only subjectively. Being here (*Dasein*) as an inducted 'being-in-the-world' is reachable only by anthropocentric mechanisms of perceptual mediation. As such, *Dasein* always exists outside itself—it cannot be dislocated from a world and thus be a 'thing-in-itself'. Nothing is objectively present for us (which is to say not that there is nothing objective phenomenally but rather that we can never know it—the ontic—as such).[1] In fact, for us, 'world' disappears with objectification. Obviously, 'things' are or can be at hand, but, as soon as they are made present as 'objects in the world' by or for us, the world itself is rendered absent.[2]

Reaching for a 'Real World'

The point to be made here is not a refusal of 'the real' but rather an acknowledgement that, for us, world is reachable only via some form of reduction that delivers an illusion of external observation. This follows a history of reduction whereby *phusis* was diminished as 'nature'—so it is with 'world' as 'the world'.

For us, the notion 'world' is constantly, and mostly unknowingly, mobilized as a heuristic device, but one that misleads rather than enlightens. 'World' is ever encased in, to evoke Fredric Jameson's notion, the 'prison house of language'.[3] Although language seems to deliver 'world' as a sensible entity of view, what it does is 'hold' us within its manner of making it present. Likewise, other modes of expression (image, music, dance) either stay encased in an individualistic hermeneutic experience or get negated via translation into language to be re-presented. Across cultures, 'world' does not exist as a singular view, a hermeneutic commonality. Notwithstanding continual appeals (not least by the media) to 'the world', there are only plural worldviews or a void. Difference thus always stands between 'world' as the ontic and ontological engagement and modes of making 'it' present.

Here is the locus of a dialectic whereby 'the world' and 'the human' constitute each other—the one cannot be seen independently from the construction of the other.

The notion of language as supplement, mobilized by Jacques Derrida, helps us see the difference between the world that 'just is' and what it is that we actually bring to presence when we use the name of 'the world'. How its presence, as 'now', is disclosed is always dependent upon metaphysical inscription—one that writes over, covers over the trace of a prior moment (the past) and forms an illusion that the signified is actually present when the signifier is evoked.[4] All we are saying here, as Heidegger also made clear, is that the phenomenal world is never actually reached (and not just by language).[5] So, for instance, all the knowledge of 'the world' created by the natural sciences is both a metaphysical manufacture of 'a world made present' and an ontological sending away. The world of 'man' is not the being of the world.

That, ontically, there is 'a world' is beyond question—this 'world' conceptually stood for Heidegger as the totality of beings actually present within 'the world'. The idea of 'having a world' is a world ontologically made present, acquired and experientially known—here is the culturally relative and perceptually framed 'world' into which we are inducted and which we get to know. So, in a globalized sense, it is clear that there is no general, single and reachable common world. But within our familiar culturally constructed world—the world we have—we do share common perceptions of what is 'real', what functions, what are aesthetic forms, and so on. But, contrary to this situation, the Other always invades the familiar. Thus, the whole history of colonialism, modernity, ethnocentricity and Eurocentrism ruptures the integrity of the 'world we have'. Moreover, while the world of/as difference extends over planetary geopolitical configurations and exposes lived worlds as plural, 'otherness' is now no longer delimited by specific geographical locations—it is of the everywhere.

The de-familiarization of the world begs re-emphasis. We are not and have never been purely external observers of 'the world': we are of that which we are within. 'To be born is to be born of the world and into it'—we exist as both 'in and of' at the same moment. Biologically, we are born, but equally we are brought into being by the ontological designing of the particular world into which we arrive. We are equally an object of determination and a condition of possibility.

No matter what we become, we are not born into the same world, the same worldhood (a specific being of that entity we call world).[6] Put simply: to be born into the environment of a European city rather than a village in a jungle in Borneo is to arrive into a dramatically different, ontologically designing condition generative of another kind of becoming. Clearly, the worldly difference of such becoming (coming to be what we are over time—our slow progression to adulthood and death) is not just a biocultural formation in the spatiomaterial environment (the environing world) within which we are nurtured. *Rather*, it is the beginning of a worldly transformative event emanating from our being-in-the-world (this, no matter whether the transformations are minute or huge). So, in essence, we are all, in significant part, changed by 'our world' but, and by varied degrees, we all also change the world in some way. It follows that two people can never be born into the same world. The temporal character of 'the world' (the world we have) is always changing and being changed, and thus time always flows unevenly.

Existence here is among and dependent upon other beings and nonbeings—'the world' is shared. Relationality is the condition of this sharing. As Nietzsche puts it, 'the World is at first relationally and affectively present: it affects us and we act in and through it.'[7]

The 'stone, the animal and the human' exemplify the relationally connected whole (another definition of 'world'), and, in this respect, Heidegger's issue of deprivation, of poverty of world, does not arrive. If it is not known or felt, it has no presence other than for the agent of designation. Deprivation really arrives only when anthropocentrically framed, that is, when the idea of 'world' is evoked purely to name a condition (world) that can and does exist only for us. World for us, then, is a registration of a manifestation of being (in-the-world) in difference.[8] In order for a knowable world to be, there had to be beings present to know and name.[9] De facto, 'world' is always affirmed to be, via multiple perspectives. Notwithstanding the agency of globalization, it is not spoken via any single voice (and never can be); thus, 'it' is the expression of a socially constructed field of plural existence.[10] As modernity expanded its global reach (under colonialism's banner of 'the bringing of civilization'), as was the case with earlier forms of imperialism, worlds were both destroyed and created. For hundreds of millions of people, such a violent shattering and transformation of 'their world' changed time and being for them. World, then, was and is, not simply a formation of a knowing in place, for it was and is always also historically prefigured with futural intent. Not only was it the present; it was equally the given time to come from the past.

The exploitation of colonized people was only half the story—the other side was the plundering of natural resources, animal (including the human 'animal'), vegetable and mineral. So framed, colonialism, in the service of capitalism, marked a quantum leap in the advance of unsustainability (at the level of both the subject and objective conditions). If we actually bring *unsustainability* and *colonialism* together, under the unification of the Enlightenment, we see that its product, Eurocentric anthropocentrism, served them both in negation. As such, these relations of negation are but subsets of the 'dialectic of Sustainment' as it expresses the indivisible relation between creation (the colony) and destruction (the colonized).

Being thrown (born) into 'the world' is to arrive in a dual condition where, as we have seen, self and world formation jointly occurs always in the company of Others: embedded in them is what we have already been and are yet to be.[11]

No matter our cultural difference, our history, its trauma or privilege, we all share a condition of worldhood—which is how Heidegger described our existential condition of 'being-in-the-world'.[12] This condition is precisely convergent with *Dasein*. Being here is being-in-the-world, which is equally being-in-time. For us, 'the world' is thus not merely a place but indivisibly the locus of an event (being). However, we have exposed 'the event of our own species being' and 'its' world formation as ambiguous. Rather than simply being an event of making, it has equally been one of unmaking. In creating our selves and our worlds, we have been destroying a world of biological dependence for numerous species (including ourselves). The defuturing action of unsustainability is not destroying the planet. After we have done whatever we will do, at whatever cost to our species and our nonhuman Others, the planet will 'live' on in some transmogrified form. What is really at risk, what will not survive, are some, if not all, of our worlds. At this point, we would do well to remember, some 293 million years ago, almost 90 per cent of all species on planet earth were wiped out. But life changed and flourished. This can happen again. The mantra of environmentalists—'Save the Planet'—manifests a profound lack of understanding.

We have already reached a moment and 'level of material development' (cf. destruction) in which it is no longer possible to distinguish between 'the natural' and 'the artificial'. Genetic engineering and nanotechnology are the advanced edge of this (con)fusion. Cultures have formed and are forming in this domain of hybridization. This, of course, means that worldhood and perception of a 'world' of human dependence will remain continually in flux. What exactly is it that we, as increasingly autotransformative animals, will end up depending upon? Will we transcend our current biological needs? Who knows? Is humanity unwittingly at war with the animal that it itself is?

We enter the material world through a body and gain our initial knowledge of this world via our embodied relation to the world wrapped around us as animal. It is only over time that our biophysical 'being-in-the-world' comes into the human via a 'world of object-things' and experiences able to brought into meaning by induction into language (delivered out the care of the social ecology of that absolutely Other being from which we came). Social construction and ontological designing converge at our moment of birth—we arrive into 'a world' of other beings, language and object-things all at the same moment.

The bodily inscription of object-things becomes an environment of language and, together with movement, seeing, and hearing, enables the animal's passage from 'being of the world' to 'being in a world' wherein the human as event occurs. The human/animal development is thus never just the coming of a being with a sense of its self but the coming of a being with an actual sense of (its) world. Making sense of our experience of 'the world' cannot be divided from the acquisition of knowledge that dominantly miscasts the relation among us, our own and other worlds.

As Merleau-Ponty indicates:

> The thing and the world exist only in so far as they are experienced by me or by subjects like me, since they are both the concatenation of our perspectives, yet they transcend all perspectives because the chain is temporal and incomplete. I have the impression that the world itself lives outside me, just as absent landscapes live beyond my visual field, and as my past was formally on the earlier side of my present.[13]

For us moderns, at some point the world becomes abstraction, idea, image and projection—it then collides with and sometimes even overwhelms the status of experiential worldhood. In placing 'my world' in the frame of 'the world' as projection, it may become more or less meaningful or simply completely trivialized.

For the vast majority of people, the world now arrives fully imaged. Increasingly, the worldly mediations of these (dominantly televisual) images arrive prior to the gaining of direct 'world-shaping' experiences. Certainly, for children, much of this experience of prefiguration, an experience of being mediated by the image, is effectively 'designing' (the perception of) the world. At the same time, it is also a designing that acts to direct the actual seeking of experiences. In an enormous number of cases, the 'desire' to explore 'the world', relationships, sexuality, a particular career, extreme sports, military life, exotic food and so on are seeded by the image so encountered. The agency of the image is never neutral. For many people, and in the not very distant past, the arrival of the image of 'the modern world' was an imposition that threatened to annihilate the being of their identity and its 'world'. This was certainly the case for many indigenous peoples, orthodox Muslims and marginal religious communities. Not only did it throw their view of the world into turmoil; it also undercut what they believed themselves to be (especially as it failed to coincide with the idea and image of 'the human' of their cultural induction).

One dramatic example of the designing power of the 'the world as image' is that of the map. The mapping of territorial boundaries, during the period of Western nations' imperialist expansion evidences the violence of the drawing of 'the line'. For instance, when, at the 1884–85 Berlin Conference, European nations 'carved up' Africa into colonial possessions (which later became nations), politicians just drew lines on a map, lines that paid no heed to topography, natural resources, tribe, community or kinship.[14] Such action was accompanied by an imperative to 'civilize savages', which in turn triggered forms of genocide and ethnocide (the negation of the value of a culture to its people and thereafter its destruction by neglect or its deliberate destruction by legislative and violent means by the banning of languages, religious practices, songs and ways of life, and ecocidal destruction).[15] The consequences of these actions still resonate (especially in anomic, dysfunctional deeply damaged indigenous cultural communities). In this context, and writ large, modernity was just a global imposition of an image, employed as a figure of reference, to legitimize the establishment of a world that conformed to a particular mode of authority, human being and exchange.

The antagonistic relation created between the world of the West and that of indigenous peoples globally mirrors, but in reverse, the more general conflict unknowingly established between the ontic ground of human existence (the biophysical world) and the physical world of human construction.

The processes unleashed by productivism are not under the control of any individual, social, economic or political body. Currently, there is nothing to obstruct the processes of defuturing productivism. This loss of control has been intrinsic to technics from the beginning and is now lodged in the ever-accelerating speed of global exchange and production of object-things. The expenditure resulting from unchecked conversion of natural capital to the suspended matter of biologically nonconsumable commodities is a negation of that mode of exchange we call 'life'.

Somehow, the irony of the 'world within the world' that is continually being made actually taking time away from the future of the people for whom it is being constructed escapes us. In the darkness of our anthropocentric vision, we are unable to see that the more excessive our immersion in a 'world of goods', the more fated we are to have less.

Thus, 'we' lose time, and we become ever more autonomic (technologically colonized instrumental beings) as we become further distant from the animal that we are as it most essentially cares for us. So while our animality in its contained form lives on, the human is in retreat as technology ontologically invades—not materially but as (an) ontology. The loss of time, the ascent of a technical mode of being, the retreat of the human and its corresponding loss of agency all converge on the unceasing progression of nihilism. Continually, the question of our becoming returns and exposes the inadequacy of pre-sented Eurocentric abstracted posthuman futures.

Thinking in time, there is much to suggest the days of *Homo sapiens* are numbered. What, then, can be the ontologically designed replacement able to counter the unrelenting march of technics? The unavoidable question becomes not so much one of 'our' survival but, rather, what, via a postevolution-ary technological mutation, will be the 'being' that will survive (and in what numbers)?

The issue is held in 'our hands'. Not God, technology, nor evolution will deliver us (as a human/animal) into the future. In order for there to be a future for us, we have to make it by overcoming our negation—'we' have to overcome the unsustainable defuturing being that we are. In our commonality and our difference, we cannot do this unless we remember what we were and have become and that which threatens us.

There is a conundrum to break—on the one hand unknowingly we are agents of change; and on the other we have a sense of lack of agency, of helplessness, and so live nihilistically. With this in mind, we can see that our species' future rests with an ability to break with:

- The notion that 'we humans' are a unified whole (irrespective of biological commonality, the cultural differences we have created have undone the species as a singularity)
- Dominant conditions of compliance ('doing one's job as worker, citizen and family member') perceived as means of advancement and self-realization
- Acceptance of power as inscribed in a constantly expanding technofunctional world
- The assumption that agency purely resides with individuals or collective subjects and that change depends on action by 'the masses'
- The assumption that the goals of life should be freedom and happiness

Thus, we need to make:

- A repository for memory that counters the ways it is being eroded
- Countertechnologies of world formation and deformation (materially and semiotically) based on a new *habitas* of creative redirective (design) practice
- Regimes of contingent meaning predicated on what needs to become true (in contrast to foundational truth)
- A foundation of thought in which we can think and act as self-recognized relational beings (as beings interrelated to object-things, animals and a social ecology)
- Ways to dwell Otherwise

If 'we' are of the privileged and therefore able to recognize the force of nihilism inherent in our everyday culture, then we are ethically bound to face this situation and act. The challenge is ontological. It is a matter not of 'consciousness raising' or individual token action but of radically reforming and redirecting the form, content and output of one's constructed world—on the basis of the *praxis* of a new design paradigm.

To become other than we are, we have to become futural, and to do this we have to make the world that will remake us. This is a project of making not an idealized world but a workplace world of arduous labour—a space of the renewed political, predicated upon the creation of a new political imaginary.

As shown in earlier chapters, the transformation of early hominids into *Homo sapiens* and the formation of their worlds was indivisible and circular—as the human made a world, the world made the human. So understood, change is inherent in our being, and ontological design is not a new invention but a recovery and amplification inherent to our becoming and very being-in-Being.[16] More than this, it is also potentially a reanimation of Nietzsche's 'will to power'. So, although dangers proliferate from our lost potentiality, 'we' remain an uneven and 'unfinished animal'. Our future, as we make it, may well reside in unexpected places.

Mark Warren characterized Nietzsche's understanding of 'will to power' as being within 'a view of the world from the "inside" of our structures of action'.[17] Our structure of action constitutes our world. Like Heidegger, Nietzsche understood 'world' as our being 'in-the-world', and, like Marx, he saw our being as a practice formed under historically determined conditions of existence. The 'will to power' therefore is everything to do with our inherent world forming and transforming propensity and nothing to do with the pursuit of power in a politico-egoistic form.

The world for Nietzsche can be characterized as the ontic, the world of *phusis* and the world of worldhood, all existing as independent structures in time and constructed space.[18] The difference of this world centred on discrete cultural identities united in difference under a common category of being. There are two issues with this understanding: first, being imposed on difference here is an abstraction, as there is no position outside the difference, and so being is itself not a resolution of difference; second, commonality is that which has to be created rather than claimed (and it can be claimed only on the basis of that which exists in difference being able to be shared in common—which is understood here to be the need to continue to be in difference, which itself defines a state of Sustainment as process).

World Making and Un-Making

As we have seen, the world changes what we are, and we change the world. Not only is this true for the species *Homo sapiens* as a whole, but it also holds true for every single human being.[19] Such a process of interaction is the means by which our animality is subordinated to our humanness. But we should not overlook that many animals also form a socioenvironing world. The key point is not that the animal forms 'a poorer world' than our world but, rather, that our world-making is an extension of (our) animal actions. Our transition to the human is an animal-to-human progression. As has been said, we are born into animality and become human. In our initial state of animality, we are totally captivated, totally helpless. Captive to our environment, our life, our being, is no freer than a chick in a nest or a blind rat at its mother's nipple.[20]

Of course, besides the ontologically designing agency of things, there is also the socialization associated with a paediac induction into humanness—learning to be human from the instruction of others, arriving as a continuum from language, ritual and object to action. All these forces clearly fuse—learning to eat with a spoon requires the spoon, a guiding hand, a choreographed action and the word of the person managing the act of feeding. Learning to speak, learning to act (for oneself and others), is learning to be human. In every case, instruction is never merely functional but is socially performative—a manner of acting towards beings-in-common.

From childhood, our world and self-forming actions are merely an extension of the ontologically designing nature of 'the object-thing' that commenced when the animal first picked up the stone, turned it into a tool and started to form a world and itself as human. For all our difference from the very first hominids, we still in some ways remain the same. As Leroi-Gourhan indicated, in making a world materially (by the use of tools) and symbolically (by the use of language, image, sound and ritual), *Homo sapiens* established 'a means of taking control of the outside world' and began to create 'a completely humanised universe'—an anthropocentrically authored cosmos.[21] At least, this is what appearances seem to communicate, yet this picture distorts. The 'taking of control' is illusory. The 'outside world'—like 'the return of the repressed'—returns with a vengeance. In contemporary parlance, 'we' are on the edge of a tipping point. We cannot say we have lost control because, in reality, we never had it.

In our anthropocentrism, our relative and graduated proximity to our animality continues. One does not need to read Freud to know this. One does not need to look beyond oneself to know that levels of repression of animality vary. Certainly, what animals recognize in us is not our humanity but an animal kinship, whether in empathic or antagonistic encounters. The further we are spatially removed from animals, the less do we have a sense of our proximal relation to them. Yet many people in the most urbanized of environments desire to be close to an animal (that is, to own a pet). This desire does not as much register a feeling of loss as indicate a wish for presence. One could also ask: does not a child's attraction to and emotional proximal need for animal contact indicate a need unable to be met by a human?

Our future does not arrive only from the past via our acquisition of language, memory and desire; it also comes, as with the world, from an 'ecology of the image'—as it constitutes an environment of our becoming and delivers images that get taken, wholly or in part, as designing templates for what we might become. As said, the way we 'learn' to see 'the world' has a direct relation to the world we form as part-actors in and of world formation. Likewise, our self-image and our worldview both become framed by the manner and form of the 'world picture' encountered as a metaphysics and ecology of image. By implication, a great deal of 'our' world formation arrives preformed. Effectively, we are 'thrown' into the designing of a defuturing past as our futuring destiny. Thus, nihilism has now taken a more extreme turn so that we are forming a world that effectively is negating elements of itself (including us).

In truth, nihilism *has* turned. First we lost agency; now we acquire agency, but only insofar as 'being here' is being with our intrinsic but heightened disposition to destroy. Against this backdrop, late modernity has countered the directional impetus indicated in Heidegger's exposition of world formation.[22] As outlined, deformation now always accompanies formation. The dialectic of Sustainment (the inseparable relation between destruction and the act of creation) is breaking down. Destruction has destroyed the dialectic's dynamic equilibrium.

Questioning 'what are we' remains before us as a challenge. We could say we are both more and less than we were, and we could give ourselves another name (as with *zoon technica*), but it is not enough. It does not do the job.

As we form and deform the processes of 'world-formation', we are equally transforming what we ourselves are and will become as human beings. As Heidegger pointed out, 'things stand with us'.[23] The problem of the world growing out of us is the 'problem' of the anthropocentric construction of 'the world' as something that is unaccountable to human ownership. The world human beings have formed is 'deworlding'. This has become a phenomenal condition of our being-in-the-world, which is to say that the negation of our fundamental conditions of being has itself become elemental to our mode of being. The combination of our numbers, technology and profligate use of planetary resources ensures the continued globalization of the nihilistic character of our world (de)formation. While this observation has been made via other terms (the diminishment of our finitude, defuturing and 'the taking of time away'), to know this, to really know it, is to stand before the task at hand determined, fearful and motivated in the knowledge of the historicity of the survival of the animal that we are. We know there has to be another way and that all we have to do is to make it—but the question is how?

As has been argued, there has to be a move out of world-formation based on naturalized ontological processes (intrinsic to evolved modes of earthly habitation) toward structures of transformation created by overtly adopted ontologically designed strategies and objects. The very nature of the 'things' human beings bring into the world that change 'the world' therefore has to dramatically change.

We must again emphasize a concern with proximity and specifically our proximal relation to 'world'. We de facto live twice removed from that ontic entity that *phusis* strove to name. Heidegger again helps us illuminate this situation.

> By the term 'world', and here perhaps more strongly than anywhere else, we initially try to seek something that is present at hand in itself and ascertainable, something that we can always appeal to. We must appreciate from the very beginning that this is not how things are, even though we are tempted to make just this mistake. Or to put it another way: philosophical knowledge of the essence of the world is not and can never be an awareness of something present at hand. It is rather a comprehending disclosure of something in a specifically determined and directed questioning, which as a questioning never allows what is questioned to become something present at hand.[24]

Our world (as the sum of the organized matter, meaning and knowing of our design and construction) exists as it is embedded in 'the world' itself in a relation to troubled and dislocated forms of exchange. Reiteration—we do not have direct access to either world. Whatever our senses put before us is mediated by what we experientially and metaphysically know; even though we have direct physical contact with that which seems spatially close, this does not imply that it is actually near (this condition of the remoteness from that which is close was named *Ent-fernung* by Heidegger and has been variously translated as 'deserverance' and dis-tance).[25]

As noted, language stands between us and world, both as an immediate naming that brings a supplementary form of the named to us with a representational claim and as that which allows the experienced to be made sensible and brought to memory and reflection. Sound, touch, smell and sight all reside in that reactive un-knowing that is the limit of animal 'knowledge'. But we have a prefigurative ability, imagination, thought and language. While 'language and world stand in an intrinsic connectedness', they fold back into and mirror our being as we are equally in and of 'world'.[26] In the company of the tool, language facilitated 'our' passage from 'the world' to (our) world. It was and is primary as a means of world formation and *redirection.*

We are now in a position to directly restate the duality of being in/of the world—world is unambiguously our place of being, while, at the same time, world is also a manifestation of our being itself. Recognizing that how we are is a product of world and that world is a product of how we are, ontological design, in the age of defuturing, now needs to be taken out of an extant worlding and posited with futuring form in 'the project' of that world-reformation that is Sustainment. Sustainment is the essence of futural worlding wherein a viable exchange relation between 'the world' and '(our) world' is made possible, but simply making an appeal to it delivers nothing. It is essential to grasp what is needed to turn the idea of Sustainment, as a project and process, into a *praxis.*

10

Imagination in a Blink of an Eye

We do not consider animals as moral beings. But do you think animals consider us as moral beings? An animal which had the power of speech once said: 'Humanity is a prejudice from which we animals at least do not suffer.'

—Friedrich Nietzsche, 1903

Out of Animality

The relation between the stone and the animal in the emergence of the hominid has been presented as decisive, because it delivered the ontologically designing agency of the tool as a force in 'our' becoming. But something else was needed to bring the human into being: the 'transcendental power of imagination'. To adequately grasp what this means requires that we trace back how Heidegger read Kant's engagement with imagination in both his *Critique of Pure Reason* (1781) and his *Anthropology from a Pragmatic Point of View* (1798).[1] If we do this, two major points are exposed. First is the crucial part played by imagination within an ensemble of factors that's been designated 'world formation'. The second is present but understated and actually masked in Heidegger's analysis of the difference between Kant's first and second editions of the *Critique of Pure Reason.* In essence, the observation, part stated, part implied, was that Kant had turned away from following his own thinking through to its final conclusion, which was that, via the power of imagination, 'man' was a product of his own creation.

Kant feared that his thinking would unleash a destruction of belief—an uncontainable slide into heterodoxy, which would expose him to the charge of blasphemy. If this had happened, Kant's overall project, which centred on morality, as well as his private and public persona, would have imploded. So, while he recognized that imagination was more than just the essential ground of all knowledge, what he discovered 'frightened him'.[2] (Similarly, Darwin was reluctant to speak on his discovery of the absence of God in the 'making of man'.) Kant's recoil from the radicality of his discovery had significant consequences for him.[3] It prompted his turn to a preoccupation with pure reason and, in so doing, laid much of the ground of modern metaphysics—his 'turning away' was thus as much 'a turning to'. One can take Heidegger's remark as a partial recognition of this:

> This original, essential constitution of humankind, 'rooted' in the transcendental power of imagination, is the 'unknown' into which Kant must have looked if he spoke of the 'root unknown to us', for the unknown is not of which we simply know nothing.[4]

Kant effectively turned away from the question of *how we came to be* toward the question of *how we came to know,* of which Richard Kearney provides a neat summary:

> Kant announced that the two 'stems' of human cognition (understanding and sensation) both stood upon reason; and nothing could be known about the world unless it was first performed and transformed by the synthetic power of imagination (*Einbindungskraft*).[5]

From the perspectives of our concerns, what Heidegger's extensive and controversial reading of Kant makes clear is that the transcendental power of imagination established 'the faculty of intuition'.[6] That is, it initiated and then established an ontological ability to learn and act on the basis of experience gained in the world. Intuition was equally seen as a 'faculty of forming' a worldview.

Imagination can now be placed alongside the self and making as elemental to the forming of a world-within-the-world. This is not to suggest that a vision informed by imagination actually triggered or prolonged an act of making that was materially world-creative. Rather, the performative power of imagination was first of all a representing, a making present, that was independent of a seen object (a referent) that could be carried into an act ontologically, rather than consciously. What this meant was an ability to see some object-thing other than how it immediately appeared. Here we have to understand that imagination is underpinned by intentionality. It has to have an object (of focus—the intentional construct), which can, of course, be 'a seeing of a thing as other than it is'. Thus, the stone as a tool is imagined as such before it is made into a tool because the stone is seen to be something it had never previously been seen to be. Imagination was both gaining the ability to see something that was absent and something that was present as it was yet to be.[7] With imagination so understood, it becomes lodged in memory, with an intuitive relation to an action. The spacing that separates the seen, the remembered and the act affirms that time is also elemental to the nexus between imagination and intuition.

What we can learn from Kant's idea of the 'transcendental imagination' is that knowledge was (and is) constructed on the ground of ontological knowledge (i.e. knowledge that is embodied and practically enacted) and that imagination was a productive force in the cognitive development of makers and their world-making ability. The ability to make another world from within the world was thus indivisible from seeing the potential of 'the world'—in its immediacy and local presence—to become in some way other than it was through an act, informed by imagination, of bringing something new into being. While, initially, such action was on a minute scale and was likely to be devoid of any reflective consideration, what undoubtedly happened was a rupture in the patterning of 'the same' (as the intergenerational repetition of behaviours that characterizes animal life). In other words, the process created a difference within the animal to become the human/animal, which itself facilitated the formation of the active identity of the proto-human (as a plural form of being). Thus, animals have stayed as they are because they never developed imagination, and, sadly, they couldn't, because the emergence of our imagination is in part due to physiological development—the 'free hand'—that enabled us to move things, handle and transform them and thus see them as other than they appeared to be—hence the stone becomes *and is* a tool (while remaining (a) stone).

What is being traversed here is the fundamental ground of design in being.

Over tens of millions of years, 'mind', as we characterize it, emerged as imagining turned to thinking reflectively and, as such, to reason. Again, Kant's placement of imagination within his understanding of 'transcendental deduction', with its ability to synthesize the seen and the known, would affirm this view.[8] In moving from mind to language, there is no consensual view on its origin. Positions vie among the zoological, biological, cognitive and social models of the development of either mind or communication. In line with our thesis of our *relational* evolution, the idea that there was a single cause that brought language into being is thought to be unlikely. There had to be prefigurative audio gestures, the biological ability to speak, the mind that could select and direct sound and social structure wherein shared meaning was possible.

One can place the arrival and development of imagination as a key factor in the emergence of a mind able to reason. Likewise, the transcendental power of imagination is also credited as being the ground upon which the very possibility of human subjectivity was created (and thus was a construction, a product of making, rather than a discovery of the intellect).[9] Moreover, meaning was itself de facto deemed by Kant a 'product of the imagination' and thus of mind (rather than being posited in world or in objects and things). As such, meaning became seen as a representation of the human subject.[10] One can now read all of these 'developments' as examples of the result of the constructivist nature of anthropocentrism. They thus add to a more developed, if still emergent, picture of our self and our world 'formation'. Imagination prior to reason is also verified anthropologically (e.g. creation stories, practices, myths, as well as objects).

With the development of language and culture, regimes of meaning in different environments became increasingly diverse and complex. Knowledge became differentially created both at a microlevel and more generally and thus became an object of exchange (social, symbolic and practical) transported between immediate and dispersed communities. Thus, an ecology of mind was formed.

In the proto-modern West, truth lodged in belief, as given by God, eventually had to give way to an onto-theological faith in truth as delivered by reason. Specifically, in the medieval age, truth became based upon a 'referential correspondence' between the referent and the representation, the subject and object wherein 'being' became objectified and truth was confirmed mimetically. Kant rendered such a position philosophically untenable, but, more than this, he massively undermined the authority of empiricism.

Nietzsche took this undercutting of truth further. He extended Kant's notion that imagination belongs to 'the Nothing' (a nonbeing that is not to hand). He viewed it as free-floating, as will, as desire, and, as such, positive. Imagination for Nietzsche thus became freedom from direction by higher values; it became a source of risk, the path to freedom.[11] Imagination's vocation was to make life liveable in a meaningless world. But this very constructivist projection of the power of imagination produced a turn of Kant's transcendental claim. Whereas what we see via Kant is the self and the world-forming power of imagination, what Nietzsche added is the world re-forming (*palingensic*) power of imagination. Thereafter, Heidegger, with due acknowledgement to Kant, took an understanding of the existential imagination further by grounding it in *Dasein* as it itself embodies imagination.[12] For him, our being arrives out of nothing (but imagination) and goes to nothing (death). It is out of this nothingness that we come to be.

Notwithstanding Nietzsche's critique, from Kant onward until the mid-twentieth century, imagination was 'deemed capable of inventing a world out of human resources, a world answerable to no power higher than itself'.[13] This world eventuated with an enormous cultural, technological, material and geopolitical complexity, but it ended up being unaccountable to the very material of the world out of which it was formed. Making a futural world within 'the world'—one able to counter the defuturing character of the world that human beings have created to date—is without doubt the greatest challenge to imagination that humanity has yet to face.

Living in the Pre-Imagined

The earliest exercise of proto-human imagination had nothing to draw on but the given world around it, as it created the most modest evidence of 'our' world-forming actions. Now, dominantly, to imagine is to imagine the already imagined; to dream is to dream the already dreamed. Imagination is not dead, but the agency of the televisual and the late-modern 'creative industries' strive to saturate it. The mind is loaded with the already imagined. When one considers the overload of imagery and the intertextual relations of the contemporary global cultural media, what one is witnessing is the industrialization of imagination and its induction, like memory, into technology. Yet imagination survives, perhaps structurally diminished (with reified forms now lodged in the 'third order of the simulacra'—the order of simulation).[14] Drawing on imagination industrialized from 'creative industry sources', the 'creatives' (not least designers) simulate the act of imagination via the construction of assemblages of the already imagined. At the same time, the importance of imagination ever increases before the challenge of species survival and accompanying Sustainment.

Notwithstanding that imagination has undergone numerous stages of transformation as the 'world-forming' and 'the formed' world has dramatically changed—from the first coming of imagination (as the animal that we were became the human/animal that we are) to the current moment in which imagination has been appropriated to serve a world of sustaining the unsustainable status quo (projected as a simulation of sustainability)—*yet* in another direction, imagination is demanded to bring the very possibility of Sustainment. This is a challenge that significantly changes the objects and ambitions of imagination, and it cannot be met by utopianism.

The utopias of the nineteenth century were overtaken by a dystopic reality—as Kearney puts it, 'romantic fiction could not be translated into fact.' Such fictions had even more tragic consequences as they unfolded in the twentieth century, as an idealized spirit of humanism was extinguished by a festival of inhumanity and violence. After this moment, while imagination continued to create grand images of the future, the means to realize them withered as world-transformative political ideologies surrendered to capitalist market forces and the pragmatics of the everyday. It is in this context that we find the existential subjectivism of creative industry 'creatives' (including designers) stranded in a situation that echoes Nietzsche's nihilist pronouncements. Imagination is and will increasingly become a site of contestation.

Crucially, the making of the vital project of 'Sustainment' (the project of futuring that must come to be as the post-Enlightenment project) has equally to embrace a remaking of the power to imagine. Seen in this context, recognition of the unsustainable—the world-within-the-world as a negation of time—offers an unsurpassable challenge to imagination. Bluntly, what is at stake is the very future of 'human' life, as it has been known to date to be, as a plural actuality and potentiality.

The televisual (the cultural technology of all electronic audiovisual media within the culture industry) colonizes imagination through its forms of disclosure—it fragments 'the picture' of the unsustainable in a way that not only conceals what needs to be seen but also presents its real 'imaginary world' as reality. The actuality of the unsustainable is the sum of its relational complexity. Yet what is made to appear are merely newsworthy symptomatic fragments of an unspoken and un-imaged overarching condition that authors fear, desires, expectations and reactions. So, rather than representing a crisis, the projected televisual appearance of critical conditions actually covers over the scale, relational make-up, and depth of what is really critical (as it is lodged in 'us').

'Environmental crisis' is made present via this 'ecology of the image', which, in its seductive horror (as image) backed by rationalist science (as assurance) and in its totalizing pervasiveness, ontologically designs our seeing/understanding of 'the problem'. This has real consequences, especially in terms of how 'we' knowingly and unknowingly act in and on 'the world' within-the-world—the world where negative impacts defuture. In this setting, the exercise of imagination must be posed against its industrialization, and this requires a sufficient degree of alienation to trigger an ability to 'see things otherwise'. This ability comes not from 'looking' or from 'information' but from the application of critically informed theory (not to be confused with 'critical theory') able to expose the concealed.

From our very beginning, imagination has been deeply implicated in a struggle for being, it ever remains so. 'How we are' and 'what we will become' continue to rest with the agency of imagination, but what is now clear is that imagination is a figure of contestation and has to become more so. Its agency cannot simply be taken for granted. It is one of the victims of nihilism and, as such, has been significantly externalized from mind. This externalization (as imagination's industrialized presence) becomes the location of the contestation. It does this by necessity though one of its late 'products': critically informed theory, as a force of clearing, acting back on imagination's simulacra, and also by that *praxis* which making otherwise names as 'Sustainment' opening a new space for imagination to occupy.

Reason as Pause for Thought

We recognize that imagination prefigured reason, but what does reason itself prefigure? To answer this question, we first have to understand the nature of reason itself.

We have two closely linked demands on our understanding to meet: (*a*) the demand to understand the 'Principle of Reason' and (*b*) the demand to understand the 'discourse of reason' and its agency. Both demands, of course, bleed into each other.

Between 1955 and 1957, Martin Heidegger gave thirteen one-hour lectures on the 'Principle of Reason', which were published in 1957.[15] Almost every one of the lectures opened with a restatement of the 'Principle of Reason'— 'nothing is without reason.' This does not mean that reason is posited within everything. Rather, it goes to the 'Principle of Reason' as it has become structurally embedded in thought and so directs the way 'we' think. This statement will be qualified in a moment, but first the 'discovery' of the principle needs acknowledgement.

In 1671, the twenty-five-year-old Gottfried Wilheim Leibniz presented a treatise (*Theoria motus abstracti*) to the Paris Academy of Sciences, which Heidegger tells us contained (at the end of one of his propositions) 'the most familiar and eminent Principle': *Nihil est sine ratione* (nothing is without reason).[16] He also tells us that it took Leibniz five years and a visit to Baruch Spinoza to get what was meant by this principle adequately explicated: 'nothing exists whose sufficient reason for existing cannot be rendered.'[17] Here, then, is the mode of thinking that got inscribed in Western thought as a means to think. Obviously, it did not mean that reason was taken as the underpinning of the way all people thought; rather, it rested on the assumption that everything could or eventually would be explained by reason.

The power of reason, so characterized, was taken as an act of faith by the Enlightenment (thus firmly establishing a *faith* in reason). This is to say that reason became an object of belief posited with transcendental power to rise above the irrational (which reason itself defined and alone can name). Like all powerful beliefs, reason became institutionalized and, as such, became enshrined in a particular discourse.

Reason, as it moved from being viewed as an expression and gift of God to an acquired characteristic of 'man', became the unifying core of the Enlightenment project and of modern metaphysics as it was presented scientifically, philosophically and politically. As an idea of 'self-revealing', reason was deemed to have the power to reveal absolutely truth and to conquer reality.[18] Reason's search for truth was and is inscribed in 'the command of nature' or, as Nietzsche put it, the 'lust of appropriation and conquest'.[19]

Knowledge grounded in reason, it is claimed, brings power and control over nature, enabling it to be manipulated and exploited, as well as the more ambiguous human celebration of 'the power and wonder of nature' as revealed through science. The unlocking of nature's 'secrets' became a continuous activity of use and/or abuse. Nietzsche's views on science here capture almost a contemporary view; he simultaneously saw science as an objectified ideal that transcended moralist systems of belief and as an instrument of nihilism.[20]

According to Warren, this seeming contradiction was based on a thought that assumed the ability of science's empirical truth to displace a Christian moralist claim to knowledge while overlooking that science too could be viewed as, an ideology.[21] Affirmatively, Nietzsche viewed science as a creative force and a form of life wherein 'we must all become physicists'.[22] Yet, unquestionably, the limitations of science beg exposure: can it look beyond objectification, create value or transcend its hyperreductive interpretation of 'world' as materiality? Such questions can never be answered by opinion, for they stand at the feet of a practice that is deemed just 'method'.[23]

Heidegger offers a counterview to Nietzsche's, illustrated by his statement that science constitutes a determinate and everyday view of truth.[24] These positions provide one backdrop against which to think about the way science exercised its authority and claimed ownership of truth. They also fold back into how the nature of animals is determined by 'scientific and metaphysical truth'.[25]

Just as reason was made integral to science, so it was bonded to the State—in particular by Hegel.

Hegel viewed the idealized State as 'absolutely rational', as the actuality of the 'ethical Idea', as ethical mind.[26] But, so configured, it could also be a means to subordinate society. More than this, reason and the rational state also served to assert the claim that human intelligence (as defined by reason) was a constant and common feature of all peoples. As such, reason was advanced politically as offering a ground of common appeal—one able to unify all difference. This notion lives on, spanning political ideologies and underpinning geopolitics. For instance, it informed and mobilized the universalist discourse of the United Nations and its characterization of the human. Likewise, the ethnocentric character of 'human rights' (based on a Eurocentrically authored designation of 'the human') is an example of what underscored the formation of that institution as it adopted and deployed the power of reason as the foundation of its form and function.

Obviously, the history of reason occupies a massive place in the history of philosophy and thus has a huge literature. Clearly, we have no intent here to trammel this well-trod path, but there are still a number of observations that need to be exposed, especially the fundamental character of reason, its agency and its place in a critique of metaphysics. But let's start with a few words on the dual crisis of reason.

As already observed, reason became an object of faith. As such, it eventually revealed its limitations but still remained trapped within them. War provides a clear illustration of the point. All the means to wage war arrive by virtue of reason instrumentally applied, whether to the design and manufacture of weapons, logistics of supply, strategy, and so on, but the 'reason for' and 'the conduct of' war are infused with and mired by the irrational. Weapons of mass destruction are the most extreme instance of this: their creation depends on the application of reason, but their use can but be totally devoid of it. Moreover, war itself exemplifies a general trait of human action whereby chaos, disorder and dysfunction are concealed and repressed by reason.

Likewise, reason appears powerless to overcome conditions that, in the extreme, even threaten the very survival of humanity. The geopolitical failure to appropriately respond to the dangers of climate change is a clear instance of this. Here and in myriad other examples, the insufficiency of reason can be made apparent. Underscoring this insufficiency is the presumption of a subject able to be directed by reason alone. Yet this notional subject, even when seemingly fully comprehending what he should rationally do, often acts in a completely different way. This is because he is overwhelmed by, among other possibilities, the power of fear, ambition, greed or carnal desires. Irrationality, as indicated, cohabits with reason.

Next, any discussion of reason is trapped in the very discourse of reason itself. Getting outside reason and into its abyss is thus an issue of critical concern.[27] This is especially realized as reason simply falls back into the very space it itself has cleared—as said in the shadow of Kant, reason cannot step outside itself to judge itself. To counter this tendency and in full knowledge of the original agency of transcendental imagination, an appeal to imagination is made. But, as John Sallis has pointed out, this has the potential to undercut metaphysics itself—something viewed by philosophy with both horror and delight.[28] At stake, of course, is the power given (or not) to 'the faculty of intuition' that, as we have seen, is constituted with a primacy from imagination and experience, rather than via reason. The relation between imagination and metaphysics still begs more consideration.

While imagination prefigured metaphysics, the relation became contradictory. To make the point, Sallis uses the example of Descartes, who railed against imagination while employing it to create the very rationalist thought he strove to protect from it.[29] Sallis goes on to say that 'imagination can be neither simply excluded from nor simply appropriated by metaphysics.'[30] Part of this recoil against imagination was based on the fact that it was seen to be unable to be disciplined. While philosophy fed upon imagination, it also put it at risk—for imagination also 'corrupted' philosophy with its 'vanity and wanderings'.[31] For some, it was even demonized as a 'monster', arbitrary, and a means that enabled illusion to be taken as truth. In contrast, it was also viewed as both a quality to be discovered or invented and a means to freedom to be celebrated.[32]

Notwithstanding the legacy of Kant's transcendental imagination, metaphysics (as the all-enveloping frame of philosophy, rather than just a disciplinary arm) has significantly repressed imagination, yet, as the repressed, it always returns, not least via the Romantics.[33] But the form of the return and its subsequent appropriation cut across a division within reason itself between the theoretical, where it empowers, and the practical, from which imagination is excluded. Effectively, this division migrates to the instrumental where imagination can act generatively, but only when constitutive of object or agency (otherwise, it becomes totally excluded)—as it mostly does in the realm of professional design.

Instrumentalized rationalism became a pronounced feature of the *habitus* of modernity, as can now be seen in the way in which contemporary forms of managerialism act to contain how imagination is appropriated while controlling its appearance (especially when it is deemed a threat to the status quo). Increasingly, one can say that there is a need to place imagination in the realm of the political. So placed, it can shatter the illusion of truth that the instrumental claims of institutionalized politics assert. In an instrumentalized society (the kind of society most of us live in), imagination is not only repressed within its historical relation to metaphysics but also held at bay politically, for it opens up the space of an Other. The repression of imagination realizes a nihilist danger of reducing a (human) potentiality to conceptualize another future in the specific situated context at hand. In so doing, this deepens defuturing forces in the present.

The repression of imagination directly links to how the end of metaphysics, as final closure, can be understood. As again Sallis points out, the end of metaphysics equates to that end which is death. It is final. However, the fate of metaphysics travels in two directions.

Heidegger made clear in *The Question Concerning Technology* that metaphysics was destined to become technology.[34] By this he meant not that it was to become a quality of any particular or even all technology but, rather, that metaphysics turned into instrumental thought would become hegemonic. In other words, it simply became how 'we' thought. Since he wrote this, in 1954, this prospect has become generalized and much closer to realization—not least because technology has become an extension of the central nervous system and has industrialized memory and modernity has been displaced by its less idealized and more instrumentally pragmatic offspring: globalization.[35]

At the same time, both Heidegger and, later, others, including Jacques Derrida, saw what came after the end of metaphysics as 'intuition'—which is to say, knowledge become ontological and enacted via the being of (a) human being, rather than just as the human mind exercised. Now here is a conundrum. Metaphysics has become an experientially grounded ontological condition; as such, it can be viewed as being with intuited 'good sense' (which is how Antonio Gramsci redefined 'common sense'), but it can also be seen as the intuitive expression of technological being. What is decisive here is the locus and status of imagination. 'We' now live with reason without reason (as reason, at the end of reason, has become enacted as and is within instrumentalism). The task and challenge now is that of transgressing the closure of metaphysics become technology, thus:

> Any opening to the future must intervene in the recurrence, must disrupt the operation of closure, transgressing its limits. Inasmuch as the figure of closure belongs intrinsically to metaphysics, such a move will also disrupt, dislodge, displace metaphysics itself. Such transgression, deconstructing metaphysics itself, will continue in Heidegger's phrase, the task reserved for thinking at the end of metaphysics.[36]

So, at the end, imagination is discovered as the intelligence able to generate a beginning (again) of a thinking of the yet unthought. Crucially, the future (for us) is a matter of thought. It is not assured, for it is unthinking that has created the defutured. What this means is that the future has to be made in the face of that which is actively taking it away.

Imagination so framed is not a matter of image, utopian projection or a visualized future. Rather, it is having the possibility of a future contemplated against the threat of its negation. It is imagining life after a loss (external-internal); thus, it is looking into an opening, rather than upon that which fills the void. It is imagining the very continuity and presence of Being itself as a *now, eidos* and *idea.* Imagining things as other than they are takes place against how metaphysics has fundamentally brought 'what is known' to presence. A consideration of the relation among the permanent, the finite and the impossible is just one case that makes the point clear.

The notion of 'permanent presence' was exposed by Kant as merely 'a product of the temporalising projection of man's finite existence'.[37] The past, present and future are a product of the limitation of a finite perspective of a specific life living toward death, as is the impossible. What is able to be seen/imagined is circumscribed chronophobically. As a result, humans sought to arrest time as a permanent moment. An aversion to time as 'becoming and change' became a feature of modern chronophobic subjects—subjects who wished for permanence where none was possible.[38] For Nietzsche, this disposition toward time was a mark of the decadence of Western metaphysics. The way time has been projected and deployed in the West has negated recognition that 'time is nothing' but change. As we will remember, Aristotle told us that time is but a perspective on those events 'that take place within it'—the 'reality' is unpunctuated change (flow) of Being as being.

As chronophobes, our sense of finitude and the finite is perverted and lodged in a form of subjectivity that removes us from confronting our 'being in time'. More than this, the chronophobic subject is inherently inauthentic in so far as she lives trying to avoid her own mortality/death by searching for 'fame, wealth and power'.[39] Living this condition of limitation not only inverts the significance of (our) life as event but also undermines the possibility of grasping the future as an ever becoming which, for us (in our impermanence), has to be secured. This is to say that a sense of time and finitude came out of imagination, as imagination prefigured reason. But, while it was reason that made time and finitude present as idea (for us), it was also reason that removed the existential recognition of time and finitude as a means by which to comprehend our own lives and life in general.

Viewing the presence of 'the world' (that our anthropocentric being cannot transcend) and the 'world-within-the-world' (that our world formation has made), we find metaphysics and reason have hidden, rather than bridged, this separation. As Kearney says, 'pure reason could not reach the object of experience except through the sensible intuition of time and space.' What this comment marks is the passage of time and space into subjective intuition via the agency of metaphysics. Such 'knowing' acted as the taken-for-granted, thus the 'object of experience', is both made present and exiled to be eternally out of reach. Thereafter, the ontological always in the end folds back into the unknowability of the ontic.

The project of Sustainment cannot resolve this divide, but it can be informed by it as imagination is called upon to go beyond the defuturing force of structural unsustainability.[40] While it engages how structural unsustainability is made present experientially—not just as reified techno-environmental scientific phenomena but also as a feature of mind, culture and conduct—the project of Sustainment does not posit agency solely with imagination. It also recognizes that experience has to be made intelligible by ontological practices that turn defuturing into an object of view that can then be engaged by futuring redirective action. Of this form of making, Warren writes of Nietzsche's thinking of 'will to power' as a practice that makes experience intelligible.[41] But, in light of earlier comments on metaphysics, technology and the deepening of the lived condition of structural unsustainability, 'making experience intelligible' needs even more focussed engagement—this via the creation of technological alienation able to prompt action beyond Heidegger's call to know technology as a 'saving power'. This capability depends not on voluntary induced interpretative and reflective acts but on produced experiential encounters with breakdowns in/of technology and its destructive ability revealed as a major feature of structural unsustainability.

Making the problem present gets us only part of the way to gaining agency. Equally important is creating a form of agency able to effectively engage the problem. Bringing imagination, technological alienation and ontological design together has the potential to deliver this agency.

To mobilize ontological design as a postmetaphysical practice requires grasping how it undercuts the notion of the primacy of the human agent. We have already seen how design as agency was active in the very coming into being of the hominid in that moment of relation that joined the stone, the animal and the human. Brought to the modern moment, the entire designed environment (designed object-things, material and immaterial) collectively act as the stone did in world-formation via a world-forming being—but it does this at a level of complexity mostly beyond our grasp.

As we now know, we are born into a designed world that designs a great deal of our mode of becoming and acting. The imposed patterning of other humans, the clothes we wear, the furniture we use, the homes we live in, the technologies we employ, the industries we create—we literally live in a designed and designing world of designed object-things. Without ascribing determinism to any particular designed object-thing, imagination, as it prefigures ontological design, has the potential to mobilize (or redirect) object-things of this made world-within-the world so that they are able act toward Sustainment and against the defuturing force of the unsustainable. Two qualifications now follow.

First, such action needs to be demarcated from modernist materialist determinism whereby, for example, a home was thought to be able to direct the way of life and, in so doing, constitute the conditions of a conscious modern subject. Ontological design, in contrast, is concerned solely with the redirection of action. It does not have to be introduced, as it is already omnipresent for us and always has been (as the power of the stone testifies). But ontological design brought to the service of Sustainment has to be posited with a futuring capability—which means that what is absolutely critical is how it comes to be and acts to make time. By implication, ontological design must not destroy anything that enables being to be. So configured, the essence of ontological design is performative as an enacted ethics. In contrast, the intent of modernist materialism was the realization of an idealized form of life—the modern. Sustainment does not give a damn how we live or act, so long as it makes time.

At its most basic and important, ontological design in the service of Sustainment is a political counterforce to the given 'designing of the world'. At the same time, it begs to be viewed as means by which the very possibility of (a new) knowledge (a knowledge of Sustainment) is created (with the coming of new agency) as the prospect of a new knowing.

Again we emphasize, Sustainment cannot be reduced to an instrumental domain. The project is 'the future' from the perspective of a 'superhuman'; it is 'time'. Without time, we have and are nothing. It is also thinking and acting in an ongoing moment as process. As *praxis*, it aims to open into the third epoch of human earthly habitation—unsettled posturban nomadism (the first epoch being the eons of nomadism, the second being the brief moment of settlement). Bringing ontological design to this conjuncture cannot be divided from the very coming of a moment that redefines the identity of 'the human'.

Nietzsche made clear that all knowledge and knowers are historically conditioned and thus perspectival. Constructivism is unavoidable, as Hilary Putnam put it:

> We don't have notions of 'existence' of things or the 'truth' of statements that are independent of versions we construct and of the procedures and practices that give sense to talk of 'existence' and 'truth' within those versions.[42]

We discover from sources as diverse as W. C. Heisenberg, Derrida, Einstein and A. N. Whitehead that truth (including truth about 'the world') is plural and, as such, is always predicated upon interpretation. The claim to truth problematically folds into an attempt to claim permanence in a world in flux, a world always becoming. Existing, as we do, in an unfolding epoch of rapid change, one can expect significant transformations in the nature of what is known to be true. The issue is not that 'nothing is true' but, rather, that the means to verify truth are never certain and always anthropocentrically grounded (for, as with all meaning, truth is 'our' fabrication).

Consequently, the sociocultural and political domains of power, where agency is exercised and subjectivities are formed/deformed/abandoned, is without any fixed form or true foundation and so will always change. In the unfolding of contemporary conditions, it is interesting to note that Nietzsche's view of what drives the production of knowledge is 'destabilization'—a condition rendering all the aforementioned domains problematic.[43] We live towards destabilization. Reason, itself relative to context and institution, is not clearly immune from such disruption. Yet the 'self-confidence of reason' is never shaken; its self-belief knows no barrier that it cannot scale.[44] It has total faith in itself—it is faith![45] Reason stands on a faith in reason itself and in its positing of universal, uniform human intelligence. As a 'system of metaphysical closure', reason cannot see its Eurocentric nature and fabrication.

Like a ghost, metaphysics ever returns to haunt. The very rhetoric of limit, closure and end ensures its return. Yet its return is not eternal. An abyss beckons. But its nature is undecided. If metaphysics becomes utterly and completely technological (that is, if it and what was once the locus of anthropocentrism become fully transferred and embodied 'within' technology and so totally autonomous), then the human will never re-emerge from the abyss. But, if 'how humans are' is *palingenically* turned by ontological design, then to fall into the abyss will be to arrive into a condition of becoming otherwise—a condition at the end of man and the birth of another (among the others) that remembers the human/animal.

There are still a few things to say on metaphysics and reason. Thereafter, 'the problem' of what comes after the limit of metaphysics will be considered.

Limit has been recognized conceptually as a commencement; Heidegger reminds us this was how the Greeks understood it.[46] In practical terms, design can do nothing without the imposition of limit(s). Closure and end can be viewed in a similar way—opening follows closure, and beginning follows end. Brought to metaphysics and its relation to intuition, limit has to arrive to arrest its closure, while a process of remaking is enacted via the agency of ontological design. Here design operates as an agent in the service of intuition in order to constitute the form and context of a new region of imagination (for the 'stone, animal and human' now read a new but essentially the same ontologically designing relation: the fabricated object-thing, human and posthuman—the *Übermensch)*. The limit is not regarded as a 'limit in time' (that is, in the medium of time and in response to the urgency of the moment).

John Sallis exactly captures how the overcoming of metaphysics can be grasped, and what he says makes a clear concluding point, in that there needs to be:

> an overcoming of metaphysics not in the sense of simply getting rid of something and leaving it behind but rather in the sense in which, for example, one overcomes profound grief over the death of a loved one, overcomes it by taking it on and yet still opening oneself to the future.[47]

As Sallis forcefully states, metaphysics cannot simply be rendered closed; it cannot simply be brought to an end. What it supports, its trace and the institutional forms of its materialized presence cannot be vaporized. Yet a process of disintegration is there for all who care to look. Nietzsche saw modernity abolish the 'true world' (the intelligible) and, in so doing, abolish the apparent world (the sensible). What remained was 'the world' as image; it is this world that environmentalism purports to save.

To conclude, let's again remind ourselves that the biophysical world has saved itself already many times (remembering that, 293 million years ago, 90 per cent of all species were wiped out and that 'we' and all other animals, aquatic life and the biota around us are a product of that remaining 10 per cent). As 'the most dangerous of animals', as a species, we are spinning out of control and failing to recognize that what is in danger is 'us'. We just cannot see ourselves in time. It is not so much that we are many but, rather, that we know no limit and thus continually damage so much of what we absolutely depend upon. So, just as we live in the 'shadow' of metaphysics become technology, we equally live in the shadow of the world become image.

Our task, against this background, is one of gathering and progressing the project of Sustainment. Whatever this designing brings into being has to be understood as never simply being a present-to-hand and object-thing of use but, rather, an object-thing, like the stone, that uses us while we use it in mutual acts of construction. However, unlike the stone until it became tool, the object-thing/agents-in-use have themselves been prefigured (designed). We live amid, create and are created by, the designing of the designed as we design.

II

On the Subject of the Subject

The subject... that which can contain itself in its own contradiction.

—G.W.F. Hegel, 1807

Our aim is not to gloss the huge literature on the subject—a task already done numerous times by many others. Rather, it is to consider the ontologically designing forces that constitute subjects with diminished agency and the reverse: an ontologically designed subject beyond the subject. To do this, we must revisit the issue of power in a contemporary context as it transmutes and shifts how the subject needs to be viewed.

* * *

The animal that became human also eventually became a subject—that is, became subjectified by the exercise of a power—initially by the power of a moral or transcendental force (the power of God exercised theologically). But, by implication, the human/animal is more than mere subject.

As has now been stated a number of times: nihilism is a negation of human agency. It follows that to have any degree of affirmative transformative agency requires resisting both the colonization of subjection and the negation of nihilism. The other major implication of what has been presented here is that the subject is not independent but is inextricably connected to and prefigured by the ontological designing of object-things. Our passage from animal to human/animal was, as has been explained at length, significantly determined by the 'thinging' of the object (tool) from our very beginning. Moreover, from this original, formative moment on, our becoming subject has always been the product of the ontological designing of object-things and social relations of power as they arrived out of the structures of culture, religion, economy and the political. There was never a subject prior to and distinct from the agency of the object. Whatever the notion of a coming of a 'subject after the subject', this subject cannot be any more independent from the object than was its prior form.

The subject is both a creation (of a specific historical and nonuniversal project) and a projection. Demonstrating the relational interconnectedness of our being (as it includes the relation to object-things and social ecology) does not erase the efficacy of the projected identity of 'being a subject'. As we shall show, the specific can be layered onto or accommodated within the general in more ways than one. Along with this, the idea of a postsubject subject is to be addressed and qualified as *Das Übermensch Anhaltend* (the 'super-being'— now 'humax'—sustained), but, before it's possible to do this, qualification and clarification are needed.

The Nature of the Subject

The subject is not reducible to the self (which is a multiplicity of subjects).

For all that has been written on the subject and subjectivity, initially in Roman law and then from the start of the Enlightenment on, it has to be understood that these are not fixed or theoretically resolved entities. Yet one common thread weaves its way through this history—all subjects, as they are brought into being, are subjected to a power that demands obedience—the very nature of being a subject is obedience.[1] Power, Eurocentrically framed, was not given or taken but created of and for itself.[2] It now reigns by virtue of obedience being ontologically inscribed (in large part via inscribed service relations to communication and industrial technologies) as *habitus,* rather than externally commanded by an authoritative voice.

The modern subject was dominantly a project of the Enlightenment—to create a modern being via the sum of its discourses, implicitly articulated as the stated intent of every specific discourse (the rational subject, the civil citizen, the educated subject, the worker are all instances of this). Thus, we can say that the general condition of 'being a subject' arrived from the convergence of what was created for specific and different ends.

As indicated, the form of the subject so far considered is essentially a Eurocentric construction that has been projected universally (as has been the human) to define Others. As a result, the way the Other is seen, named and understood does not necessarily correspond with its own and its culture's self-understanding. For example, within globalizing political culture, an orthodox Muslim may be viewed and engaged as a political subject on the basis of a secularized Eurocentric understanding of the human as a social and thus 'political animal'. Conversely, the orthodox Muslim may see herself in purely theological terms as a servant of 'Allah on Earth' and, as such, a spiritual (rather than a human) being. In this instance, to be addressed as a political subject can be a negation of one's fundamental identity, if not also a threat to the very being of whosoever is addressed.

Contrary to the various forms of imposition, the modern subject was elevated and philosophically presented by the Enlightenment as 'not a thing but a general self understanding' directive of how we humans conduct ourselves.[3] Equally, and in contradiction, the subject became deeply implicated in the establishment of a position from which not only could the world be objectified as a 'standing reserve' (able to be treated and reduced to that available for technological appropriation) but also, within this position, the subject itself could be reified as another pure resource (*Bestand*) deployed as labour power able to be designed elementally into a production system. Here Marx's theory of labour folds into Heidegger's view of the way material resources came to be designated.[4]

The perception held for a long time that 'everything is an object for the subject' falls by the wayside.[5] In an age become technologically hegemonic, the destiny of the modern subject is now toward becoming hollowed out and diminished. Former firmly held beliefs about the nature of the subject now start to dissolve. For instance, how firmly held is the notion that, to become a subject, one has to have freedom to lose—by implication, neither the slave nor the serf could become subject—yet is not the incarcerated prisoner who has lost his freedom still not a subject? What of the belief that, as transcending beings, bound in the world, we could become aware of object-things and of our selves as subjects?[6] But, as we learn from onto-logical design, the self can be as much a product of the agency of design as are nonbeings (objects). Human being itself is based not on a subject/object *division* but an *articulation*.

The forms of subjection of the subjectivism of the subject are many. The sovereign subject of the state, the subject of knowledge, the patriarchal sub-ject, the interpellated subject (of the text), the subject of desire, the worker subject and so on—whatever the subject, 'it' is always subjugated to some object or force of power, yet the subject is relative and exceeded (clearly the politically disenfranchised subject is more subjugated than a citizen subject with enshrined constitutional rights). Effectively, the subject is more accu-rately understood as a variety of trans-individual subject positions constituted by different discourses, practices and object-thing relations that defy totaliza-tion (any theory of the subject that reduces 'it' to an 'it' can be assumed to be a misrepresentation of the plural nature and complexity of the subject).

We tend, of course, to think of ourselves as specific individuals who get gen-eralized as subjects. In reality, we are never outside the regimes of dispersed power and exist as identities always under erasure (whatever we 'are' at any given moment will always be displaced by an arriving identity—consumer to worker/worker to husband/ husband to father/father to motorist and so on) and as relationally bound figures with hardly any sense of this. These regimes have undergone major changes, not least as modernity broke the power of 'God' (and placed the subject under the disciplinary rule of the modern state and its institutions of law); identity has been turned into stereotypical images, into signs, and the Enlightenment-inspired production of the individual has driven social relationality further into concealment.

Another Cut

Subjectivity presumes a sense of self, with a degree of autonomy and a desire for exercised, self-realized power. Nietzsche would have it that 'the will to power' in fact authored subjectivity. If we ask what the source of this power is, rather than positing it in vitalism, the argument that has been put here suggests that it emanates from the practice of world formation converging with imagination. Thus, the exercise of power, as applied practical knowledge of and/in the world, precedes its recognition and social exercise. The distinction being made, then, is between an animal's application of brute force and directed energy as it ontologically acts back on a hominid actor—which experiences itself as having agency (and losing it).

The subjugated animal is harboured in the self. Instinctively, we know this, but we seldom admit it as other than a notional biological residue. That commonality—of fear, affection, pleasure—indivisibly shared between the animal and the human within the self has no voice. The human refuses 'the animal that it is' in the very designation of (other) animals. More than this, what constitutes the primary self goes unnoticed: this is the self composed from the human (with all its capabilities), the animal (as that interconnectivity that cares) and the nonhuman (that object-thing in being that facilitates and extends our becoming).[7] Our very being and survival depend on these linked relations. So contextualized, the subject, in its condition of obedience, is a middle ground between the internal instruction of the human over the animal and an external application of sociopolitical and ontologically designing power.

Notwithstanding remarks made so far, the relation between subject and object has been an enduring preoccupation of metaphysics. Positions abound, including a 'metaphysics of the subject' wherein the subject is merely generative of a 'surface effect'. The domain of the subject is considered one of the key competing ideas between almost every Enlightenment and post-Enlightenment thinker. To give just a hint of the complexity, let's take a single example: the relation of the subject to representation and reason.

The relation of the self to the subject raises the issue of whether it (the subject) 'represents its self'. Posing this issue creates a string of problematic questions. What proximity does the subject have to the self and its identity, especially when it's recognized that the subject can never be in full correspondence with the self (is it always, and at best, less than the self or, at worst, a nonidentity)? Is the subject simply a surface appearance? Is the subject purely a moment in time, of which there was a before and will be an after? What exactly will forge the link among self, subject and representation? The thing about such questions is not merely their complexity but that any answer provided will be contested, for there is no firm figure of reference, no uncontested ground upon which any claim to a 'truth' can stand. Echoing the exchange between Jacques Derrida and Jean-Luc Nancy two decades ago, one can simply say, 'everything becomes problematic in this discourse.'[8] Nonetheless, a certain certainty of the self can be claimed.

> Because care characterizes the self as self, and in this we see the fundamental trait of man, we must say that man as we encounter him and as we experience him—as the you, I, we—is grounded in the fact that that man is a self. The characteristic of Being a self is the condition for the fact that man is an I, and not vice versa. The self is the originary source that makes I and you possible. Only on the ground of the self is there the struggle for priority between I, you and we.[9]

Crucially, events do not wait until a mind is found that can answer these crucial questions.

The issue of the subject needs to be placed before the face of defuturing.

To continue to be, as a being we recognize as a being, we have to move beyond the way scientific techno-rationalism constitutes a subject as 'user' (that is, as a self-subordinated being not just using a technology but being used by it—who is overtly ontologically designed by it). Now the mechanism that delivers obedience shifts out of the metaphysical into the completely ontological. It is a matter not of knowing of the power that subjugates and thereafter acting in compliance—be it at the direction of God, the king, the law, the corporation and so on—but rather of coming to terms with human beings who are being used by a technology to complete *its* functional 'needs'. Examples abound: acting on the instructions of an algorithm; responding to the head-up digital diagnostics system controlling, say, the energy distribution system of a power station; or the compliant architectural drafter automatically conforming to the creation of sections by an Autocad software package. Here are 'subjects who in their objectification are no longer subject' and who have become designed, in their instrumentalized actions, as nonidentities.

By implication, the 'true self'—the unified being that we think we are—not only never appears but is driven evermore into exile even as a possibility. Increasingly, our mode of being 'thrown' into 'the world' is by the force of what Derrida, drawing on the ideas of Antonin Artaud, called the "subjectile" (which we can view here as the force of the theatre of the technological).[10] As has already been pointed out, power is ever being transferred to technology—as the power of technology continually inducts technology into beings (as metaphysics and memory) and thereby adds to its ontologically designing capability. Here another kind of subject after the subject arrives—subject in its lost freedom and the absolute instrumentalism that overwhelm the self. Such a subject is 'a principle of calculability' and, as such, a principle that can be taken to indicate the 'production' of a subject as a result of a calculated creation.[11]

We cannot critique that which cannot be reached (the ontic entity that we are); the self is a facticity that invites comment but not criticism. In contrast, the subject takes many forms, all of which are historically constituted under specific conditions and which are thus (and have been) open to criticism. Clearly, the criticism has been not so much of the subject itself as of the agent/agency which created it and which it obeys. So, rather than being what Michel Henry calls 'a specific and autonomous reality', the subject is 'a specific representation of a general reality'[12]—a state of being, economy, culture, psychology, pathology and so on—and of a specific expression of a human condition—anthropocentrism.

On writing on man as subject, Henry asserts: 'inasmuch as he is identified as this subject that man appears as a "super-being" to whom everything has entrusted its Being'.[13] On the contrary, one can firmly state that nothing was entrusted to 'man'. All that man has was taken from 'the world' to make 'a world'—a world in which the subject was created. All subjects act in obedience to anthropocentrism as they act in obedience to 'the power of man'.

The Subject Reborn: Reconsiderations

The question of 'what comes after the subject?' has been posed by many heterodoxical thinkers, but there has been no definitive answer. Generally, the answer is said to be another kind of subject.[14] However, the question can be recast; in fact, it needs to be recast as: what will 'we' become as what is coming toward us from the future (as it has been thrown into the future) 'eclipses the self'? Put another way, the question 'what comes after the subject?' cannot be answered in itself, because what can be expected to 'come before the subject' will decide what comes after it.

Nietzsche saw the future coming and addressed it in a very particular way in the mid-1880s in *Thus Spoke Zarathustra*. He contrasted the *last man* and the *Übermensch* (the overman, the superman) in the context of the growing wasteland and famously warned 'woe to him who harbours wastelands within.' The wasteland, of course, is the devastation of the spirit. The twentieth century saw the wasteland materially realized, in one form via the mass destruction of cities (including by a single bomb), the slaughter of millions on battlefields and the death of millions in camps wherein the inhumanity of the forces commanding them dehumanized the inmates to levels beyond the imagination of all civilized peoples. In another form, the wasteland arrived as the aesthetically glittering but vacuous forms of the diminished meaning of modern life—the elegant city, fashion, designer products—where appearance became the concealment of the unsustainable and the surrogate for meaning with substance. In this setting, we equally discover that ontological design, as design after the subject, travels in two directions: delivering the subject's erasure (just as, as we have seen via design and tools, it delivered its creation) and moving toward the enactment of a new mode of (super)human being (the 'humax') by bringing 'futuring things' into being. Here is but another acknowledgement of the primordial and futural relation wherein the self and the world are unified in one being.

In naming 'the last man', Nietzsche was calling up 'everyone' and 'no one'. Such a (wo)man is weak, decadent, decomposing and fated to oblivion, a being slavishly following 'the herd'. As such, she is a parasite on the power and values of the Other; all she takes is taken from elsewhere; she is empty. Even her dreams are borrowed.

We now live in this world of borrowed dreams with, as we have seen, a 'creative industry' having been created to deliver them. It tells us what to do, *and we do not even notice.* Unless 'we' collectively rise above this commodification of imagination, we risk falling into emptiness unable ever to be filled—the abyss.

Standing before the wasteland, we (that is, those of us—an indistinct community—who have some retained potentiality to act) have a choice. We can go on doing what we are currently doing (which is essentially refusing to recognize the defuturing of the objects of our own creation), or we can simply go on dealing pragmatically with symptomatic problems as they arrive while looking away from the future (at best, all we do here is to sustain the unsustainable). Alternatively, we can start to do what Nietzsche suggested, which, notwithstanding the enormity of the task, is, in the end, the only real affirmative act—to begin to change 'the nature' of our being. The dangers of trying to do this and the ease with which the project can get perverted are well recognized, not least by the intellectual history of the project in Germany in the 1930s (which, of course, included Heidegger's great error of judgement) and the crass, monstrous form it was given by the Nazis. But let it be stated baldly—the notion of the transformation of being to a higher order in not inherently fascist. If anything, it is an enduring onto-theology shared by a large number of cultures over a vast expanse of time.

Nietzsche used the notion of the *Übermensch* to name our self-overcoming. Translated as superman, as we realize, it has become an unfortunate term that somehow has to be dealt with because of its crude, misplaced appropriation by Nazi rhetoric in Germany from the 1920s on and because of its association with the 'End of the West debate' triggered by Oswald Spengler in the same period [wherein, for example, Arnold Toynbee argued that the rise of a 'superman' leader was fraught with danger but also asserted that 'higher religion exists to save civilization via the "Transfiguration of Saviours"' (claimed as a means to transfer the supersensory to the 'Kingdom of God')—a process whereby 'man' becomes 'superman' (evidenced by the figure of Christ)].[15] Finally, and more recently, *the* 'superman' degenerated into a figure of science fiction and mass culture. Added to this situation is, of course, the general debased use of 'super' as a prefix.

Yet, despite this history, the notion of 'superman' retains critical importance and has been radically recast, not least by Heidegger:

> The 'superman' does not simply carry the accustomed drives and strivings of the customary type of man beyond all measure and bounds. Superman is a qualitatively, not quantitatively, different form of existing man. The thing that the superman discards is precisely our boundless, purely quantitative non-stop progress. The superman is poorer, simpler, tenderer and tougher, quieter and more self-sacrificing and slow of decision and more economical of speech.[16]

More recently, Bernd Magnus had this to say:

> As an idealised type, one may view the *Übermensch* as the highest possible integration of intelligence, strength of character and will, autonomy, passion, taste, and perhaps even physical prowess...*Übermensch* is to be understood as the expression of ascending life, overfull and effortless.[17]

Yet, as we shall later see, these elaborations remain insufficient, bound as they are to a humanism and thus structurally to anthropocentrism. Miguel de Beistegui problematically says:

> The overcoming of nihilism through the shaping of the overman is at bottom a humanism, indeed the last phrase and the fulfilment of humanism, where 'man', albeit in the form of the overman, becomes the centre of all things and the absolute value.[18]

One can reply that 'man' has already become the centre of all things (this is exactly what anthropocentrism names) and that overcoming nihilism requires our being other than we are without a loss of memory. Just as, in our transformation from animal to human, the animal (by necessity) lived on, so on becoming 'superman' ('humax'), the human will remain, but subordinated to that greater than 'the subject'.

Part V

Now-ings

Photography: Peter Wanny / Illustration: Tony Fry

> However ready we are to rank man as a higher being with respect to the animal, such an assessment is deeply questionable, especially when we consider that man can sink lower than any animal.
>
> —Martin Heidegger, 1929

The telos of humanity as it is dominantly presented to us by humanist histories of civilization, nations, science, technology, commerce and the arts is one of continual development wherein both 'we' and the world-within-the-world we created have continually advanced. But the dialectic of Sustainment tells another story: yes, there have been numerous examples of progress, but often indivisibly linked to regress.[1] Likewise, for all the wonders of human creation, humanity has also wrought a terrifying amount of planetary destruction. If one thing is clear from even the most casual reflection upon this history, it is that, for the most part, human beings have had only a very marginal concern with and understanding of the consequences of their actions—both for themselves and for the world upon which they depend. What most distinguishes us from other animals, then, is not just our intelligence but the extent of our violence upon our own kind and our capacity to destroy other species and their environments. It seems we find many ways to celebrate our smartness but ignore the depth of our destructiveness and stupidity.

Knowledge is not external to the dynamics of the dialectic of Sustainment. Notwithstanding the accelerating growth of especially scientific and instrumental 'how-to' knowledge over, say, the past century, a great deal of knowledge has also been destroyed (not least from indigenous, artisan and contemplative cultures). Likewise, so much of what is seemingly known goes unexamined, and, certainly, knowledge, understanding and wisdom do not equate. Just to cite three examples: 'globalization' carries no element of choice—whatever its humanitarian claims, it does not arrive by its recipients' choice; environmentalism projects itself as action to 'save the planet', but it is actually we that are at risk because of the damage done to our conditions of dependence—the planet will recover from us or transmute as it has done before; and, as technoculture has proliferated, concern with the cultural and psychological impacts of technology has actually diminished. In contrast is the unknowing of much of what we are in our animality, as it is directive of the *nature* of our human being and, as such, remains the same.

What should be clear to all of us (no matter who or where we are) is that we can no longer remain as we are and have a viable future.

From the most deprived to the most affluent, changing the nature of our being is not a matter of choice but is becoming an absolute futural necessity. How we act in relation to one another, individually, interculturally and internationally, and upon the biophysical world is actually a determinant of the nature and possibility of our actually having a viable future. The call for change cannot be made by appeal to a humanistic agency (raised consciousness, a new morality or a new subject). Rather, it demands a *praxis* that liberates a transformative, ontologically designing force. The call for the creation of this force has to break through the noise of the everyday. Its urgency must be heard. For in the oft-cited words of Walter Benjamin, we in are in a storm, 'a chain of events...which keeps piling wreckage upon wreckage', and, as Benjamin reflected with regard to Klee's painting *Angelus Novus* (an angel of history), we are being propelled 'into the future' to which our back is turned 'while one single catastrophe which keeps piling wreckage upon wreckage and hurls it in front of his feet...while the pile of debris before him grows skyward'.[2] This storm around us is creating darkness, not just for a moment but also for an age to come and for the people who will populate it.

How do we get to another future? Ontological design has and will continue to be argued as means toward this end. But it is not enough. We need critical thought (theory), as well as imagination, but of a particular form, one that can link to ontological design. Design fictions gather and meet these needs.

What has to be imagined is what can and has to be designed. This itself is a designing.

Yet it cannot be written fantasy. Design fictions have to be subjected to critical interrogation. They may not announce themselves as fiction, can appear as speculation or may hide in authoritative projections. However, what they affirm is that the possible can and often does follow the improbable. Are design fictions different from theory? The answer to this question turns on the reader's view of theory as truth or not, which in turn is an epistemological issue. Positivists would refuse theory as fiction, realists might argue the toss, while constructivists have no argument—constructivism builds its reality on fiction, on a world of projected imagination of the nature of things.

12

Living in Darkness

In this immeasurable darkness, be the power.

—Rainer Maria Rilke

Darkness here is used literally and as a metaphor. To speak of darkness is to speak with and of uncertainty. This chapter is full of uncertainty. In speaking in such a way, I do not claim speculation as truth, and thus opinion will not be silenced. Thinking is what is sought, rather than agreement.

Humanity is travelling toward the prospect of living with a loss of light, with permanently grey skies, and with the loss of a key source of enlightenment. These losses possibly mark the coming of a new 'dark ages'. This is not just a rhetorical trope. Unlike the past Dark Ages, what is now unfolding is characterized by knowledge overwhelmed by information—with the result that vast numbers of 'knowing spirits' die. How this event will unfold remains uncertain, but the dangers are real and have to be confronted.

It's worth briefly touching on the first of the Dark Ages so that we may see how its shadow still falls over us.

The moment characterized by European history as the Dark Ages spanned a period of around five hundred years from the fall of the Roman Empire (this places it from around the fifth to the tenth centuries). In this period, geopolitically, power reverted to the East (China and Japan) and the Middle East. The dominant figure in Europe during this period was Charlemagne (724–814 AD), King of the Franks (a Germanic people powerful in Europe between the third and the ninth centuries) and ruler of the Holy Roman Empire (an empire that aspired to emulate the lost power of Rome and was underpinned by the power of the Church—a power that was violent, corrupt and degenerate). Crucially, knowledge at this time was dominantly secured by those monastic orders that isolated themselves from the turmoil.

An opening into the Middle Ages was created by the reform of the Christian Church, especially during the eleventh century. This reform led to the rise of Scholasticism in the twelfth century, culminating in the influential thinking of Thomas Aquinas. While cultural darkness started to lift in Europe, it was lowering elsewhere. At the call of Pope Urban II, the Crusades in the Holy Land began. The first commenced in 1096 and was conducted over forty-eight years; the eighth and final Crusade started in 1270 and lasted twenty-one years. While mostly forgotten in Europe, the consequences of these events still remain powerfully present and so have influenced the cultural and political life and destiny of the Middle East.

Clearly, the prospect of living in a period where tyranny is widespread and where past knowledge survives only under the protection of the few (as it was in the Dark Ages) may seem remote. Yet any sense of security we harbour that such circumstances cannot return could well be misplaced. Certainly, in evoking a New Dark Age, one would assume that it would have little in common with the first. But there are global dangers present that could well converge, and, if they do, the metaphor will not be out of place. Many of these dangers are connected by one factor—climate change.

The idea of a New Dark Age travels with the prospect of fear—fear underscored by the unthinking of instrumentalism and the actuality of hegemonic technology as both 'liberate' dangerous technologies over which there may be almost no control.

Certainly, one can read Nietzsche's view of nihilism at the end of the nineteenth century as a fear of what was to come. Oswald Spengler's polemic *The Decline of the West,* published in 1923, was a symptomatic text registering fear at the imminent loss of thinking. Spengler argued that the young and future generations would turn away from philosophy (thinking) and poetry (the poetic and the arts in general) and instead gravitate toward technology and an aestheticized nationalist politics based on celebration of distant past glories in which the German people rose up against the first Dark Ages. Spengler's view of technology was Faustian—it was a devil to employ for one's own ends. As such, perverting Nietzsche, he cast it as a means to exercise a 'will to power' best able to be 'creatively expressed' by war. His mythological politics was bonded to technology as a romantic force; it also provided a key conceptual foundation to Nazi ideology. De facto, the Nazis viewed technology as an instrumental means to reinstate a crude, mythologized, idealized version of the politiocultural order of the Greek past.[1]

The prospect of a climate-change-induced 'New Dark Age' turns on political and technological convergence.

Politically, it would arrive as the consequence of the failure of governments to act globally with sufficient urgency. The expectation here is that this failure would have dramatic and dire consequences for biological life in general (from the loss of biodiversity—terrestrial and aquatic) and thus equally for human life. This situation needs to be seen in the context of other factors stemming from the continued growth of the human population (for at least another century), especially as they are linked to climate change impacts. These factors, which will express themselves in numerous scenarios, include pressure on food production, stress on natural resources, fresh water crises, the collapse of some types of ecological systems, economic breakdown (including of the carbon economy), the probability of a rapid increase of environmental refugees and the increasing likelihood of regional asymmetrical conflicts. Every one of these scenarios will be extremely complex. Many of them already exist in their early stages. As they unfold, they will become relationally connected, more serious and much harder to deal with.

What is evident is the fact that there is no overall picture, discourse or analysis that comprehends and presents what is actually happening and where consequences will lead, biophysically and geopolitically. This failure cannot be separated from chronophobia as it marks both a fear of time and an inability to 'think in time (as a medium)'. Obviously, this situation is likely to unfold in many different ways, but one expects that in each case they will generate political, social, cultural and technological responses that themselves will present huge challenges everywhere.

As outlined earlier, human beings everywhere, know it or not, are moving into an age of unsettlement. That said, much that has been taken as certain and fixed will be seen to be uncertain and fluid. The idea of continual progress and of human development having direction staggers on, but it will fall. The view that 'the environments of our dependence' can and will continue to provide security and a sense of permanence will also disappear. Likewise, and more problematic, the notion that technology 'will save us' will not survive. It is by no means impossible that whole nations will disappear, that disease and famine will cull vast numbers of people globally. Moreover, as military think tanks around the world are recognizing, it is almost certain that, as vast numbers of climate-displaced people cross borders uninvited and conflict ensues, large numbers of people will be killed.[2]

As such, events fuel the feeling of unsettlement, both for people directly affected and for observers, the very nature of human psychology will start to change. For an indeterminate period, life will come to be lived in darkness. As has already been said, we shall examine the assertion of the arrival of life lived in darkness in two ways: technologically induced darkness and psychosocial darkness. Before doing so, we need to be clear that what is being considered here is not being posed as certain. Presenting these negative scenarios serves two functions: to potentially identify what has to be avoided so as to prompt the pursuit of means of avoidance and, if avoidance action is not taken or if it fails, to prompt the planning of designed responsive action.

Darkened Skies

'Geoengineering' (generally now understood as a technological intervention in the climatic system to reduce global warming) is an idea that has been around for more than half a century, but now it has moved from fiction to fact. So, although design fictions can still be generated from speculation about particular geoengineering impacts, its status as a fictional technology has ended. Geoengineering is heading toward becoming a 'respectable' area of scientific enquiry. For example, both the Royal Society in Britain and the US National Academy of Sciences have made calls for research to explore possible geoengineering impacts on the planet. The issue is also receiving attention in other countries, including Australia.[3] It could actually end up marking a quantum leap in the anthropocentric impetus of humans to dominate nature. Reportedly, in 'saving humanity' from global warming such technology might generate another kind of disaster which kills the life of the oceans, turns blue sky a permanent grey and transforms human psychology—all issues to consider in more detail.

Driven by pragmatics and the possibility of short-term, high-yielding financial returns, geoengineering illustrates the application of 'capital logic' to direct the future of the planet. But, to start with, what we shall examine is the prospect of the implementation of geoengineering, not just from the perspective of technology but equally as its development demonstrates the irrationality of instrumental reason.

Geoengineering is the most overt example of such irrationality since the Manhattan Project, whose development process was driven by instrumental reason at a key moment of the Second World War. This project reconfigured how risk was viewed. The imperative of realizing the Manhattan Project's goal meant that major risks were taken: effectively, while risk was calculated, expediency overwhelmed reason, and actions were taken with a lot of hope but without real knowledge of consequences. Experimental underground testing of the atomic chain-reaction process is a dramatic example of just how high the stakes were—for, if controls had failed, the chain reaction could have been uncontainable.

At a more fundamental level, the creation of atomic weapons rested on an enormous application of instrumental reason and, in so doing, brought something irrational into being which still has the potential to destroy the entire human race and much else besides.

It is no coincidence that an advocate of geoengineering, Jay Michaelson, writing for the *Stanford Environmental Law Journal,* titled his article 'A Climate Change Manhattan Project'. In so doing, he exactly captured the scale and madness of the enterprise.[4] His basic argument was that the politics of emissions reduction is too difficult, so the way to go is to become totally economically pragmatic. Unlike more recent supporters of geoengineering, he sees it not as complementing emissions reduction but as the more viable alternative. In fact, he asserts that geoengineering can 'minimize the time between sacrifice and reward, it minimizes the discounting of that reward and the deniability of the need for the sacrifice'.[5] In cavalier fashion, Michaelson leaves 'nature' to pay the price:

> Even if 'geoengineering' were expensive, and even if it were not superior to climate change regulation in terms of its effects on elites, it may yet be the cheapest available strategy in terms of political economy because it carries almost no social costs whatsoever. No one need change lifestyles, take a bus instead of a car, or pay more at the gas pump to combat climate change, if 'geoengineering' can offset the climate effects of business as usual. Consumptive patterns of life, which the majority of Westerners seem to enjoy, can continue unabated.[6]

He believes that:

> the need to mitigate climate change may simply outweigh the aesthetic valuation of the natural world. The costs of coping with dead forests and shifting agricultural zones are not scare tactics, but serious concerns that may outweigh eco-aesthetic (or even religious) reservations about a man-made sky. If the consequences of global warming track the more acute predictions of greenhouse 'doomsayers', this is certainly the case: few may insist on the integrity of Gaia if millions of people (and animals) will starve.[7]

Hyper-pragmatically Michaelson concludes by saying:

> A 'geoengineering' project may be expensive, unreliable, dangerous, ugly, and unwise—although I attempted to answer each of these objections...But so are many cures for a desperate situation.[8]

While these views have been around for a while, the pragmatic spirit they represent not only still holds but is gaining ground. Typical are some comments made at the first conference in Australia on geoengineering, in September 2011.

The overall view at the event was that such 'measures need to be part of a global emergency response if all else fails when tackling climate change'. The view of Dr Graeme Pearman, senior research fellow at Monash University, was that 'there needs to be a global approach to putting geoengineering on the table as a back-up option'—this as a kind of insurance. Another speaker, Dr Greg Bodeker, said that 'firing sulphate aerosols into the stratosphere is one option; the technique would create a semi-transparent umbrella that would shade the planet from the sun, thereby reducing global temperatures.' But he went on to say: 'It's very effective but the risk associated with that is very high.'[9] Thus, not only does this triangle of prospective need, potential and risk denote the character of this conference; it also indicates the overall state of debate on the issue.

At the Asilomar event, on the Monterey peninsula in California, between 22 March and 26 March 2010, there was a major deliberation by scientists on geoengineering—which was defined as human-directed change of the world's environment. Some of the scientists who attended wished to start preliminary experiments or supported such action. They wanted a clear regulatory framework to be established. As a report of the event made clear:

> There are two broad approaches to 'geoengineering'. One is to reduce the amount of incoming sunlight that the planet absorbs. The other is to suck carbon dioxide out of the atmosphere and put it somewhere else. The second of these approaches is not particularly in need of new regulation. Whether the carbon dioxide is captured by real trees, as some would like, or by artificial devices, environmental problems caused by the process would be local ones at the site of the sucking...Even the most potentially disturbing

suggestion, which involves fertilising the oceans with iron in order to promote the growth of planktonic algae (in the hope that they would sink to the seabed, taking their carbon with them), can be covered by the London Convention on marine pollution, which regulates dumping at sea.

Reducing incoming sunlight, by contrast, is fraught with danger. While it is possible to imagine doing so in a way that cancels out the change in average temperature caused by an increase in carbon dioxide, such a reduction would not simply restore the status quo. Local temperatures would still change in some places, as would ocean currents, rainfall patterns, soil moisture and photosynthesis. Sunshine reduction, then, clearly needs to be regulated.[10]

The kinds of sunlight reduction experiments discussed in Asilomar were of a small scale. One was based on propelling plumes of various sulphurous fluids into the stratosphere to find out which would produce the best haze of small particles (similar to those that cool the planet after a large-scale volcanic eruption). Another would attempt to whiten clouds over the oceans by seeding them with tiny salt particles (these clouds would, in theory, have more, smaller droplets in them, which would mean more sunlight reflected away from the planet. Such stratospheric aerosol injection technologies, along with 'sunshades in space',[11] have the greatest potential to cool the climate but also carry the greatest risk.

The Asilomar report noted that 'a team of scientists and engineers that calls itself "Silver Lining" is working on this idea, with some of its research paid for with money from Bill Gates'.[12]

Importantly, as James Hrynyshyn points out, 'the more feasible the idea, the smaller the contribution it can make.' For instance:

the pyrolysis (oxygen-free) burning of organic waste, which turns it into 'bio-char' that can then be buried, for example, has been widely touted as one of the most promising proposals to sequester carbon. James Lovelock is talking it up as one of the only realistic options we might have to forestall catastrophic climate change.[13]

But Hrynyshyn also notes that it will bring down CO_2 levels by only 34 ppm. He goes on to say (totally counter to Michaelson's views) that geoengineering really 'only makes sense as a part of a larger strategy that includes cutting back hard on greenhouse gas emissions'.[14]

In addition to being very costly and dangerous, geoengineering has the potential to undermine both the vital task of reducing greenhouse gas emissions and human-based adaptive action. Its development message is 'business as usual'.

As far as the global media are concerned, the issue of climate change has 'gone off the boil'—displaced by a preoccupation with an ongoing financial crisis. However, as reports on the Durban climate change negotiations in December 2011 made clear, even in a period of economic decline and stagnation in many parts of the world, the level of emissions continues to rise, and the situation continues to get worse.[15] Of course, one could expect that any economic recovery would significantly add to the problem. So there is growing cause for concern not only about the rate of rise of emissions but also about the widening gap between rhetoric and action. Effectively, as the Durban event indicated, setting targets and getting agreements are becoming substitutes for action, rather than leading to it.

Yet everyone who knows anything at all about climate change recognizes that it will now take a gargantuan effort to reduce emissions, and the longer the wait to take action, the harder it will be. Yet, somehow, this simple and powerful message still does not arrive universally or penetrate the popular and political consciousness. If it does arrive, it may well be at a time when disaster has become unavoidable. What is clear is that the nearer we get to disaster, the greater the danger of adopting untried and questionable geoengineering measures. One can even contemplate that, in a moment of panic, there could be a resort to a disastrous a large-scale intervention in the Earth's climate system.

Moving our focus from the sky to the ocean—the other domain of geoengineering—a recent study from the University of Western Ontario in Canada found that adding iron to the world's oceans in order to capture carbon and fight global warming could do more harm than good. This is because the mineral appears to boost the growth of plankton that in turn produce a deadly neurotoxin—a chemical that actually kills brain cells.[16]

Whatever action is now taken, whatever the eventual level of emissions reached, the problem of a transformed climate is going to be with humanity for a very long time. As Susan Solomon, a scientist at the US National Oceanic and Atmospheric Administration, has demonstrated in her modelling, changes in surface temperatures, rainfall and sea levels are largely irreversible for more than a thousand years after CO_2 emissions have stopped.[17]

Darkened Lives

The darkness of the New Dark Age, if it comes, will arrive in three forms. As outlined, it will come from the skies, but also from ignorance and the soul. Geoengineering would likely bring darkness to the skies; ignorance as darkness arrives as a failure to see and thus a failure to act preventively in the face of danger; and darkness casts a shadow over the soul and, in so doing, diminishes the very being of our being.

Re-Framings

Following on from earlier characterizations of relational impacts of climate change, here are some of the key interconnected factors: heat and heat islanding; rising sea levels; drought and desertification; extreme weather events; resource stress; a crisis of food supply combined with an ever-growing global population; and rapid urbanization, bringing huge concentrations of people (and creating endless cities).[18] All these well-documented problems and more will converge, along with, as already noted, social and political conflict (likely to be violent) as climate-displaced people cross borders in search of livelihoods in new settings. These problems are already beginning to unfold for millions of people in the most impoverished and vulnerable nations, especially in Africa.

The security afforded by settlement over the past ten thousand year will be significantly reduced. People will not be able to return to the nomadic way of life that existed for millennia prior to the age of settlement (even if they tried, they would be ill-equipped in body and mind to do so; moreover, the planet could not support the chaos and the ecological demands of billions of people living this way).

These scenarios need to be seen 'in time' and in the context of (*a*) the climatic cycles of heating and cooling of our planet (the next cooling has been projected to occur in twenty-five thousand years, but anthropogenic climate change brings this projection into question) and (*b*) past climate-induced planetary transformations, which have been on a scale beyond our comprehension (not least the six major ice ages). For many hundreds of thousands of years, great swathes of the planet were uninhabitable. The last glacial episode spanned from around 118,000 to 18,000 years ago.[19] During this period, the population of *Homo sapiens* was reduced to just a few thousand, yet 'we' survived. As detailed in an earlier chapter, it was only a few thousand years later that human settlement began, predominantly in the Fertile Crescent of the Middle East. If this history is any measure, 'we' will survive out into the future. What is harder to predict is how many of us will, in what ways, and in what kind of world.

To gain a sense of the significance of the changes that lie ahead, to see in them plausible danger, and to rightly fear them require that we shift away from viewing events in human-centred time to geological time. A few centuries are a long time to us, but in geological time they are a mere blink of an eye. In our time, climate change appears to be occurring moderately slowly, but in geological time it's travelling 'at the speed of light'. Perceptually, our epochal time is a product of modernity as event (it brought the geopolitical world into one moment of time—the modern measured time of 'now').[20] It is not unlikely that 'modern time' will break down in more distant decades as the relation between the local and the global and between different technological cultures fractures. Unquestionably, much will fragment.

There are, for instance, estimates that sea-level rises will displace seven hundred million people.[21] Added to this, there will be people displaced by heat, the loss of water, extreme weather events, and violent conflict. Thus, it could be that, within a century or so, more than 10 per cent of the human population of the planet will be homeless, nationless, and displaced. Just having this number of people moving in huge numbers, often in a hostile physical and security environment, will in some way affect everyone, everywhere.

With such events as context, it is not beyond the bounds of imagination that the systems of governance of many nations could easily implode as the borders of nations (which are, of course, no more than artificial creations) cease to function as policed boundaries to contain the mass crossings of populations. The systems and structures of economic exchange in and between nations could equally fragment as environmental disasters bankrupt nations.[22]

Unless there are major global directional changes in the next decade or so, the 'age of unsettlement' *will* ensue. As indicated, human psychology will change (as it would have done a number of times in the past). There has always been a link between climate and psychology, and this, of course, never more so than when major changes are experienced.

One can conjecture that, with the coming of climate changes, some societies and communities will split. Those regions where the changed climate is beneficial, leading to increased agricultural productivity, may well get an unwanted influx of people from regions where the reverse is the case. Clearly, many people without the will or means to adapt will suffer despair and a feeling of hopelessness. Conversely, for those who are able to adapt, aggressive protectionism, short-term self-interested action and long-term pessimism can all be expected to be rife. Realistically, it's likely that huge numbers of people will live with their hopes and dreams dashed and a sense of the future as darkness. Conversely, the minority will find the courage, determination and leadership to start the task of building the form of the future at the opening of the new epoch. Additionally, there is also an economically powerful constituency that will acquire the most habitable of places and exploit them.

In such a setting, civilization as we know it is unlikely to survive. Likewise, how freedom is currently understood and enacted will not survive. The notion of the 'end of man' could shift from a philosophical judgement on the death of a particular discourse to an actual socio-anthropological and bloody reality wherein savagery becomes widespread. Insecurity, physical hardship and omnipotent fear might well again be the dominant human condition. Here, then, is the reality of the darkness of the soul. Yet, against this backdrop, lessons of the past will confirm that a possibility will open for the birth of another future. As ever, making this future will equally make its makers. What is also certain is that, across all our difference, we will not remain as we are (just as now we are not as we were). There will be a moment of *palingensia*—a moment of re-creation.

In solidarity with change agents of the present working toward Sustainment (future makers of the yet-to-be), it behoves us to think the future not as void to fill with fantasy but as a partly delineated space/time populated by the problems already pitched into it. In so doing, we span two modes, one imagining what has to be prevented or avoided and another imagining what has to be created. To illustrate the point, the possible fate of cities will be revisited (initially as outlined in chapter 8) and elaborated as a series of generic types within a notional time frame of about two hundred years. Their order of presentation is not intended to be read as a linear progression from one to another. As is always the case, different forms of cities will coexist at different times and places. The futural forms will not be architecturally, socially or economically uniform but obviously will reflect local climatic conditions, available knowledge and material resources, plus demographic and sociopolitical circumstances. Circumstantially, these cities can be expected to exist in varied conditions of crisis.

These generic cities are not being presented as developmental end-points to realize. They are merely figures to prompt discussion of their possible forms. It is important to understand that, while the entire activity is instrumentally presented, it is indivisible from ontological design. Whatever future action is taken or whatever form is created, it will be transformative of both people and the(ir) environment(s).

Of Cities and Posturban Futures

I will comment on seven city forms of a possible future. Some already have a nascent form and invite immediate action. Others await particular circumstances to bring them into being. All these city forms have a specific relation to the movement of people, events and climate—this not least because, as said, it is very likely that freedom of movement will change dramatically in the future. Climate-displaced people (the possible 10 per cent of the human population—which, if things go badly, eventually may be a billion people by 2100) will constitute a new transit class. Conversely, those people living in secure environments will be less mobile across, outside and beyond their city (in a more dangerous and divided world, fear will likely be a powerful anchor holding people in place). Electronic communication and associated forms of telepresence can be expected to assume even greater importance in the everyday life of these people.

The Metrofitted City

The metrofitted city[23] is the city of the present brought to a condition where it can have a more viable future and futuring capability. Subject to circumstances, some such cities will have a future of one or more centuries, others, those in high-risk environments, much less. At the highest level of risk are, for example, cities on the Bay of Bengal, the Ganges, the Mekong, the Irrawaddy, the lower Amazon, and the Parana, as well as New York, London and Shanghai.

The conceptual basis of metrofitting is to take retrofitting to a much higher level—to the metropolitan scale. It would include conventional building-based retrofitting approaches, applied to an entire city's building stock. However, metrofitting goes beyond this and starts with comprehensive time-based risk mapping, along with a programme of transforming education for and the practices of design and planning. This programme could include, for instance, design to combat heat islanding, cyclone-protection shelters, and the transformation of built structures to enable them to withstand the coming climate (heat, extreme weather impacts, reduction of energy load) while improving thermal comfort. Equally, it would include water conservation and recycling, the modification of energy infrastructure to meet an increased load while reducing impacts, urban food production, and low-impact transport modes. Metrofitting can again go much further and engage: fashion for the future; modification of work and the working day; the management and planning of refugee influx and resettlement; emergency shelter and signage (signage that identifies 'safe to shelter in an emergency'); and evacuation pathways for use after a disaster.

The intent of metrofitting, besides lowering the negative environmental impacts of urban fabric and infrastructure, is obviously to give increased viability to a city over time so that its population does not have to move. Crucially, the selection of a city to metrofit must be based on a rigorous assessment of location, climate risk exposure and quality of the material fabric of the city and its infrastructure. More than this, the approach can be brought to existing programmes of urban transformation (like the 'transition town' movement).[24]

The Abandoned City

Since ancient times, cities have been abandoned because of environmental change, fire, disease or war; what can be expected to be new is the scale and number of such abandonments. As already suggested, many of the cities that will be affected are currently very important, extremely large and well-known. But, in many cases, their fate was decided at the very moment when they were inappropriately sited. Perhaps a few of them may be reconstructed at some future time, but most will remain as ruins. Certainly, all will have an afterlife in popular memory.

Some cities will be abandoned in response to impacts that arrive gradually (like rises in sea level, multiple extreme weather impacts, or heat/heat islanding that make them totally or partly unliveable). Others will be depopulated as a result of the impact of a single disaster event. Then there will be those that will be devastated because of conflict. The duration of abandonment may be extended, well-planned and orderly; however, some cities will be depopulated very quickly as hundreds of thousands or millions flee from danger. In some instances, a totally depopulated city may be deliberately razed (by being blasted, bulldozed or bombed). It is almost certain that these cities, if left in ruins, will be reoccupied in a dysfunctional condition by the incoming dispossessed. Likewise, it is also possible some cities could be 'mined' for material resources.

For the lucky, movement from an abandoned city will represent a flight to another, temporary, informal, or new city. For those who are not so lucky, the expectation will likely be a displaced-persons camp, and, for the very unlucky (of whom there will be many), the future will simply be an endless search for food and shelter wherever they can find (or take) it.

The Informal, Rapid-Construction City

In almost every newly industrializing nation, there has been rapid growth of informal cities.[25] These are cities built without planning, building regulation, utility services or adequate infrastructure. They have very inadequate (or no) public health facilities and have a high fire risk; some harbour crime, *but* they often have a strong social fabric and a highly developed community structure.

The abandonment of cities will unquestionably accelerate the number and size of informal cities. Such cities—of which there are many types, from the liveable to the hellish—are very vulnerable to extreme weather events, yet structurally many can be easily rebuilt after they have been destroyed. A number of lessons come from informal cities. First, a common culture and circumstances, needs, and high density are generative of cooperation and community. While this has been recognized and is undoubtedly true, in many circumstances it also gets romanticized and even treated in a patronizing manner. Increasingly, cooperation and strong social bonds will become even more important to human survival. This social capability and knowledge are vital to capture. Second, developing the ability to build semi-informal/temporary cities at a low cost, with rapid construction methods and available material and using mostly unskilled labour, will be essential to meet future huge demands for shelter. Knowledge of how to do this exists and, with workable systems of power, water and sewage infrastructure, rests as much within informal cities as it does in the advanced building industry of orthodox cities. Third, in some locations, the most appropriate form of building new permanent cities could be with sacrificial lightweight elements combined with secure high-specification protective-shelter cores. Learning from informal cities could well inform the conception and technology of new cities.

In the past, informal cities have occurred mostly as a consequence of rapid urbanization, where large numbers of people abandon a life of subsistence agriculture in the hope of earning money. If unsettlement arrives at the scale expected, then, in all its forms, it will drive the creation of informal and semi-informal cities. Movement in this context will be determined by population redistribution, the growth in transitory communities and the movement of people to new temporary or fixed settlements.

Moving Cities

The moving of cities is again not a new idea or practice.[26] But, for the most part, cities have been moved badly and even violently (not least in China).

The choice between moving and abandonment will confront many governing authorities in cities in coming decades. For a city to be moved, four things have to move: a sufficient volume of the original building fabric for a claim of continuity to be made; the transfer of a viable social fabric to ensure social continuity; linkage to forms of cultural life, especially those able to enhance community; and the relocation of an existing economy or the creation of a new one that utilizes available existing skills and knowledge. The key to the success of a city move is a clear and desirable destination combined with a good system of governance directing both 'the move out' and 'the move to' over time. This system must embrace all vested interests to the city: its economic interests, its political culture and the interests of its various communities. Good logistics and realistic timing are also crucial.

Moving cities takes time (one or several decades), not only because of the scale of the task and the need for the idea of the new (city) to gain the momentum that brings it to life but also because of intergenerational difference. Even moving a part of a city, which again is an established rather than a new practice, takes many years if done with due sociocultural considerations.[27] In essence, older people often have strong attachments to place and resist moving. In contrast, if the new city presents opportunities, young people will embrace the prospect. Time planning has to take this into account and, in so doing, deal with the generational middle ground. Obviously, moving a city requires both conservation and change. Key to such change is reducing and editing out as many problems as possible that are intrinsic to the existing circumstance so that they are not transported into the new.

While moving a city is hard, it can, in some circumstances, offer a viable alternative to abandonment and the breakup and dispersal of a 'community'.

The Urmadic City

As opposed to the movement of an existing city, the urmadic city[28] is a city specifically designed to move. It is an opening into thinking a posturban future, especially as conditions of unsettlement grow. Moving through a number of prototypical forms, urmadic cities could start to be created toward the last quarter of this century.

The concept is based on the fact that, although the majority of the planet's population is now urban, for nearly all of *Homo sapiens'* existence, life and survival depended upon being nomadic. In the conditions that will emerge, many urban cultures will be forced to learn how to become mobile and thus partly nomadic (hence ur(ban no)madic). The urmadic city is not the kind of 'high-tech plug-in/walking city' characterized by Archigram in the 1960s. It does not have a particular architectural form, except that it would be technologically overdetermined: it would have to be easy to move—and moving would take place in from one to several decades. The idea centres on the creation of many small cities (with populations of around sixty thousand people). In addition to favouring certain construction methods and materials because of the need for mobility, urmadic cities would have a different system of land tenure, and their dwellers would have quite different relations to property and goods than are common today; dwellings would also be much smaller than is currently the norm in most European cities. Likewise, there is the expectation that much of life would be immaterialized (meaning that people would own far fewer material goods). However, what people owned would be created to be far more aesthetically and functionally significant. Such changes presume major legal reform and industrial transformations that are as challenging to introduce as the creation of the city itself.

What would direct the movement of a city would be precautionary actions in the face of clearly identified risk (climatic or conflict). By implication, the distance moved could be small or great, as well as being preplanned strategically, physically and legally. The actual mechanism of movement would be based on something like railway infrastructure, with advanced design for disassembly and rapid reassembly with supplementary prefabricated construction. The elements of the city would likely be rationalized: public services and utilities; a 'lean' retail sector; industry and commerce; dwellings and community facilities. The dominant form of such cities would be immaterial and centre on community and self-governance. The urmadic city would not presume fully operational national, state or regional government. The security of such cities would be delivered by perhaps their own defence militia (exclusively defensive), for which all adults would be trained and serve for a certain number of days per year. Movement would always be a means to avoid conflict.

What the urmadic city represents is an opening into the future where some kind of foundation to build a quality of life could start to be contemplated and created.

The Fortified City

The response of some cities (and nations) to the prospect of the arrival of climate-displaced persons will be to try to keep them out. The tendency of people in many wealthy sections of cities (especially those with large poor communities) is already to fortify their places of privilege (the so-called secure 'gated communities'). This disposition will extend to larger areas or to the totality of many cities. Likewise, new fortified cities will be built; signs of this are already appearing.[29] Less confrontationally, fortification will also extend to 'climate-defensive architecture' (and, as such, will arrive more generally).

Historically, fortification has a mixed history, and it often fails. The population of fortified cities can become prisoners of their own construction. Provided the attackers have good logistics, the odds favour those who besiege these cities. Even with the support of modern technology (e.g. helicopters, advanced weapon systems, electronic surveillance), the need to move matter (goods in/waste out) and, in many cases, water and power will mean that fortified cities will always remain vulnerable.

The Underground City

Underground construction technology is already advanced. Many cities already have large underground areas (for example, Toronto, with its harsh winters, has 28 kilometres of underground arcades linking fifty major buildings and many major facilities; there are around '1,200 underground shops and services, such as photocopy shops and shoe repairs, employing about 5,000 people').[30] Going underground will likely be a widely used climate-defensive urban strategy. But it requires a lot of equipment and a great deal of money. Living underground also brings long-term psychosocial problems. Variants could be created: semisubterranean structures (as the protective core); underground zones in which all key services are located (e.g. schools, hospitals, food storage, emergency services, telecommunications); hypershelters; and, at the other extreme, totally robotic industrial cities. One of the advantages of such cities would be a massive reclaiming of agricultural land. The image here could be enclosed cities beneath and protected farms on the surface, with the underground population being required to undertake a number of days of farm work or farm defence service per year. Movement of people, in this context, would mostly be between above and below ground.

13

Postpolitical Prospects

The contest is not one of vengeance but one of endurance. It is not those who can in-
flict the most pain but those who can suffer the most who will conquer.

—Terence MacSwiney, Irish hunger striker, 1920

As we have seen, there are a number of major climatic and geopolitical forces in prospect now and at least over the next century that will have profound consequences for human earthly habitation. As we have been saying, these forces are likely to seriously destabilize not just the political order that underpins existing forms of governance but the very fabric of contemporary life everywhere. There is no way to be exact about the actual form of these or the exact moment of change, but major change there will be.

To reiterate—risk grows from two directions: from the human-induced amplification of those environmental impacts that threaten life in general and from an increased concentration of human lives in vast, dense, inappropriately located cities. The first cities had tiny populations (Ur, for instance, was home to approximately twenty-five thousand people), whereas there is now talk of endless cities of one hundred million people.[1]

The point of looking at some of these possible changes here is to register the scale of what can be expected and the necessity of thinking about consequences and responses.

Fragments of the City and Nation

The fragmentation of the idea of what a city is was considered in the previous chapter. What was not addressed in any detail was what might happen if this occurs. But, before we start to do this, we must offer one important caveat.

Relational climatic change occurs continually in incremental, geographical and chronologically uneven ways as the planet moves through its cycles of heating and cooling. These changes are beyond the human capacity to imagine in time—they escape us—yet they nonetheless have determinant consequence for our species. For example, as mentioned, the planet is headed toward a massive cooling in approximately twenty-five thousand years time (subject to the still-unknown impacts of anthropocentrically induced warming on this cycle). Taking the point a little further, geological time frames are outside the grasp of our thinking. The case of Britain illustrates the point.

Britain was not a continuous home for hominids until twelve thousand years ago. For the previous hundred thousand years, it was visited by hominids only when the climate permitted—which was only about 20 per cent of this time. In fact, in that period prior to seventy thousand years ago, it was so cold that what we know as Britain was totally abandoned—initially by Neanderthals for more than one hundred thousand years and a little later by *Homo sapiens*—a latecomer species.

Changes associated with current global warming are not awaited but are under way. Currently, the greatest changes are occurring in poor and vulnerable countries—places that the world media pay scant attention to. Things will not remain so. History suggests that most people in most places do not face change until it is unavoidable. We view the transitory world around us, the world of our making, as having permanence. Yet there is nothing of human creation, including cities, that is permanent. As Karl Marx memorably remarked in the *Communist Manifesto,* 'all that is solid melts into air'. Certainly, as individuals and as a species, we are but objects of a passing universal moment.

Cities are not merely dynamic sociocultural and economic formations with a particular constructed metabolism, for they also function as nodes in the operational structures of a nation and beyond it. They serve as intersecting organizational hubs of commerce, industry, culture, administration, law, medicine, communication, private and public life and so on. The city in history, over a period of nearly eight thousand years, has both remained the same and dramatically changed. To say that its future is not assured is not to say anything new. Lewis Mumford opened his seminal *The City in History* by asking: 'will the city disappear or will the planet turn into a vast urban hive?'[2] If the city ceases to function as an element within the matrix of the nation (while still operative in the global economy), both nations and cities as we understand them may break down and transmute.[3] Although it might be difficult to imagine this situation, it is not impossible. Both were products of human invention, as will be future modes of life and political organization. One newer form of organization that has received some attention is the idea of a 'network society'.

The form of a network society, as outlined and developed by Manuel Castells a decade and a half ago, does not have to be predicated upon information flows that break the sequences of events upon which the recognition of the passing of time (change) depends.[4] Rather than being the substrate of a postindustrial globalized economic community, network societies that emerge out of 'a coming wasteland' could be a means of clustering the fragments of cities (or fragmentary cities) via local sociopolitical organizations and energy power grids (national power grids are unlikely to survive the breakup of nation-states). Such societies could be the proto-structures out of which new formations of collective life could be constituted.

The second and coexistent possibility is a remaking of tribal societies.

The challenge of survival always divides cultures: some fall, and others rise. There is a strong prospect that tribalism, as a coming together to constitute identities and action motivated by a will to survive, will be a crucial futuring factor for hundreds of millions of people. Clearly, they can take benign or aggressive forms. The rise of armed tribes that cross borders to plunder and seize land by force to grow food is one real possibility. But so is the reverse— some tribes could be affirmative social clusters setting out to reconstitute a viable way of life in the absence of any other form of identification and, as such, work to establish collective solidarity based on mutual concern and protection. More than just local groupings, regional tribal formations could well work together strategically to reconstruct some kind of civil society. Lest all of this sound like fantasy, it is worth noting that there are already dysfunctional states where governance is no more than whatever communities can constitute for themselves; also, there is the previously discussed example of the self-created functionality of existing informal cities.

Nevertheless, what is clear is that the prospect of political certainly will likely evaporate. From a time where political hegemony seemed to be firm (although the fall of the USSR belied the difference between appearance and reality), we are, as is being indicated, moving toward a situation of uncertainty, of unsettlement. The rise of the structure of the modern state made what is now taken to be the normal conditions of social and economic life possible. With the demise of the viability of the nation-state, a reversion to 'societies without a state' may take place. As Pierre Clastres pointed out, citing J. W. Lapierre, this is not the end of the political, for, whenever social innovation takes place (and with it a reconfiguration of power), so also does the political re-emerge.[5]

Future societies may well extend across a spectrum from the residually functional to the dysfunctionally brutal. Between these poles would be those societies working to create micro-economies, workable means of exchange, operative social structures, forms of protection, new kinds of institutions and administrative structures and legal and ethical codes. Trying to think and imagine all of this is a considerable challenge. Many of these features are mirrored in the form of the 'urmadic city' discussed in the previous chapter.

Without making any deterministic claim, the exercise of imagination can serve to prefigure how such a political situation might be engaged. In so many ways, the future will demand thinking what, at the moment, seems unthinkable (and saying what, if convention were to dictate, would remain unsaid).

Cull Times

We have a choice: we can ignore the likelihood that huge numbers of human beings are going to die because of the forces of defuturing which we humans ourselves brought into being, or we can confront it and find an ethical position from which to view the situation and to act.

If the kinds of extreme weather events that have been predicted happen (floods, fires, cyclonic storms, extreme heat and drought, extreme cold and consequences that follow, including famine and vector-borne diseases) and if the amount of conflict related to climate change that is feared by informed strategic sources actually occurs, *then* the human global population could suffer a very significant cull. It has happened at a catastrophic level before. As remarked earlier, *Homo sapiens* was almost wiped out in the last Ice Age. Disease in the past has also reduced populations, not least the 'black death' (bubonic plague), which killed between a third and half of Europe's population in the fourteenth century. Famine equally has devastated humanity in many places and times.

Ambiguity frames this prospect, as it has framed much of our existence for the past ten thousand years. Essentially, once 'we' started on the path of trying to dominate 'nature', we began to render ourselves homeless and destined to become unsustainable. We failed to remember what our ancestors recognized for tens of thousands of years—'the world' is our home. Unless we contemplate this prospect, we cannot confront the ethical issue—that is, choose between acting to avoid or alleviate those means that could kill great swathes of humanity and doing nothing on the basis that having a substantial percentage of the human race culled will enhance the prospect that survivors will extend the life of the species.

Farewell to Democracy

As I have argued at length elsewhere, democracy as an overarching international political ideology in support of capitalism will fail.[6] It is able neither to prevent the still-unchecked crisis that travels toward us (as the defuturing force of unsustainment) nor adequately to deal with the crisis once it pluralistically arrives (as it is starting to do). This is not to say that the political processes adopted by, for instance, tribalism cannot be informed by the democratic process. It is to say that the ballot box will not vote for the future. Proto-societies may well be of a scale where they are able to operate with direct democracy.[7] However the limit of direct democracy is that it works only with a small constituency that has been educated to understand the issues to be decided by direct contact. Once the size of the constituency grows beyond a certain point, it becomes impossible to manage the creation of this situation. So, while the Internet can provide the communication vehicle for such a political practice, what it cannot do is to ensure the level of engaged and informed decision making that direct contact with people brings.

Another key problem for democracy (one that has always undercut its efficacy) is that, in order for responsible and informed decisions to be delivered by its process, a significant level of educated opinion is required. In the past, this has been provided (albeit often inadequately) by the formal education system, the media and public debate. In conditions of national breakdown, actually learning what is happening in the immediate and wider world around you is very hard. Rumour runs rife. Two implications follow: the form of operational direct democracy could well become a basis for 'day-to-day' decision making, and, in the longer term, the reformation of society will need a new political imaginary[8]—one able to deliver the kind of unpopular changes the democratic process has never been able to make (but without reverting to any of the failed political ideologies of the past that have underpinned the economic and political systems and institutions of capitalism, fascism and totalitarianism).

If events unfold in a way anything like those indicated here, then there will be a need for a totally new form of human development. This will need to be one predicated on forms of re-creation across very many practices and knowledge (essentially, a *palingensic* project in which there is a reversion to and a modification of, those ontologies that were based on structural common interests and interdependencies that existed in the distant past and the traces of which are still seen in some indigenous cultures). It cannot be assumed that the kinds of beings we currently are and recognize as human will populate or even survive in this changed, much harsher world. At best, the nature of human being is itself likely to undergo radical change—the key issue, however, is whether this change will be driven simply by circumstances or by design. As indicated, such change itself maps onto the transformation of politics, and there is no way to currently know how this might play out.

People of the Future

There are those things one says with a true sense of certitude, those things one says with conviction that may have the appearance of certainty, and those things expressed with a degree of doubt. What follows are two statements, one said with certitude, the other with conviction.

As we move into an age of unsettlement created by the biological success and intellectual limitations of our species, we will come to recognize that we are at a moment unlike any other since human settlement commenced—a moment in which the future of our species at large can no longer be assumed. We have a future worth having only if we make it. The problems to overcome have to be faced, and to name them is not to be negative. That some of these problems are less defined than others in no way undermines the claim. Critically, we need to understand that problems (contrary to the way they are presented to us and the way we characterize them) do not exist independently but are always relationally connected. Thus, the actuality of the problem may have very little in common to the way it is represented.

Now to the statement of conviction—as has been presented, the claim that 'we' are headed toward becoming increasingly fractured subjects is said with a good deal of certainty. This is based upon recognizing three factors: (*a*) the error of how the subject has often been thought in the past as if it were unified and independent from object-things; (*b*) evidence of what has already happened to disrupt the sense of the unity of the subject over past decades via the loss of the authority of the discourse, the rise of the power of the 'technology of the world picture', geosocial mobility and the subsequent disruption of fixed identities; and (c) uncertainty about the forms of our futural being in conditions of 'our' uncertain becoming (what is assured is that we cannot 'be' as we are).

Notwithstanding the qualifications just given, we can speculatively contemplate the kinds of subjects that the radical changes outlined might generate. The list that follows is merely suggestive and doesn't claim to be exhaustive or even credible. What it does strive to communicate is that the fiction of a globally unified notion of the human (the human of universal human rights) is a humanist self-deception. The form of the human subject will fracture well beyond past processes of the pluralization of the self. In attempting to imagine some possibilities, we can perhaps recognize that what will emerge will in significant part simply be an extension or amplification of qualities already lodged in people of the past and present. There will also be difference. This being said, we can consider 'design fictions' based on the arrival of people who are both like and unlike us (in our difference)—insofar as circumstances in the future are likely to amplify those positive and negative characteristics that 'we' already have.

The point about these design fictions is not that they can claim to be predictive representations of what is to come but, rather, that they first of all support and communicate the strong likelihood that the being that we are and that we call 'human' will increasingly ontologically fragment (which means differences between 'us' will increase and any claim to a unified species will break down). Second, the fictions deliver the necessity of imagining what is to become. In one sense, this implies a designing, a prefiguration, whereby, in those circumstance where there is choice, what 'we' become is what we imagine is possible to create (here is the same proposition that de facto underpinned the Enlightenment and modernity). In another sense, the act of imagination has the potential to bring into relief the negative other that will threaten our inchoate becoming(s).

These fictions are presented as short sketches, evoked in socioeconomic and, to a lesser degree, psychological terms; so, inevitably, they are caricatures without existential and emotional depth. Moreover, though they struggle against the science-fiction tropes of novels, movies and comics that frame all images of the future, they remain captive to a Gibsonesque semiosphere. Yet, it is to be expected that questions about the forms of our becoming can arrive with the prospect of enhanced engagement. The fictions are put forward as provocations to reflect and think, thus inviting acceptance, qualification, modification, additions or rejection and displacement.

Seven possible beings and an outline fictional future are put forward.

Homotecs—these are fully instrumentalized human beings for whom technology has become a totally internalized, metaphysically framed worldview. Such people are now not just science-fiction fantasy, yet they display an uncanny correspondence to some of the dehumanized qualities of characters famously portrayed in the novels of Aldous Huxley (*Brave New World*) and George Orwell (*Nineteen Eighty-Four*). These subjects are arriving out of and appearing in technoculture. They are extensions of an extant mode of systems compliant subjectivity—one that has been amplified by and inducted into an absolute faith in reason and technology's ability to engineer futures. They will live mostly in a light-engineered, electrobiological, technological bubble, emotionally existing in a condition of deep repression, with feelings dislocated from rationalized actions. One can imagine their compliant way of life folding into, serving and extending the will of a dominant administrative class. History (not least the history of totalitarianism) affirms just how dangerous such people, in their lack of empathy and remorse, are.

Neo-nomads—in contrast to the majority who are sedentary, these people see themselves as travellers of the future. Over time, they have learnt to read the weather and the environment, travel with seeds, develop adaptive agricultural skills and grow crops according to the nature of the seasons. They depend on light horse-drawn transport, live in yurt-like villages, produce a surplus of food when they can and trade it. They expect to slowly create very simple but viable ways of life and are able to continually remake the services they need (e.g. health and education). Their way of life is directed by a very basic moral code: if you cannot recover from a sickness to travel, you die; whenever faced with the option 'fight or flight', you flee; if you have to fight, it's 'all or nothing'; whatever you have or know you share, or you die. Their emotional being has reinstated that collectivism that was intrinsic to all nomadic peoples whereby wealth was not a material measure but the qualitative character of a social condition.

War-takers—this is the collective name of a cluster of barbaric, violent criminal classes and tribes that survive by raids on any kind of established community (big or small). They will take anything from anyone: food, clothing, animals, tools, whatever. They also capture people to use and sell as slaves. Many of them are former mercenaries and professional soldiers; as such, they were already, by degree, dehumanized. They build semipermanent fortified camps from which raiding parties journey (sometimes for several months) and return. They are always well-armed with assault weapons. Some will group into well-organized and well-disciplined units, while others are just a wild rabble treating the lives of others with complete disdain. Yet one must recognize that, for the most part, these people will be fated as they will produce nothing and will depend entirely on what they can take from others. So, in the end, they will be defeated by the intrinsic unsustainability of their way of life—even if with some kind of trace remains.

Hoarder survivalists—rather than tribes, these are mostly extended families that, influenced by knowledge of (and, in some cases, experience in) 'alternative communities', created ways of life centring on hidden dwellings and a network of storage facilities. Many of these people have been shopkeepers or wholesalers. They live an emotional illusion based on a faith in the possibility of creating 'a world' outside the instabilities of 'the world' around them. But most are likely to be doomed—they are prime targets of *war-takers*, who will hunt them out, and even those who remain hidden can expect this fate, for their large store of goods (tinned food, clothes, bedding), in the end, is finite—and, thus, so are they.

Scavengers—sadly, these people, from the poor and neglected of the once-developed and developing world, have become the waste-pickers of the wastelands. Scavenging will become a dominant way of life for an underclass living in the ruins of the abandoned cities and detritus of the lost modern world. They will lack the organization of a tribe and gather mostly in small mixed groups. Ignored by most, hated and killed by *war-takers*, these often disease-ridden people will have no future. A small number of lucky ones may break free of this way of life and join *neo-nomads*, but most will not. Most scavengers will be permanently haunted by hunger, and there is a good chance that there will be a minority who will practice cannibalism. Here, then, are the once-humans become inhuman—like the 'Muselmann' of Nazi death camps, these beings are the living dead.[9]

Gatherers—they may appear to have something in common with scavengers but in fact are very different. The gatherers of the future replay some of the functions of gatherers of the past but go beyond them. There is evidence that 'gathering' predated making—a practice so important in hominid evolution, wherein an initial 'world-within-the-world' was created materially and symbolically from an assemblage of what was found in 'the world'.[10] Gatherers of the future are going to continue to be tribal communities, collectors and re-makers. They will continue to extend their critical capability of seeing the reconstructive potential in things found. In so doing, they will have the ability to elevate recycling to a new kind of technology. Already they 'feed' off things from the old world (from any domain of manufacture, in any material) to make something quite new. Remarkably, in their care for and of the world around them, they feel themselves to be 'futural'.

Palingensiaists—here is our final category. These are the people of 'the remotes'—distant places, hard to reach and without any discernable attractions (islands, valleys high in mountain ranges, far-flung desert oases). These people will live very modestly as keepers and re-creators of knowledge. More than this, they will travel in time, not in any science-fiction sense but just by living and reproducing in the knowledge that a moment of need will eventually arrive once the age of stabilization arrives. They will recognize that, in its technologically diminished, fragmented and numerically reduced (and still reducing) form, humanity has significantly lowered its defuturing agency. Not unlike monks of the 'Dark Ages', *Palingensiaists* will feel that they are carriers of knowledge of the past to the future. They will be caring but beleaguered and so, in some ways, joyless.

Against this backdrop, depending on the size of the *Homotec* population and providing they do not dramatically extend their capabilities beyond their lifeworld, planetary recovery, not least atmospherically, will be just a matter of time. One of the key factors here is the fragmentation of the species, leading to 'a world' in which there is almost no manufacturing capability (the only culture that has this will be the *Homotecs,* who will make only for themselves). The key determinant of this situation is the loss of markets for new, industrially made goods (rather than of productive capacity). A future mode of making will thus be dominated by neo-craft production at various levels of quality and quantity. Predominantly, as it was in the past, production will be directed toward meeting material needs, rather than guided by aesthetics.

At this moment, the process of the re-creation of human being to become posthuman (humax) can be seen as the product of a successful and not necessarily violent conflict led by a minority against the inherent forms of nihilism of the now-fragmented species of *Homo sapiens.* Key to this attainment is a process of worldly rematerialization, enabling the 'being otherwise' of these beings. Effectively, such 'humax beings' transcend what they are while finding ways to live alongside and to enable those others less fortunate. They will be without overidealized expectations and be able to value one another and life in general while also recognizing the imperative of living futurally. For them, fundamental needs will be defined by collective interests and will be met but not exceeded. Likewise, their creative fulfilment could be recognized in numerous ways (e.g. attainments in the advancement of futural knowledge, the creative art and craft skills). Yet, in a world of residual conflict, where hardship is inescapable and damage done in the past lingers, utopian and idyllic dreams will have no agency.

As indicated, the rise of 'humax beings' will be a matter of ontologically designed evolution triggering their becoming and actions. This is to say, it will depend on neither their 'will to power' nor biological determinism. There is no implied claim of perfection projected with this future, only of substantial incremental improvement of 'making time', thereby making an age more fu-tural than the present.

In the Face of the Negative

Of course, there is no intent here to try to imagine exactly what the people of the future will be like. However, from what has already been said, it has been possible to put forward some broad categories, as said, *as provocations to reflect and think.* In one direction, what frames this tentative endeavour comes from a question in response to Nietzsche's warning on the danger of the growing wasteland (within and without). The question is: what constitutes the form of the wasteland as we look toward it from where we currently now are? Even more significant is the fact that the circumstances in which we humans find ourselves (including the circumstance of political silence over what has to be faced) demand that we think the future and act directively.

Certainly, we are likely to see a breakdown of homogeneity between and within nations, regions, cities, organizations and communities; along with this, dysfunction will become widespread. But there will also be some forms of regrouping, with new cells of social, cultural and economic functions emerg-ing. Many existing subject identities may totally disappear, but again one can expect that new ones will be created. Against this background, one can expect people of the future to be distributed across conditions of, at one extreme, rel-ative order and control and, at the other, fragmentation, conflict and chaos. In the context of this design fiction, it is impossible to say what the proportions of people living in functional or dysfunctional circumstances will be.

At one extreme, one can expect that aggressive warring 'communities' will emerge, but almost certainly there will also be those who are innovative and future-affirmative. The past tells us that, no matter what the circumstances, there will always be adventurers and the pathfinders toward the new. Once such people cease to exist, all people will be fated.

The wasteland may also have spaces, cultures and people of denial enjoying whatever they can find to enjoy before it goes—this encompassing both 'a beautiful and an ugly decadence'. Privileged classes will find their enclaves, with huge numbers of people trying to find ways to hang onto what they already have. At the other extreme, a vast underclass will grow and envelop those people dispossessed, directly and indirectly, by climate change. Maybe new kinds of tribalism will then form. There will be people, organizations and nations that will covet and hoard, but, counter to this, there will be new political cultures, conservers of old knowledge and producers of new, protectors of memory and technological advances and regress (which may or may not be the same thing). Enormous numbers of people will be physically and psychologically damaged by many kinds of traumatic events. Yet the extent and quality of the survival of our species remains significantly in our hands, with the Sustainment absolutely and directly in opposition to that defuturing carried by the New Dark Age.

❋ ❋ ❋

What is being recognized in these very brief fictions is that both biological and hominoid life always transmute, have great recovery capability and change over expanses of time in ways totally disconnected from human existential means of measure. To say this does not imply an assured future—humanity clearly has an auto-destructive ability. But it does indicate that what is currently at stake is the conservation of its potential. Here it is a matter of investing not in hope but in action.

14

The Rise of Another Other

I flew too far into the future: a horror assailed me.

—Friedrich Nietzsche

Just as, in our transformation from animal to human, the animal (by necessity) lived on, so, on becoming 'humax', the human will live on, but subordinated within its maximized condition.

'We' can become what we need to be only via the efficacy of the ontological designing of a materiality of change (even if initially through small-scale experimental projects). Utopian schemes, theoretical proclamations, political manifestoes will not deliver—they just don't have the agency or go the problem. There has to be:

- a narrative (the story of the attainment of the (im)possible)
- the action of a designing agent of change (creating 'things' that ontologically design change) informed by rigorous historical and situational analysis and a theoretically underpinned future projection
- experimentation linked to critical reflection to modify the change process

All of this has to come together to constitute (a) *praxis*.

But, equally, there has to be an engagement with the two structuring determinates (nihilism and anthropocentrism) as they structure the ground upon which stand the symptomatic aspects of defuturing (unsustainable productivist capitalism, liberal democratic pluralism—as both serve pragmatic globalization and nationalism). As these forces of defuturing continue, they constitute our very being (as it becomes totally instrumentalized) as standing reserve. The creation of economic wealth, as it has been made the theological mission of humanity, thus travels toward the inevitable loss that comes from bringing (our) finitude near.

The story to tell is of the creation of Sustainment—a narrative travelling in two directions that enfold each other. The first would tell of the beginning of the human endeavour to redirect its forms of world-making. The second would give an account of this project, what it can produce and how it will have an ability to change us. What unites these two narrative elements is simply what has constantly been asserted here: that, while *we have always been partly formed by the way we form our world* (as a 'world-within-the-world'), what we have never done is to make such action a conscious, directed and deliberate transformation of the self. It is an understanding of ontological design that gives us a capability to do this.

The creation of Sustainment—coming out of unsettlement, in full recognition of the depth of the unsustainable in the human psyche, and a consequential worldly unmaking—requires a process of ontological design at its core. So enabled, Sustainment has no choice but to embrace the imperative of making time and a new human becoming. The only other, unacceptable, option is to give way to the defuturing force of the unsustainable. It is vital here to again acknowledge Sustainment as project of a scale beyond that of the Enlightenment and counter to that project's dark heritage.

A Culture of Relearning

Unsustainability and its defuturing trajectory do not occur without their relational agency: 'us', our values, knowledge and institutions as they deliver material forms, structures and technologies of negation—all, in significant part, assisted on their way by our 'education in error'. Thus, we are not unsustainable by accident but learn how to be so through the direction of our 'essential nature' by our inculcation into 'human being' and by much of what we are taught from primary school to graduate school. This action—the ontologically designed, defuturing essence of much of our education—acts back on us negatively. Education, diminished to the level of instrumental functionality, becomes ever more vocational and bonded to supporting the status quo. It 'produces' compliant, service-orientated subjects and displaces the essence of learning and, in so doing, erodes our ability to be critical—understood as a facility of judgement able to disclose the world (given and made) so that directional responsibilities can be adopted. These 'attributes' have been 'dissolved' by the corrosive qualities of defuturing embedded in hegemonic capitalism, with its reduction of culture to entertainment. Education, as *paideia,* has to be reclaimed and taken out of the service of capital, wherein it has been simply reduced to a 'use value'.[1] Named here *Neu Bildung,* it does not become layered onto the educational status quo but displaces and remakes it. As with Heidegger's notion of 'ontological education', it centres on the disclosure of 'the essential in all things' as the means to inform 'the what and the how' of ontological designing as the designing of that which performatively 'cares'.[2]

Such affirmation rests with advancing Sustainment and its process—which means bringing ideas, knowledge, practices, object-things and environments into being with a futuring capability.[3] It equally means waging 'war' on the time-negating forces of defuturing. These two actions converge in and as 'design as politics', with its essence being the rescuing of 'the political' from institutionalized politics *and* the creation of design-led futuring practices.[4] This, in turn, means establishing a *Neu Bildung*—the remaking of learning via the creation of a new culture of relearning—as an imperative.[5]

Neu Bildung carries recognizing and taking responsibility for (our) anthropocentrism, engaging critically with technology, learning to deflect violent conflict, going beyond democracy (as we know it) and sacrificing for the common good.[6]

Unquestionably, there is a crisis of education that to all intents and purposes is evidenced by 'learning' being destroyed.[7] Educators have been unable to resist this, and most of what all students know is what they experience in their 'being-in-the-world' in this time. Nowhere is this more evident than in the humanities. It is not just that the humanities have been diminished in volume and status but that their very function has been instrumentalized. The implication is not that an ideal model has been destroyed but, rather, that the ground upon which the futuring of education could take place has been made part of the wasteland.

We need to see education, especially the university, in the historical frame of the end of the Enlightenment. As it is, it cannot deliver us to futuring. The modern university is in its dotage. Just as we need to become Other than we are in order to be futural, so it is equally the case with the university. Both it and we need to constitute a third epoch of becoming. In making this appeal, one can first note that the university as it currently exists is unable to deal with the defuturing world of human existence—how could it when it is in servitude to the status quo? Certainly, there are individuals who know this, and pockets of authentic learning, but the managerialists who now run universities everywhere have no horizon beyond the instrumental. They, in their 'servicing', have turned teaching against learning and are liberating the defuturing of technology as metaphysics. Universities are without vision. They are mostly dying or dead places. Yet, in coming to an 'hour of need', a *Neu Bildung,* a new kind of university (an urmadic university),[8] may well offer content 'open' to be appropriated.

Ontological, design-led change is obviously going to arrive not as a mass uprising but through the formation of a change community that liberates the idea and through practice that delivers futuring solutions to actual problems. Such leadership has little in common with avant-garde deterministic design or constructivist 'social condensers'—it is not about creating iconic forms with a discernable aesthetic but about transformative material cultures. As the knowing inheritor of the process that transformed the animal, via its turning the stone to tool, the 'humax' would know itself to be both a product and directive agent of ontological designing. As such, it would have little in common with modernity's formation of a modern subject. The aimed-for 'humax', as a plurality, has to recognize itself to be far more attuned to other beings and to be aware of its indivisible relation to object-things and their form, so long as it's futural.

This creation of the Sustainment and the 'super-being' will be seen as an impossibility. But it can happen. The history of humanity, in all its difference, continually asserts the attainment of the impossible. In so many cases, the impossible is purely a limitation of perspective that rests with the available knowledge at any particular time. One could write a certain kind of history of humanity as a history of the realization of the impossible.

To realize how we became what we are is to recognize that, in large part, we are the consequence of our own invention. 'Man first implanted values into things to maintain himself—he created the meaning of things, a human meaning! Therefore he calls himself "Man", that is: the evaluator.'[9] The tool, the act of making, the giving of value to the made all mark moments of transition in the making of 'Man' and the subordination of his animality. 'Man' thus made himself and has to make that which he will become as a self-overcoming, for 'he who cannot obey himself will be commanded.'[10]

Ontological design affirmatively deployed takes this characteristic of our being in hand. To realize this is to realize the political at the most fundamental. Essentially, it tells us that the political choices we make about the material world in which we live have a significant determinate consequence over what we become. Let's be absolutely clear: to become the 'humax' (the 'we' that could be), we would need to undertake our own re-invention by designing the processes of our own ontological transformation.

The term 'humax' obviously must be treated with caution. It would not name the ultimate state of our being. Like all else, we will eventually disappear, and, unknowingly, it can be characterized only as a marker between our 'being, becoming and end'.

As acknowledged, the *Übermensch*/overman/'superman' was deemed by Nietzsche to mark an overcoming of what 'Man' already was and is as an eternal recurrence. He saw 'Man', as he currently is/was, as the 'the last Man' (the end of the process of evolutionary development). So confronted, 'we' have realized that we are collectively challenged to either rise above ourselves or fall. Nietzsche believed that our overcoming demanded a fundamental break with those forces that perpetuated the recurrence of 'Man' as he is. This required, in his view, a radical transformation of culture—a recasting of fundamental values, including those underpinning 'science, nobility, morality and art'. The necessity of becoming other than extant 'Man' was posed against his current mode of being, seen as decadent, increasingly technological and lacking in meaning. These negative qualities folded into Nietzsche's understanding of nihilism as life without agency. One now asks: does this judgement resonate with the 'masses' living in the televisual era as 'cultural consumers'? Certainly, there are active members of all societies and communities, but passivity is the norm. To become a humax (super-being) implies, as Michael Tanner has pointed out, living in exile, outside the norm, with a great deal of self-sufficiency.[11] Life so lived has to be made rewarding, provide pleasures, be attractive and not rest on idealism or moralism. It has to be designed to work as an agency for all.

How could such a process of transformation be enacted? According to John Richardson, it centres first of all on 'a self' obtaining insight into the ways her values are created.[12] More interestingly and realistically, to have substance, these insights have to be incorporated by design into the very being of her 'drives and habits'; thereafter, they can give rise to a totally new ontological disposition.[13] As indicated, Nietzsche's view asserts that the 'superman' arrives via new values that power a higher level of 'self creation'. He projected the attainment of such a being out into the future in circumstances that negated the possibility of generalization and, in fact, posited the claimed agency with what would transpire to be an elite.

Nietzsche names what we need to become: 'superman'. As we saw in chapter 11, Heidegger, echoing Zarathustra ('Man' is something that should be overcome)[14] understood that this being needed to be a negation of the former essence of 'Man' as well as the form of what 'Man' should become. Heidegger very clearly stated his projection as humanism humanized[15]—here deemed as the condition of the humax.

Against this backdrop, the voice of Zarathustra speaks as and for the 'super-man'. He asks, 'How may man still be preserved?' 'How shall man be *overcome*?' He says: 'The Superman lies close to my heart, he is my paramount and sole concern—and *not* man: not the nearest, not the poorest; not the suffering; not the best.'[16] He speaks not merely of his own plight but of ours as we move toward and look at a world made ever more unsustainable, knowing that 'but nowhere have I found a home; I am unsettled in every city and I depart from every gate.'[17]

In the contemporary moment, as it is gathered by unsustainability and as-serts the imperative of Sustainment—as a process where, once again, at a fun-damental level, imagination confronts finitude and the necessity of a higher being—the 'superman', recast as the 'humax', is the prospect of transcending the anthropocentric rule of 'the last Man'.

The actual or aspirant globalized and globalizing 'Man' of the present, the 'Man' who wants everything and strives to get it, is a being out of control. There is no material limit to the accumulative habits of this 'Man'—he is truly the last of a kind.

Unless this being can rise above itself to become other than it is, it (that is, 'we') has no future. The call to become super, to become 'humax', is no invita-tion of and to arrogance but the voice of 'a will to continue to be'. The language used to evoke this being is absolutely appropriate. The drive to advance, to be-come superior, is indivisible from accepted ambitions of self-improvement as-sociated with becoming cultivated, civilized, educated—it is the very project of a culture of modesty and thoughtfulness appropriate to its age. It is the culture of Sustainment. It's time to put the abuse of Nietzsche's language behind us.

A Rising Potential

The notion that one can appeal to 'humanity' in general has been a longstand-ing Eurocentric illusion. The biological commonality of the species does not override fundamental difference in culturally constructed senses of the self—senses based upon a belief in one's nature of being-in-being as it defines one's relation to things and Others (human and nonhuman animals). As already noted, notwithstanding the efforts of modernity and globalization to counter this difference, not least by the continued universalization of 'Man', commodity culture and humanistic notions of rights mark the trajectory of structural unsustainability.

All prospect of species homogeneity is receding, and a (re)fragmentation of humanity is more than likely.

As has been postulated and elaborated, the greater climatic instability and its multiple relational effects, the greater will become the difference between 'us'. Whatever the forms 'we' take, whatever the environments that we end up inhabiting, we can be assured that events will take one of only three possible courses: they will deteriorate, stabilize or improve. In all cases, change will occur in a time frame at odds with how 'we' view change. So what can be expected? Again, three ways present themselves: (*a*) tipping points will be reached, prompting rapid and perhaps unexpected change; (*b*) slow and virtually invisible change over time will occur; or (*c*) long-term change beyond the reach of our current ability to predict or imagine will happen.

The idea of a 'tipping point' goes to a dramatic transformation of climatic conditions once a particular and not easily identified threshold has been crossed. Such change is thought to have the potential to trigger short-term or enduring climate chaos. However, its meaning can be broadened beyond the climate system to include any climate-change influences that produce serious and unexpected consequences, especially those events that initiate a chain of events that we cannot manage. To give an example obviously undermines the proposition that such events and their consequences are unexpected. So said, one could contemplate the scenario, as does Gwynne Dyer, of vast numbers of climate-displaced people (CDPs) crossing the border into a hostile state, precipitating a nuclear war that escalates globally.[18]

Slow and virtually invisible change might significantly affect our own biophysical being over time and induce mutations in life forms in the world around us. Conversely, alterations in climatic conditions may get worse, but the prospect of improvement is far more uncertain. As was indicated earlier, some informed scientific research is now suggesting that climate change is now irreversible for at least one thousand years. Therefore, no matter what actions are now taken, the die is cast.

Long-term change, beyond the reach of our current ability to imagine or predict, by definition defies comment other than to say that 'we' exist in a condition of limitation. We literally have no idea of what our world or we, for that matter, will be like in, for instance, a thousand years. We cannot even be certain that transmogrified human beings will still be around or in what form or in what numbers. Neither biological nor technological change in the past provides any guide for us in this situation. For what 'we' have increasingly done is to speed 'the passage of time' for us (which is to say that we have accelerated technological change and, in so doing, created a disjuncture between us and the need to biologically adapt to 'the world', knowingly and unknowingly, that we have technologically transformed). As we have done this, our world (and our self)-forming actions to date mostly defuture, resulting in a continual negation of time. Such action remains unchecked. It seems that the negative agency of the technologies of human invention are likely to increasingly dissolve the distinction between the biophysical world of human dependence and the 'world-within-the-world' of human creation—the account given of 'geoengineering' illustrates this and takes the 'naturalization of the artificial' to another level.

Rather than being that which we ignore, the unknown has to be used to temper our actions as we consider the drift of events that carry us into the future. Where, how and why we do this brings us back to confront that complex and plural question 'what exactly are we?' Answering this question or at least trying to (as has sought to be demonstrated) undermines what it is we think ourselves to be.

A very different notion of what a 'humax' needs to be has already been briefly registered. To fully unpack the prefigurative ontological formation of this being, its nature and agency, is a major project in itself, but one able to be informed by the function of design in our becoming.

There are design-fiction starting points. For instance, there is the example of what was earlier called the *palingensiaist.* Such a nonutopian being could be considered and projected as more than was initially suggested (a being living in 'the remotes', living simply 'on modest means' as 'keepers and re-creators of knowledge'). So characterized, they could be posited with the kinds of individual qualities deployed to define what a futural mode of being might be. They also could be projected to exemplify one instance of what would be the formation and moment of a change community of action with the power to establish ontologically transformative conditions. Their crucial quality would be 'disengaged engagement'—meaning a 'community' formed neither as 'alternative' nor 'utopian' but rather as political design actors on the outside of the inside of the culture out of which they emerged.

As travellers 'in time', 'humax' beings would be able to face defuturing as a past still able to arrive in a present. They can be thought of as 'living, repro-ducing, thinking and acting' in the knowledge that a moment of transforma-tive opportunity will arrive. Somewhere, somehow, a space, a hiatus between 'the then' and 'the now', will open out of the power of imagination as it breaks the grip of extant knowledge.

The Rest

The unevenness of plural humanity (as has been unambiguously presented as the global population continues to dramatically increase), along with the twentieth-century notion of 'global development' and its afterlife, will eventu-ally implode economically.

All that stands between current perceptions, related values and unfolding circumstances is a chronophobic refusal to view that future which is coming toward us. Life is still being lived in the endless condition that gets called 'nor-mality' (albeit punctuated with an occasional aberrant event). The normal is equated with permanence. Nietzsche believed that our becoming other than we are turns upon 'a radical transformation of culture able to recast funda-mental values'. This view still retains its salience—but with two qualifications: that we are not one and that the agency of ontological design is necessary.

Efforts to weaken, contest, modify or replace the idea of the 'humax' would be a negation of a futural agency. The majority of humanity (in their hype-consumptive dream or reality)[19] would remain oblivious to their arrival and potential. Yet, such beings would have a huge transformative impact. So, while enormous problems can be caused by the few, so likewise can solutions. 'Humax' being is simply being futural—a being who sees her actions in time in every respect.

Clearly, the modernist proposition, that all of humanity can be unified as 'Man' and brought into one moment of time and development has already fallen. Not only is it theoretically flawed (not least by presuming humanity as a singularity), overtaken by the pragmaticism of globalization (whereby economic function overrides all humanistic ambitions), but the ambition of the universal being of one world, as it stands upon an ethnocentric paradigm of 'being modern', is inherently unsustainable. It presumes and idealizes the overt and covert utopianisms of capitalism as it extols the possibility of an economy able to go on growing eternally—a perpetual-motion economy.

Re-evaluation and redirection would be the actions of the 'humax' few. As for the rest, if they were to regard their future, it would be with 'fear and trembling', not least because the past suggests that culling has always been a visitation to our species. So informed, one must fear that the more we remain the same, the greater the scale of this negative prospect. As is ever the case, the greatest threat to our survival is our anthropocentric selfhood.

15

Last Words

In your fair minds let this acceptance take.

—William Shakespeare

Inevitably, we find ourselves again at the beginning—it is not the beginning from where we started, but, nonetheless, it is a beginning.

It can be said that, no matter what we call ourselves, now or in the future, for 'us to-be-in-time' requires two fundamental things: we need to think, and we need to act at the most basic and elevated levels. What we need to think is Sustainment (as said, this is a project more critical than and as great as, if not greater than, the Enlightenment). This thinking demands a new thinking (which is in fact the remaking of philosophy of the future). Implicit to this thinking is what Heidegger called 'ontological questioning'—which he viewed as the essence of philosophy and which is effectively 'the action of thinking' that finds a path and 'a direction into a historical future'.[1] Acting, we need to act futurally—which is other than the way we now act—chronophobically. Such acting means acting in time (the medium and with urgency); it also means having learnt what should be done and of the significance of ontological design. More than this, action requires the remaking of what we ourselves are, but with an accompanying imperative to remake the very foundation of meaning.

Darwin exposed life as meaningless; it simply was. It was never underscored by 'the hand of God' or by any other transcendental designing agent. Meaning after Darwin can never again be legitimately posited with nature, with the biological (which does not *mean* that such action of positing meaning with it ceases). Two and a half thousand years ago, Protagoras of Abdera famously pointed out 'of all things the measure is Man' (now usually translated as 'Man is the measure of all things'). This statement not only reads as unequivocally anthropocentric but leads to the recognition that all meaning is a human fabrication. Intrinsically, nothing has meaning. We also saw a reframing of meaning during the course of the Enlightenment via the assertion that 'nothing is without reason'. The significance of bringing these two declarations together is to bring us to the realization that among the fundamental actions implicit to the project of Sustainment is the remaking of meaning in an absolute sense. Cardinal to this task is the transformation of what it means to us 'to be'. However expressed, we have to come to see that we cannot be independent from other beings. Empirically, this has always been so, but an anthropocentric construction of meaning created a falsehood—one that so many of us lived by. Fundamentally, and hereafter, the world was taken as an object that existed purely for 'our' use. This was what it meant, and all that belonged to it could be treated as something at 'our' disposal—as a standing reserve for our material and aesthetic use. As meaning came to take on an existence of its own (as theology, as philosophy), it in itself began to function as an environment, one in which 'we' come into being (for example, this is seen with Derrida on language and Luhmann on system); as anthropocentric causality is carried by our language, so our actions are, in a sense, prewritten, prespoken.

Where meaning ends up resting does not negate the significance of where it came from. The prosthetic extension that is language ever remains connected to its (per)formative source, as does system to the mind of its representational projection.

In fact, meaning is always found 'at home' in the historico-conjunctural space and time of our hermeneutic dwelling. But it is also rendered homeless as it is posited in object-things. Meaning-full things are never communication: they cannot mirror the content of mind nor arrive without the filter of interpretation.[2]

Western metaphysics has been deeply implicated in the construction of not only 'self deceptive' but also destructive perceptions. From his reading of Heidegger's understanding of the ontotheological structure of Western metaphysics (an 'ontological holism' that historically defines what we are), Iain Thomson comments: 'For by giving shape to "what is" metaphysics determines the most basic presuppositions of what *anything* is, ourselves included', and then: '"What is" is not an "externality" created for us.'[3] Whatever we are, whatever we do, we are elemental to it. So understood, language is indivisible from our 'nature' and, thus, from our way of being human, as affirmed by the power of the word (Lacan) and the text (Derrida) and in the creation of (a) world (Heidegger). But as a locus of (our) being, language, together with design and making (technics), now exists as a rift from 'what is' that Sustainment must bridge.

Complexity defeats us. Second-order systems theory claims to overcome our representational failure with the way it characterizes: observation of the complex; contingency; self-organization and emergence. But, in folding into a space of pure abstraction, it fails, as all systems building fails (the fundamental lesson of Hegel). The nature of complexity entertained and presented by Luhmann undoes his very own explanatory decentred systems theory.[4] It ever remains stranded, in Jean Baudrillard's terms, as a simulation. It is simply another immaterial world—albeit one with evocative and illuminating powers. Claiming its authority via the power of the narrative (hence its appeal to literary theorists),[5] its agency remain arrested. Such thinking does not fully embrace the complexity of uncontainable relationality, order, disorder and any organizing principle. Rather, it sets out to create a particular representation of semantic closure via a process of selectivity by which a constructed 'complexity reduces complexity' (the system). It does this by seeking to establish a means of containment (as with *autopoiesis*) between system and environment, organization and structure (which itself is subject to a reduction).[6] In essence, what Luhmann gives us is a good deal of knowledge, much to think about and an example of the ongoing human-centred error and arrogance of reason. The notion that complexity (what is) is open to be known by metaphysical means of observation doubled does not establish an external line of sight. We now cannot be what we have made ourselves to be and not be anthropocentric; this casts us eternally on the 'inside of the inside': we are subjugated to this selfhood.

What we call that being that we need to become cannot be resolved by a typology of theoretical constructions around humanism/posthumanism.[7] Our redirective action has to step out of the shadow of the Enlightenment. Our futural becoming is a matter of ontologically designed self and world re-formation *but* taken into care by, as said, a redirective way of thinking and action. This is a matter of a project, of making. It is something we have to *do*. It is a *praxis*, a constitution of change communities, an ontological designing, a delimiting of freedom so that there may be freedom. We are, all of us, know it or not, at an end or at this beginning.

So where are we 'now'?

We are at a moment of ur-history, a *Jetztzeit*, an 'everlasting now' which will last at least as long as we do.

Walter Benjamin, in what has been called his anthropological materialism, was influenced by Goethe's speculative ideas and by something far older. He brought Goethe's notion of *ur-forms* to those *urtexts* lodged in the birth of the Jewish faith. (The first extant manuscripts in Hebrew and Greek have been designated *Urtexts*. The most significant of these is claimed to be Ezekiel 36–39.)[8] He then projected this relation of origin, agency and form to understand the confluence of photography, cinema, technology and history in a composite moment of appearance.

Thereafter, what came into view for Benjamin was never just the image or one represented moment but a gathering time of past, present and potential. He grasped this through thinking cinema, wherein image, movement, time and technology all fuse into a single moment. But he refused to contain this understanding to any particular medium; instead, he generalized it as a way of seeing everyday life (its culture, economy, politics, history, technology and change). In doing this, he applied the 'ur' prefix to history (ur-history) to characterize how origin, history and phenomenal forms could all be viewed together.

Partly echoing Goethe on archetype and Plato on seeing, Benjamin recognized that the transformation of a form of thought was also a transformation of sight. Seeing was taken to be subject to determinate forces (historical, economic and political).[9]

Benjamin's somewhat idiosyncratic way of thinking influenced not only his writing but also his sensibility. In particular, he saw that things of the everyday present contain the time of everything that brought them into being from the ancient onward. All that is created thus reveals and conceals what it is and where it has come from.

Benjamin produced a revelatory mode of making the world of everyday objects appear strange and mythic. His mode of relationality brought everything associated with origins and futuring to the present moment of *ur-historical* interrogation—not, however, as transparent figures but as clues to be found, deciphered and read. His thinking exposed that what was materially present at a particular moment of history is a gathering buried in human (designed) artefacts or events. The revelation or, as Benjamin called it, 'rescue' of these objects or events he named *Jetztzeit*—the act of exposing the 'everlasting now'.[10] This has been likened to the *Nunc Stans* of Aquinas and, obviously, the '*Urphanomen*' of Goethe, but it equally resonates with the Nietzschean notion of eternal return.

Now we can read defuturing object-things. Yet, learning from what has made us what we are, from the stone to the designing all and everything of contemporary everyday life, we are left looking for what to pick up, the tool, the thing, to ontologically design us toward the 'humax' (the super-being) we have to become in order to continue to be. In this task, it is not the animal that troubles us but the human.

Notes

Preface

1. Early writing of note here includes Tony Fry, 'Designing the Future—Whose Future, Whose Design?,' *Sydney Review*, no. 21 (Feb. 1990); Fry, *Green Desires: Ecology, Design, Products* (Sydney: EcoDesign Foundation, 1992); and Fry, *Remakings: Ecology/Design/Philosophy* (Sydney: Envirobook, 1994).

Introduction

1. This process of reading has been likened to the *Nunc Stans* of Aquinas and, obviously, the *Urphanomen* of Goethe; it resonates equally with the Nietzschean notion of eternal return. See Maria Zimmerman Brendel, 'The Everlasting Now: Walter Benjamin's Archive,' *ArtUS* (1 Mar. 2007).
2. Friedrich Nietzsche, *Beyond Good and Evil,* trans. Walter Kaufmann and R. J. Hollindale (London: Penguin, 1990).
3. This view has, for example, been a longstanding one held by Bruno Latour. See *We Have Never Been Modern,* trans. Catherine Porter (Cambridge, MA: Harvard University Press, 1993), pp. 130–42.

Part I: First Pass

1. It had been getting colder in the West and hotter and drier in the East, so people converged on a place where the climate was hospitable and where there was food (especially early forms of barley and wild einkorn, a forerunner of wheat).

2. See Tony Fry, 'Homelessness—A Philosophical Architecture', *Design Philosophy Papers Collection Three* (Ravensbourne, Qld, Aust: Team D/E/S Publications, 2007), pp. 19–28.

Chapter I: End of the Story

1. See Johnson Kent Wright, 'A Bright Clear Mirror', in Keith Michael Baker and Peter Hanns Reill, eds, *What's Left of Enlightenment* (Stanford, CA: Stanford University Press, 2001), pp. 71 and 101.
2. Ernst Cassirer, *The Philosophy of the Enlightenment,* trans. Fritz C. A. Koelln and James P. Pettegrove (Princeton, NJ: Princeton University Press, 1932), p. 18.
3. Ibid., p. xiii.
4. Productivism is not merely an idea within economic theory, for it has an older and more fundamental meaning—in the ancient world of Greece, it named that way of thinking that viewed the world as a compound of structural elements. This thinking became both an analytic methodology and a projective tool—it could and did build a system of thought. As such, it travelled through to the Enlightenment and into that instrumental modality that has underpinned the rise of modern science and technology and their application to the forms of economic development that are now universalized. As such, productivism became a *habitus.* It acted as an underlying structure upon which other forms of structuring were established. Thus, and in terms of our concern with the question of proximity, productivism is absent from view in its presence.
5. See Marshall Sahlins's essay 'What Is Anthropological Enlightenment? Some Lessons of the Twentieth Century', in his *Culture in Practice, Selected Essays* (New York: Zone Books, 2005), pp. 501–26.
6. On colonialism see Margaret Kohn, 'Colonialism', in Edwar N. Zalta, ed., *The Stanford Encyclopedia of Philosophy,* Fall 2011 edn, http://plato.stanford.edu/archives/fall2011/entries/colonialism/.
7. 'Enlightenment thinkers such as Kant, and Diderot were critical of the barbarity of colonialism and challenged the idea that Europeans had the obligation to "civilize" the rest of the world. At first it might seem relatively obvious that Enlightenment thinkers would develop a critique of colonialism. The system of colonial domination, which involved some combination of slavery, quasi-feudal forced labor, or expropriation of property, is antithetical to the basic Enlightenment principle that each individual is capable of reason and self-government. The rise of anticolonial political theory, however, required more than a universalistic ethic that recognized the shared humanity of all people. Given the tension between the abstract universalism of natural law and the actual cultural practices of indigenous peoples, it was easy to interpret native difference as evidence of the violation of natural law. This in turn became a justification for exploitation.
Diderot was one of the most forceful critics of European colonization. In his *Histoire des deux Indes,* he challenges the view that indigenous people benefit from European civilization and argues that the European colonists are the uncivilized ones.' Kohn, 'Colonialism'.

8. Cassirer, *The Philosophy of the Enlightenment*, pp. 4–5.
9. Ibid., p. 14.
10. The divisions of knowledge empowered by the Enlightenment were supported by very specific protocols that gave them their identifiable form (not identified by the object of study). See Cary Wolfe, *What Is Posthumanism?* (Minneapolis: University of Minnesota Press, 2010), p. 113.
11. See Friedrich Nietzsche, *The Will to Power*, trans. Walter Kaufmann and R. J. Hollingwood (New York: Vantage, 1968), pp. 9–82.
12. On this issue of causality see Bernd Magnus, *Nietzsche's Existential Imperative* (Bloomington: Indiana University Press, 1978), pp. 6–12.
13. Mark Warren gives a full and insightful account of Nietzsche's thinking on nihilism in *Nietzsche and Political Thought* (Cambridge, MA: MIT Press, 1988), pp. 13–45.
14. Ibid., pp. 13–14.
15. Magnus, *Nietzsche's Existential Imperative*, pp. 11–12.
16. See Susan Steward and Jacqueline Lorber-Kasunic, 'Akrasis, Ethics and Design Education (Revisited)', Design Philosophy Papers Collection Four (Ravensbourne, Qld, Australia: Team D/E/S Publications, 2008), pp. 21–33.
17. Warren, *Nietzsche and Political Thought*, pp. 12–14.
18. Ibid., p. 159.
19. Ibid., p. 143.
20. These influences are detailed in full by Vincent P. Pecora in his article 'Nietzsche, Genealogy, Critical Theory', *New German Critique*, no. 53 (Spring/Summer 1991), pp. 104–30.
21. See Warren, *Nietzsche and Political Thought*, pp. 104–5.
22. Ibid., p. 87
23. Ibid., p. 80.

Chapter 2: Start of a Story

1. See Robin McKie, 'Cold Comfort for Earth', review of Chris Stringer, *Homo Britannicus*, in *Guardian Weekly*, 5–11 Jan. 2007, p. 26. More generally, what is evident from ongoing research on human biological evolution is that the picture is constantly developing; see Chris Stringer, 'Human Evolution: The Long, Winding Road to Modern Man', *The Observer*, 19 June 2011, http://www.guardian.co.uk/science/2011/jun/19/human-evolution-africa-ancestors-stringer.
2. Jeff Tollefson, *Nature News*, Report, http://www.nature.com/news/durban-maps-path-to-climate-treaty-1.
3. The study, led by Susan Solomon, a senior scientist at the National Oceanic and Atmospheric Administration, U.S. Department of Commerce, shows how changes in surface temperature, rainfall and sea level are largely irreversible for more than one thousand years after carbon dioxide (CO_2) emissions are completely stopped. The findings were presented during the week of 26 January 2009 and published in the *Proceedings of the National Academy of*

Sciences. Susan Solomon, Gian-Kasper Plattner, Reto Knutti and Pierre Friedlingstein, 'Irreversible Climate Change due to Carbon Dioxide Emissions', *Proceedings of the National Academy of SciencesS,* 106/6 (10 Feb. 2009), pp. 1704–9.

4. Intergovernmental Panel on Climate Change (IPCC), 'Climate Change 2007', Special Report on Renewable Energy Sources and Climate Change, Fifth Assessment Report, www.ipcc.ch/.

5. Ibid.

6. It is evident that the human/technology relations will become more indistinct, with human qualities increasingly being transposed into machines. Certainly, machines will arrive with the ability to reproduce themselves. It is quite clear that divisions among mechanical, biological and electronic technologies are dissolving. Bringing the notion of ontological designing to this context, it is certain that the technocentric qualities that are already present in the human psyche are going to be reinforced. More than this, some qualities that currently appear as anthropocentric will become apparent in technology (already prefigured in 'human-centred' technologies). Much science fiction in some form will become science fact. Machines will live in us; we will live in machines. Equally likely is the splitting of the species. There will be those who will deal with life in an unstable climate via machine-life; there will also be abandoned underclasses (many of whom will perish). Either way, 'we' will no longer be as we are.

7. See Gwynne Dyer, *Climate Wars* (Melbourne: Scribe, 2009).

8. The IPCC 2007 report suggested that more than 600 million people currently living in low-lying coastal zones—438 million in Asia and 246 million in the least-developed countries—will be directly at risk to potential threats of climate change in this century.

9. Such a post-Enlightenment project is dealt with at length in Tony Fry, *Design as Politics* (Oxford: Berg, 2011).

Chapter 3: Proximity

1. See Martin Heidegger, *Being and Time,* trans. John Macquarrie and Edward Robinson (Oxford: Blackwell, 1962), paras 150–60.

2. Hans-Georg Gadamer, *Truth and Method,* trans. Joel Weinsheimer and Donald G. Marshall (New York: Crossroad, 1990), pp. 269–77.

3. Emmanuel Levinas, *Otherwise Than Being or Beyond Essence,* trans. Alfonso Lingis (Dordrecht: Kluwer Academic Publishers, 1978).

4. Ibid., p. 63.

5. Ibid., p. 81.

6. Ibid., p. 82.

7. Martin Heidegger, 'Letter on Humanism,' in *Basic Writings,* trans. David Farrell-Krell (London: Routledge Kegan Paul, 1978), p. 210.

8. Jean François Lyotard, *The Inhuman* (Stanford: Stanford University Press, 1991), p. 2.

9. Friedrich Nietzsche, *Beyond Good and Evil,* trans. R. J. Hollingdale (London: Penguin, 1990), p. 55.

10. Heidegger, 'Letter on Humanism', pp. 200–1.

11. Iain D. Thomson, *Heidegger on Ontotheology* (Cambridge: Cambridge University Press, 2005), p. 151.
12. Michel Foucault, *Language, Counter-Memory, Practice,* trans. Donald Bouchard (New York: Cornell University Press, 1977), p. 148.
13. Maurice Merleau-Ponty, *Phenomenology of Perception,* trans. Colin Smith (London: Routledge, 1989), p. 326.
14. Ibid., p. 349.
15. Fry, *Design as Politics,* pp. 29–33.
16. Martin Heidegger, *What Is Called Thinking,* trans. J. Glenn Gray (New York: Harper and Row, 1968), p. 16.
17. See Hugh Lawson-Tancred, 'Introduction' to Ch. 13 of Book 3 of Artistotle's *De Anima* (London: Penguin Books, 1986).
18. Jacques Derrida, 'Geschlecht II: Heidegger's Hand', trans. John P. Leavey Jr, in John Sallis, ed., *Deconstruction and Philosophy: The Texts of J. Derrida* (Chicago: Chicago University Press, 1987), pp. 161–96.
19. Martin Heidegger, *Parmenides,* trans. Andre Schuwer and Richard Rojcewicz (Bloomington: Indiana University Press, 1992), p. 80.
20. See Heidegger, *What Is Called Thinking,* pp. 16–23, and *Parmenides,* pp. 79–84.
21. Michael Heim, *The Metaphysics of Virtual Reality,* Oxford: Oxford University Press, 1993, pp. 62–5.
22. See for instance Wolfe, *What Is Posthumanism?,* p. 27, on 'the same and sameness erases difference and identity'.
23. Hannah Arendt, *The Human Condition* (Chicago: University of Chicago Press, 1958).
24. For a full account of the agency of sign value see Jean Baudrillard, *For a Critique Political Economy of the Sign,* trans. Charles Levin (St Louis: Telos Press, 1981).
25. Karl Marx, *Capital,* Vol. 1, trans. S. Moore and E. Aveling (London: Lawrence and Wishart, 1977), p. 173.
26. Heidegger, *Parmenides,* p. 135.

Part II: Emergence over Origin

1. Stanislav Andreski, *Herbert Spencer: Structure, Function and Evolution* (London: Nelson, 1971).
2. Immanuel Kant, 'Idea for a Universal History from a Cosmopolitan Point of View', in L. W. Beck, ed., *Kant on History,* trans. L.W. Beck, R. E. Archer and E. L. Fackenham (Indianapolis: Bobbs-Merrill, 1963).
3. Ludwig Wittgenstein, *Zettle,* trans. G.E.M. Anscombe (London: Blackwell, 1967), § 608, p. 106e.
4. This is the key issue confronted by Jacques Derrida in *The Animal That Therefore I Am,* trans. David Willis (New York: Fordham University Press, 2008).
5. On these relations see Wolfe, *What Is Posthumanism?,* p. 47.

Chapter 4: Coming into Being via Natural Selection

1. Karl Marx, 'Economic and Philosophical Manuscripts', in *Early Writings,* trans. R. Livingstone and G. Benton (London: Penguin Books, 1975), p. 391.
2. For a more complex view of transposition see William McNeill, *The Time of Life: Heidegger and Ethos* (New York: SUNY Press, 2006), pp. 21–2.
3. Warren, *Nietzsche and Political Thought.*
4. The major tenets of the evolutionary synthesis are that 'populations contain genetic variation that arises by random (i.e., not adaptively directed) mutation and recombination; that populations evolve by changes in gene frequency brought about by random genetic drift, gene flow, and especially natural selection; that most adaptive genetic variants have individually slight phenotypic effects so that phenotypic changes are gradual (although some alleles with discrete effects may be advantageous, as in certain colour polymorphisms); that diversification comes about by speciation, which normally entails the gradual evolution of reproductive isolation among populations; and that these processes, continued for sufficiently long, give rise to changes of such great magnitude as to warrant the designation of higher taxonomic levels (genera, families, and so forth)." D. J. Futuyma, *Evolutionary Biology* (New York: Sinauer Associates, 1986), p. 12.
5. Warren, *Nietzsche and Political Thought,* p. 114. What this equals is moving the conception of agency from metaphysics to values, for values direct action into being as an ontological force. As such, they counter the idea of the unified agent as the originator of willed action. One can substitute design for values in this context, as design is equally an agency to which the human agent becomes subordinate.
6. On this point see Thomson, *Heidegger's Ontotheology,* p. 148.
7. See John Richardson, *Nietzsche's New Darwinism* (Oxford: Oxford University Press, 2004), for a comprehensive account of the relation between Darwin's theories and Nietzsche's engagement with them.
8. There were, of course, moments of violent and rapid change in the past, but often the time between them was sufficient for 'natural adaptive' processes to occur.
9. See www.darwinonline.org.uk/.../Freeman_LifeandLettersandAutobiography.html.
10. Daniel Dennett, *Darwin's Dangerous Idea* (London: Penguin, 1995).
11. Thomson, *Heidegger's Ontotheology,* p. 15.
12. Friedrich Nietzsche, *The Anti-Christ,* trans. R. J. Hollingdale (London: Penguin Books, 1975), § 14.
13. See Giorgio Agamben's account of Jakob von Uexküll's understanding of 'unwelt' (environment) in *The Open: Man and Animal,* trans. Kevin Attell (Stanford: Stanford University Press, 2004), pp. 39–43.
14. Ibid., p. 73.
15. See E. Delson, I. Tattersall, J. A. Van Couvering, and A. S. Brooks, eds, *Encyclopedia of Human Evolution and Prehistory* (New York: Garland, 2000), and Carl Zimmer, *Where Did We Come From?* (Sydney: ABC Books, 2005), p. 43.
16. Delson et al., *Encyclopedia of Human Evolution and Prehistory.*

17. André Leroi-Gourhan, *Gesture and Speech,* trans. Anna Bostock Berger (Cambridge, MA: MIT Press, 1998), pp. 18–19.
18. Ibid., p. 59.
19. Martin Heidegger, *The Fundamental Concepts of Metaphysics,* trans. William McNeill and Martin Walker (Bloomington: Indiana University Press, 1995).
20. Three years later (1933), Heidegger added the qualification that the human was also distinguished from the animal (and obviously the stone) via 'care'. Martin Heidegger, *Being and Truth,* trans. Gregory Fried and Richard Polt (Bloomington: Indiana University Press, 2010), p. 167.
21. McNeill, *The Time of Life,* pp. 1–51.
22. Heidegger, *The Fundamental Concepts of Metaphysics,* §47, p. 198.
23. Ibid., § 59, pp. 240–1.
24. Agamben, *The Open,* p. 52.
25. Heidegger, *The Fundamental Concepts of Metaphysics,* §49, pp. 201–9. See McNeill, *The Time of Life,* p. 21.
26. Derrida, '*Geschlecht* II: Heidegger's Hand', pp. 174 and 195, n.20.
27. Agamben, *The Open,* p. 69.
28. Bernard Stiegler, *Technics and Time 2: Disorientations,* trans. Stephen Barker (Stanford: Stanford University Press, 2009), p. 63.
29. These lines come from Jacques Derrida's magnum opus, *Of Grammatology,* trans. Gayatri Chakravorty Spivak (Baltimore: John Hopkins University Press, 1974), cited in Stiegler, *Technics and Time 2,* p. 111.
30. For a full account of this genetic journey see Chris Stringer, *The Origin of Our Species* (London: Allen Lane/Penguin, 2011).
31. On the basis of recent DNA research from material from Siberia, Chris Stringer points out that 'the Neanderthal genome strongly suggests those genes were not lost, and that many of us outside Africa have a tangible Neanderthal heritage. What these shared genes do for us, if anything, remains to be determined, but that will certainly be a focus for the next stages of this fascinating research. With much more genetic data to come, including further studies of ancient DNA from the "Lineage X" fossil from Siberia, which has yet to be matched to an ancient human species, and of recent DNA in Oceania that hints at additional archaic interbreeding there, we may yet discover new surprises about who our distant ancestors were.' Chris Stringer, 'You Calling Me a Neanderthal? You're Right', *Times Online,* 7 May 2010, www.timesonline.co.uk/tol/comment/…/guest…/article7118688.ece.
32. The Mitochondrial DNA from 147 people, drawn from five geographic populations, has been analyzed by restriction mapping. All these samples of mitochondrial DNA stem from one woman who is postulated to have lived about two hundred thousand years ago. See Rebecca L. Cann, Mark Stoneking, and Allan C. Wilson, 'Mitochondrial DNA and Human Evolution', *Nature,* 1 January 1987. Since publishing this, the three authors have looked at the mtDNA with the help of a computer program: 'they put together a sort of family tree, grouping those with the most similar DNA together, then grouping the groups, and then grouping the groups of groups. The tree they ended up with showed that one of the two primary branches consisted only of African mtDNA and that the other branch consisted of mtDNA from all over

the world, including Africa. From this, they inferred that the most recent common mtDNA ancestor was an African woman.' Rick Groleau, 'Tracing Ancestry with MtDNA', January 2001, *Nova Online*, www.pbs.org/wgbh/nova/neanderthals/mtdna.html.
33. Wolfe, *What Is Posthumanism?*, p. 35.
34. See Leroi-Gourhan, *Gesture and Speech*, p. 20.

Chapter 5: Coming into Being via Un-Natural Selection

1. Agamben, *The Open*, p. 12.
2. Derrida, *The Animal That Therefore I Am*, p. 39.
3. Sigmund Freud, *Civilisation and Its Discontents*, ed. and trans. James Strachey (New York: Norton, 1961), p. 36.
4. Our sociality, inherited from our ape-like ancestors, is one of these commonalities.
5. For a view on this issue, see McNeill, *The Time of Life*, p. 19.
6. Heidegger, *The Fundamental Concepts of Metaphysics*, § 72, p. 311.
7. On these issues see Agamben, *The Open*, pp. 73–80.
8. See especially Derrida, *The Animal That Therefore I Am*, and Agamben, *The Open*.
9. For a fuller account of both Stiegler's and Agamben's positions, see Nathan Van Camp's account in 'Bernard Stiegler and the Question of Technics', *Transformations*, no. 17 (2009).
10. As Stiegler says, 'technics does not aid memory: it is memory'. Stiegler, *Technics and Time 2*, p. 65.
11. Stiegler gives a detailed and critical account of the industrialization of memory and its relation to mind in ibid., pp. 97–187.
12. See Magnus, *Nietzsche's Existential Imperative*, pp. 190–5.
13. Leroi-Gourhan, *Gesture and Speech*, p. 146.
14. For an exposition of Nietzsche's understanding of the initial function of language (and his more general engagement with Darwinism) see his *Beyond Good and Evil*; see also Richardson, *Nietzsche's New Darwinism*.
15. Richardson, *Nietzsche's New Darwinism*, p. 83.
16. Ibid., p. 97.
17. Ibid., p. 5.
18. On this issue see Warren, *Nietzsche and Political Thought*, p. 50.

Chapter 6: Coming into Being via Design

1. Bernard Stiegler, *Technics and Time 1*, trans. Richard Beardsworth and George Collins (Stanford: Stanford University Press, 1998), pp. 141–2.
2. Stiegler, *Technics and Time 2*, p. 2.

3. As Paul Virilio points out, historically, prosthetics became an industry in the seventeenth century from the rise of orthopedic surgery as a result of war—see Virilio, *Speed and Politics*, trans. Mark Polizzotti (New York: Semiotext(e), 1977), pp. 61–74.

4. Stiegler goes so far as to say 'technics thinks'. *Technics and Time 2*, p. 32.

5. This dynamic of creation and destruction is the very nature of the dialectic of sustainment (which makes clear that making cannot occur materially without destruction and that ethical decision rides the line between the two). See Tony Fry, *Design Futuring* (Oxford: Berg, 2009), pp. 201–6.

6. Leroi-Gourhan, *Gesture and Speech*, pp. 130–3.

7. Ibid., p. 140.

8. *Australopithecus Afarensis*—an extinct hominoid that lived between 3.9 and 2.5 million years ago. See Delson et al., *Encyclopedia of Human Evolution and Prehistory*.

9. Leroi-Gourhan, *Gesture and Speech*, p. 97.

10. In the modern world, 'tool-making tools' is the domain of machine tools. Yet, at the same time, tools from the ancient world, such as the whetstone, continue in their modern form.

11. This sickle was used around eight thousand years ago to harvest wild cereal crops as quickly as possible to maximize yields. See Ofer Bar-Yosef, 'The Natufian Culture of the Levant, Threshold to the Origins of Agriculture', *Evolutionary Anthropology*, 6/5 (1998), pp. 159–77.

12. Ibid.

13. Ibid., p. 102.

14. Here is a history extending from the punchcard-instructed Jacquard loom of 1804 to contemporary robotics.

15. Stiegler, *Technics and Time 1*, p. 157.

16. Ibid., p. 178.

17. Ibid., p. 136.

18. Elizabeth J. Himelfarb, 'Prehistoric Body Painting', *Archaeology*, 53/4 (July/August 2000).

19. On Luhmann and second-order systems see Wolfe, *What Is Posthumanism?*, pp. 109–22.

20. Heidegger, *What Is Called Thinking?*, p. 22.

21. Martin Heidegger, 'The Question Concerning Technology' in *The Question Concerning Technology and Other Essays*, trans. William Lovitt (New York: Harper and Row, 1977), p. 5.

22. Stiegler, *Technics and Time 2*, pp. 97–187.

23. Heidegger, *Being and Time*, H. 68.

24. For instance, one can cite Martin Heidegger's essay 'The Thing' in *Poetry, Language, Thought*, trans. Albert Hofstadter (New York: Harper and Row, 1971), pp. 163–86, and, more recently, Bruno Latour's opening essay 'From Realpolitik to Dingpolitik or How to Make Things Public', in Bruno Latour and Peter Weibel, eds, *Making Things Public: Atmospheres of Democracy* (Cambridge, MA: MIT Press, 2005), pp. 14–43.

25. Merleau-Ponty, *Phenomenology of Perception*, p. 330.

26. Ibid.

27. Ibid.

28. John Sallis, *Delimitations: Phenomenology and the End of Metaphysics* (Bloomington: Indiana University Press, 1995), pp. 78–81.

29. Ibid., pp. 81–2. The thrust of Sallis's argument is to support the move initiated by Heidegger and developed by Derrida that disclosed the metaphysical nature of what is made present while undercutting the epistemological claims of traditional phenomenology by an engagement of things in the world.
30. Merleau-Ponty, *Phenomenology of Perception,* p. 323.
31. Ibid., p. 320.
32. Cited by Sallis, *Delimitations,* p. 76.
33. Ibid., p. 207.
34. Ibid., p. 203.

Chapter 7: Why Make the Leap?

1. Aristotle, *Physics—The Complete Works of Aristotle,* ed. John Barnes (Princeton, NJ: Princeton University Press, 1984), IV, Ch. 11, 219a ff.
2. With such an atomic clock, there was an increase in the precision of the second by four orders of magnitude. M. A. Lombardi, T. P. Heavner, and S. R. Jefferts, 'NIST Primary Frequency Standards and the Realization of the SI Second', *Journal of Measurement Science,* 2/4 (2007), p. 74.
3. The bare face of the clock can but indicate the moment of now. It is nothing without memory; it tells us nothing without change. The clock needs us and the event it is used to divide or measure. Martin Heidegger, *The Concept of Time,* trans. William McNeill (London: Blackwell, 1992), p. 5E.
4. Ibid., pp. 6E/7E.
5. Ibid., pp. 6E n.1 and 23E.

Chapter 8: The Passage from 'Here and Now' to 'Then'

1. The conventional, media and familiar scientific way of picturing 'the problem of unsustainability' by addressing particular instrumental causes and impacts is absolutely inadequate (as they range across levels and sources of greenhouse gas emissions and the impacts of climate change, like increased temperatures, extreme weather events, reduced soil moisture, reduced crop yields, sea level rises, the increase of vector-borne diseases and the potential for the creation of huge numbers of environmental/climate refugees). Likewise, so are the ways that stress on natural resources are characterized and addressed, especially water use, loss of biodiversity, deforestation, desertification and loss of topsoil, food production crises, problems of waste (including toxic, putrescent and electronic) and global population growth. The same is true of the way 'overconsumption' is presented to us.
2. On the transition from gathering 'founder crops' (emmer, einkorn wheat, hulled barley, peas, lentils, bitter vetch, chick peas and flax) to cropping them, see Robin G. Allaby, Dorian Q. Fuller, and Terence A. Brown, 'The Genetic Expectations of a Protracted Model for the

Origins of Domesticated Crops', *Proceedings of the National Academy of Sciences of the USA,* 105/37 (16 Sept. 2008), pp. 13982–6.

3. This account is informed by Ofer Bar-Yosef, 'The Natufian Cultures in the Levant, Threshold to the Origins of Agriculture'.
4. Dyer, *Climate Wars,* and James R. Lee, *Climate Change and Armed Conflict* (London: Routledge, 2006).
5. Mike Davis, *Planet of Slums* (London: Verso, 2006). Recent contestations of learning from slums (e.g. slums as sustainable) is acknowledged in chapter 12.
6. For a contemporary version of fortification see the Masdar Development designed by Foster and Partners, *Design Observer,* 6 June 2010, http://www.designobserver.com/changeobserver/entry.html?entry=13878.
7. See Fry, *Design as Politics,* pp. 67–74.
8. Tony Fry, ed., *The Urmadic City* (Brisbane: Griffith University, QCA, 2011).
9. Fry, *Design as Politics,* pp. 209–36.

Part IV: From 'Where We Were' to 'Where We Are'

1. The German term 'mensch', while used to designate 'man', dominantly signifies 'human being'.
2. See Heidegger, *Being and Truth,* p. 163.
3. Ibid.
4. Ibid.
5. Ibid.
6. Ibid.
7. Ibid., pp. 163–4.

Chapter 9: World-in-Being

1. Science cannot help us here, for, whatever it objectifies and whatever the efficacy of its actions, it is always isolated from the whole and within its own condition of representational containment.
2. Heidegger, *Being and Time,* S 75.
3. Fredric Jameson, *The Prison House of Language* (Princeton, NJ: Princeton University Press, 1972).
4. See '2 Linguistics and Grammatology' in Derrida, *Of Grammatology,* pp. 27–73.
5. Heidegger, *Being and Time,* H 64.
6. Martin Heidegger, *History of the Concept of Time,* trans. Theodore Kisiel (Bloomington: Indiana University Press, 1985), p. 170.
7. Cited by Warren, *Nietzsche and Political Thought,* p. 127.
8. See Heidegger, *The Fundamental Concepts of Metaphysics,* p. 349.
9. Ibid., p. 275.

10. Besides Heidegger's notion of 'worldhood' supporting this view, we can cite, for example, Maurice Merleau-Ponty, 'Other Selves and the Human World', in *Phenomenology of Perception,* pp. 346–65, and Dietmar Kamper and Christoph Wulf, eds., *Looking Back at the End of the World,* trans. Robert Golding (New York: Semiotext(e), 1989), pp. 49–63.

11. See McNeill, *The Time of Life,* 2006, p. 51.

12. Ibid.

13. Merleau-Ponty, *Phenomenology of Perception,* pp. 333–4.

14. In this 'scramble for Africa', the major decisions were made at the conference, and then the detail was handed over to respective government departments of foreign affairs.

15. The term 'ethnocide' was first used to describe the destruction of the culture (the way of living and thinking) of the indigenous people of Latin America—see Pierre Clastres, *Archeology of Violence,* trans. Jeanine Herman (New York: Semiotext(e), 1994), pp. 43–51.

16. Heidegger, *The Fundamental Concepts of Metaphysics,* pp. 172–6.

17. Warren, *Nietzsche and Political Thought,* p. 111.

18. Ibid, pp. 133–4, and Nietzsche, *The Will to Power,* S 567–70.

19. See especially McNeill, *The Time of Life,* pp. 36–42.

20. Ibid., p. 42.

21. Leroi-Gourhan, *Gesture and Speech,* p. 146.

22. Heidegger, *The Fundamental Concepts of Metaphysics,* p. 285.

23. Ibid., p. 281.

24. Ibid., p. 292.

25. For a discussion on the relation between *Ent-fernung,* the remote and the near, see Paul Adams, 'In TV: On "Nearness", on Heidegger and on Television', in Tony Fry, ed., *RUATV? Heidegger and the Televisual* (Sydney: Power Publications, 1993), pp. 45–66.

26. Heidegger, *The Fundamental Concepts of Metaphysics,* p. 301.

Chapter 10: Imagination in a Blink of an Eye

1. Martin Heidegger, *Kant and the Problem of Metaphysics,* trans. Richard Taft (Bloomington: Indiana University Press, 1990). It has been argued that imagination occupies a central role in Kant's philosophy as a whole. See Freydberg, *Imagination in Kant's Critique of Practical Reason.*

2. Heidegger, *Kant and the Problem of Metaphysics,* p. 115.

3. This is the claim made by Richard Kearney in *The Wake of Imagination* (Minneapolis: Minnesota University Press, 1988), p. 157.

4. Ibid., p. 110.

5. Kearney, *The Wake of Imagination,* pp. 156–7.

6. Heidegger's understanding of imagination was built not just on his relation to Kant but equally to Husserl. After his 'turn' it moved into the domain of the heterotopic. See Brian Elliott, *Phenomenology and Imagination in Husserl and Heidegger* (London: Routledge, 2005).

7. This was explicitly stated by Kant: 'Imagination is the faculty of representing an object even without its presence in intuition' in *Critique of Pure Reason,* trans. J.M.D. Meiklejohn (New York: Prometheus Books, 1990), p. 87.

  8. Ibid., pp. 113–18.
  9. Ibid., p. 118.
 10. On this issue see Kearney, *The Wake of Imagination,* pp. 157–8.
 11. Kearney interestingly reviews Nietzsche's view on imagination, ibid., pp. 211–17.
 12. On the existential imagination, see ibid., pp. 211–14.
 13. Ibid., p. 155.
 14. On Orders of Simulacra see Jean Baudrillard, *Simulations,* trans. Paul Foss and Philip Be-
     itchmas (New York: Semiotext(e), 1983).
 15. Martin Heidegger, *The Principle of Reason,* trans. Reginald Lilly (Bloomington: Indiana Uni-
     versity Press, 1996). This was not Heidegger's first engagement with the issue of reason as
     ground. For example, he made specific reference to Leibniz's notion of the sufficiency of
     reason in his 1927 lecture course on *The Basic Problems of Phenomenology,* trans. Albert
     Hofstadter (Bloomington: Indiana University Press, 1988), p. 92.
 16. Heidegger, *The Principle of Reason,* p. 32.
 17. Ibid.
 18. Ernst Cassirer, *The Philosophy of the Enlightenment,* trans. Fritz C. A. Koelln and James P.
     Pettegrove (Princeton, NJ: Princeton University Press, [1951] 2009), pp. 6–9.
 19. Cited by Kearney, *The Wake of Imagination,* p. 212.
 20. See Warren, *Nietzsche and Political Thought,* pp. 164–5.
 21. Ibid.
 22. Ibid.
 23. Ibid., p. 167.
 24. See Heidegger, *The Fundamental Concept of Metaphysics,* p. 204, and McNeill's comments
     in *The Time of Life,* p. 35.
 25. Ibid., McNeill p. 35.
 26. Hegel's *Philosophy of Right,* trans. T. M. Knox (Oxford: Oxford University Press, 1967),
     p. 155.
 27. On this see John Sallis, *Delimitations: Phenomenology and the End of Metaphysics* (Bloom-
     ington: Indiana University Press, 1995), pp. 35–6.
 28. Ibid., p. 37.
 29. Ibid., p. 3.
 30. Ibid.
 31. Ibid., p. 9.
 32. See Kearney, *The Wake of Imagination* on Nietzsche's critical view of imagination, p. 213.
 33. Here one can cite F. Schelling's *System of Transcendental Idealism* and the English Roman-
     tic poets Coleridge and Wordsworth. Ibid., p. 12.
 34. Heidegger, *The Question Concerning Technology.*
 35. See Bernard Stiegler, *Technics and Time, 3,* trans. Stephen Barker (Stanford, CA: Stanford
     University Press, 2009), pp. 97–187.
 36. Sallis, *Delimitations,* p. 23.
 37. See Kearney, *The Wake of Imagination,* for a more comprehensive account of Kant's position,
     pp. 192–3.
 38. On chronophobia (kronophobia) see Bernd Magnus, *Nietzsche's Existential Imperative*
     (Bloomington: Indiana University Press, 1978), pp. 190–5.

39. Michael E. Zimmerman, *Eclipse of the Self* (Athens: Ohio University Press, 1981), p. 225.

40. On Sustainment see Tony Fry, *Design as Politics* (Oxford: Berg, 2010).

41. Warren, *Nietzsche and Political Thought*, p. 114.

42. Hilary Putnam, 'Why Reason Can't Be Naturalised', in Kenneth Baynes, James Bohman and Thomas McCarthy (eds), *Philosophy: End or Transformation* (Cambridge, MA: MIT Press, 1987), p. 223.

43. Ibid., pp. 90–1.

44. Cassirer, *The Philosophy of the Enlightenment*, p. 22.

45. Alfred North Whitehead makes the point that in the end reason rests upon religion. See *Process and Reality*, chapter 1, section 2 (New York: The Free Press, [1929] 1978), pp. 42–3.

46. Martin Heidegger, *Vorträge und Aufsätze*, 5th ed. (Pfullingen: Neste, 1985).

47. Sallis, *Delimitations*, p. 25.

Chapter 11: On the Subject of the Subject

1. Etienne Balibar, 'Citizen Subject', in Eduardo Cadava, Peter Connor and Jean-Luc Nancy, eds, *Who Comes after the Subject?* (New York: Routledge, 1991), p. 40.

2. Ibid.

3. Zimmerman, *Eclipse of the Self*, p. 224.

4. On this issue see Thomson, *Heidegger's Ontotheology*, p. 150.

5. Zimmerman, *Eclipse of the Self*, p. 216.

6. Ibid., p. 26. Here Zimmerman is informed by Martin Heidegger's *Die Grundprobleme der Phänomenologie* (1927), p. 230.

7. These comments echo a consistent and underaddressed position adopted by Derrida that refused the human/animal binary—a binary held in place by 'the subject' as a meta-discourse. See Derrida, *The Animal That Therefore I Am*. The statement of this text was a last word that flowed back over his entire oeuvre.

8. Jacques Derrida, 'Eating Well', in Cadava, Connor and Nancy, eds, *Who Comes After the Subject?*, p.103.

9. Heidegger, *Being and Truth*, p. 167.

10. Jacques Derrida and Paule Thévenin, *The Secret Art of Antonin Artaud*, trans. Mary Ann Caws (Cambridge, MA: MIT Press, 1998), p. 157.

11. Derrida, 'Eating Well', p. 108.

12. Michel Henry, 'The Critique of the Subject', in Cadava, Connor and Nancy, eds, *Who Comes after the Subject?*, p. 157

13. Ibid.

14. Balibar, 'Citizen Subject', pp. 33–57.

15. The rise and fall of civilization by Arnold Toynbee was documented in his ten-volume *Study of History* (1934–61), in print in abridged form from Oxford University Press (1987).

16. Heidegger, *What Is Called Thinking?*, p. 69.

17. Magnus, *Nietzsche's Existential Imperative*.
18. Miguel de Beistegui, *Heidegger and the Political: Dystopias* (London: Routledge, 1998), p. 74.

Part V: Now-ings

1. One often-cited example of progress is, of course, that delivered by medical science, yet it has equally created the condition of iatrogenisis—medically induced illness. Added to this, many of the diseases of the modern world are a product of technologies, materials and environments.
2. Walter Benjamin, 'Thesis on the Philosophy of History IX', in *Illumination*, trans. Harry Zohn (London: Fontana/Collins, 1970), pp. 259–60.

Chapter 12: Living in Darkness

1. While Oswald Spengler's most noted work was *The Decline of the West* (1928), his *Mensche and Technik* (*Man and Technology*, 1932) was also significant, including for Heidegger. For an account of Spengler and his influence see Jeffery Herf, *Reactionary Modernism* (Cambridge: Cambridge University Press, 1984), pp. 49–77.
2. See James Lee, *Climate Change and Armed Conflict*, pp. 117–47; Gwynne Dyer, *Climate Wars*, pp. 1–31.
3. For example, in September 2011, a symposium titled 'Geoengineering the Climate' was held in Canberra to explore the general issues of 'geoengineering', carbon dioxide removal, solar radiation management, and governance, ethics, risks and uncertainty and their possible affects in the southern hemisphere.
4. Jay Michaelson, "Geoengineering': A Climate Change Manhattan Project', *Stanford Environmental Law Journal* (Jan. 1998), pp. 105–39, http://elj.stanford.edu/.
5. Ibid.
6. Ibid.
7. Ibid.
8. Ibid.
9. See http://www.abc.net.au/news/2011–09–26/scientists-call-for-geoengineering-regulation/29 42918.
10. Asilomar Geoengineering Report, 'Geoengineering: We All Want to Change the World', *The Economist*, 31 Mar. 2010.
11. 'If such a reduction in incoming solar radiation were achieved by placing a sunshade consisting of multiple "flyers" at the L1 point (Angel, 20 2006), it would require a total area of 4.1 million km2…given that atmospheric CO_2 is rising at 2 ppm yr-1 and converting this

to 0.0282Wm2 yr-1 using Eq. (9), a surface area of 31 000 km2 would need to be added each year. This equates to 135 000 launches per year, each carrying 800,000 space flyers of area 5 0.2882m2.' James Hrynyshyn, 'Can 'Geoengineering' Reverse "Irreversible" Climate Change?', *The Economist,* 28 Jan. 2009.

12. Ibid.
13. Ibid.
14. Ibid.
15. See note 2, chapter 2.
16. Researchers led by Charles Trick of the University of Western Ontario, Canada, found that fertilizing the ocean with iron can boost the growth of Pseudo-nitzschia, a phytoplankton that produces a component of the neurotoxin domoic acid. Humans who eat shellfish or crab that have ingested Pseudo-nitzschia can get amnesic shellfish poisoning, severe cases of which can cause neurological symptoms, including permanent short-term memory loss, which gives the intoxication its name. Amnesic shellfish poisoning can also be fatal. 'Adding Iron to Sea Boosts Deadly Neurotoxin', *Agence France-Presse,* 15 Mar. 2010.
17. Solomon et al., 'Irreversible Climate Change Due to Carbon Dioxide Emissions', http://www. noaanews.noaa.gov/stories2009/20090 126_climate.html.
18. See John Vidal, 'UN Surveys a World of "Endless" Cities', *Guardian Weekly,* 26 Mar. 2010, p. 4.
19. Brian Fagan, *Floods, Famines and Emperors* (New York: Basic Books, 1999), p. 76.
20. The First World War being the most overt instrument of this, as colonial forces brought troops from Europe, Asia and Africa into one coordinated moment of action.
21. This is the figure given at Copenhagen in March 2009.
22. As I write, my state (Queensland) is in the midst of floods covering an area greater than the combined size of France and Germany. In and around my local city (Toowoomba), scores of people have lost their lives, Brisbane is flooding and all roads in all directions out of where I live are closed due to landslides—we had 650mm of rain in four days. Some people in the region have had four 'one-hundred-year floods' in a month. The damage done to the state's infrastructure, businesses, homes and economy (especially as a result of flooded mines and lost agriculture) runs to many billions of dollars and counting. The economic impact of this extreme weather will be national. Views expressed on extreme weather, of which the preceding is only one experience in the past decade, are thus not simply statement of opinion.
23. Tony Fry, Nora Kinnunen, Petra Perolini and Will Odom, *Metrofitting: Adaptation, the City and Impacts of the Coming Climate* (Brisbane: Queensland College of Art, 2009).
24. On details on the movement see *Transition Handbook.* A free version is released under GFDL and Creative Commons Attribution-Share at http://www. uniteddiversity.com/transition-handbook/.
25. Davis, *Planet of Slums.*
26. Fry, *Design as Politics.*
27. One example of this is moving a slum in Porto Alegre over a planned four-year period, via the UN Global Compact Cities Program (of which RMIT University's Paul James is the director). See http://www.abc.net.au/rn/futuretense/stories/2011/3262513.htm.

28. The Urmadic City was a project and exhibition (shown at 'Unlimited', the Asia Pacific Design Triennial, Brisbane, 2010) created by the Master of Design Futures students of Griffith University, Queensland College of Art. See Fry, ed., *The Urmadic City.*

29. Norman Foster, *Design Observer,* 6 June 2010, http://www.designobserver.com/changeobserver/entry.html?entry = 13878, extract from review by Dominique Browning of 'Why Design Now?', Cooper-Hewitt National Design Triennial, New York, 2011.

30. See http://www.toronto.ca/path/.

Chapter 13: Postpolitical Prospects

1. Vidal, 'UN Surveys a World of "Endless" Cities'.

2. Lewis Mumford, *The City in History* (London: Penguin Books, 1966).

3. Including a reversion to 'city states'.

4. The notion of network societies was given particular profile in the mid 1990s by Manuel Castells, *The Rise of the Network Society* (Oxford: Blackwell, 1996).

5. Pierre Clastres, *Society against the State,* trans. Robert Hurley (New York: Zone Books, 1987), pp. 23–4.

6. Fry, *Design as Politics.*

7. Proto-societies may well be of a scale where they are able to operate with direct democracy (its first form), in contrast to representative democracy. Direct democracy means that every member of the tribe, society, city, or nation can exercise a vote on every issue.

8. Again, this is discussed at length in Fry, *Design as Politics.*

9. Slavoj Žižek, glossing Catherine Malabou's *Les Nouveaux Blessés* (The New Wounded) (Paris, Bayard, 2007), asks, 'If the twentieth century was the Freudian century, so that even its worst nightmares were read as (sado-masochistic) vicissitudes of the libido, will the twenty-first be the century of the post-traumatic disengaged subject, whose first emblematic figure, that of the Muselmann, is multiplying in the guise of refugees, terror victims, survivors of natural disasters or of family violence?' Slavoj Žižek, *Living in the End Times* (London: Verso, 2011), p. 294.

10. Specifically, late Neanderthals are known to have collected fossils and odd-shaped stones. Leroi-Gourhan, *Gesture and Speech,* p. 3.

Chapter 14: The Rise of Another Other

1. See Thomson, *Heidegger on Ontotheology,* p. 152.

2. See the summary of Heidegger's position on ontological education in ibid., p.101.

3. On futuring see Fry, *Design Futuring.*

4. See Fry, *Design as Politics.*

5. Ibid., pp. 187–208.

6. Fry, *Design as Politics*, p. 203.

7. The growing literature on the crisis of the university now embraces writers as diverse as Jürgen Habermas, Bill Readings, Henry A. Giroux, Stanley Aronowitz and Dominick LaCapra.

8. The notion of the Urmadic University (a university without a place) is an international project that is already under way—see http://www.theodessey.org.

9. Friedrich Nietzsche, *Thus Spoke Zarathustra*, trans. R. J. Hollingdale (London: Penguin Books, 1969), p. 85.

10. Ibid., p. 137.

11. Michael Tanner, Introduction to Nietzsche, *Beyond Good and Evil*, p. 21.

12. Richardson, *Nietzsche's New Darwinism*, p. 97.

13. Ibid., p. 101.

14. Nietzsche, *Thus Spoke Zarathustra*, p. 41.

15. 'The "Superman" does not simply carry the accustomed drives and strivings of the customary type of man beyond all measure and bounds. Superman is a qualitatively, not quantitatively, different form of existing man. The thing that the Superman discards is precisely our boundless, purely quantitative non-stop progress. The Superman is poorer, simpler, tenderer and tougher, quieter and more self-sacrificing and slow of decision and more economical of speech.' Heidegger, *What Is Called Thinking*, p. 67. Others have characterized the Superman in similar terms. Bernd Magnus, for instance, describes the Superman as a type of human being who represents an ascending life, self-overcoming and self-possession in contrast to a life of decadence, decomposition and weakness. He is 'the extraordinary being that extols autonomy, independence, power, pride, spontaneity, intelligence and passion.' See Magnus, *Nietzsche's Existential Imperative*, p. 34. More modestly, Michael E. Zimmerman described this being as an indication of 'humanity released from its drive to dominate and mastery': Zimmerman, *Eclipse of the Self*, p. 215.

16. Nietzsche, *Thus Spoke Zarathustra*, p. 297.

17. Ibid., p. 144.

18. See Dyer, *Climate Wars*, pp. 31–41.

19. See chapter 3 of Tony Fry, *A New Design Philosophy: An Introduction to Defuturing* (Sydney: University of New South Wales Press, 1999), on the global impact of the creation of the modern industrial design profession in the United States in the 1930s.

Chapter 15: Last Words

1. Martin Heidegger, *What Is Philosophy?*, lecture given in France in 1955, published in German in 1956, trans. Jean T. Wilds and William Kluback (Albany: NCUP Inc., undated).

2. See Wolfe, *What Is Posthumanism?*, p. 35.

3. Thomson, *Heidegger on Ontotheology*, p. 55.

4. Niklas Luhmann's position is most comprehensively presented in his magnum opus, *Social Systems*, trans. John Bednarz Jr with Dirk Baecker (Stanford: Stanford University Press, 1995).

5. Cary Wolfe's *What Is Posthumanism?* represents the insightful end of this tendency.

6. Ibid., pp. 13–15.

7. Ibid., p. 125.

8. Ashley Stewart Crane, 'The Restoration of Israel: Ezekiel 36–39 in Early Jewish Interpretation', PhD diss., Murdoch University, 2006, p. 23.

9. Here his thinking was inflected by his engagement with Marxism (especially his understanding of the relation between a mode of production and superstructural cultural forms, but without abandoning his mystical disposition as it was grounded in Hebrew *ur-texts*).

10. Brendel, 'The Everlasting Now: Walter Benjamin's Archive'.

Select Bibliography

Agamben, Giorgio, *Homo Sacer: Sovereign Power and Bare Life,* trans. Daniel Heller-Roazen, Stanford: Stanford University Press, 1998.

Agamben, Giorgio, *The Open: Man and Animal,* trans. Kevin Attell, Stanford: Stanford University Press, 2004.

Andreski, Stanislav, *Herbert Spencer: Structure, Function and Evolution,* London: Nelson, 1971.

Arendt, Hannah, *The Human Condition,* Chicago: University of Chicago Press, 1958.

Aristotle, *Physics—The Complete Works of Aristotle,* ed. John Barnes, Princeton, NJ: Princeton University Press, 1984.

Asilomar Geoengineering Report, 'We Want to Change the World', *The Economist,* 31 March 2010.

Bataille, Georges, *The Accursed Share, Vol. I,* New York: Zone Books, 1988.

Bataille, Georges, *The Accursed Share, Vols II & III,* New York: Zone Books, 1993.

Bataille, Georges, *Visions of Excess: Selected Writings 1927–1939,* trans. Allan Stoekle et al., Minneapolis: University of Minnesota Press, 1985.

Baudrillard, Jean, *For a Critique Political Economy of the Sign,* trans. Charles Levin, St Louis: Telos Press, 1981.

Baudrillard, Jean, *Simulations,* trans. Paul Foss and Philip Beitchmas, New York: Semiotext(e), 1983.

Baynes, Kenneth, Bohman, James and McCarthy, Thomas, eds, *Philosophy: End or Transformation,* Cambridge, MA: MIT Press, 1986.

Beck. L.W., ed., *Kant on History,* trans. L. W. Beck, R. E. Archer and E. L. Fackenham, Indianapolis: Bobbs-Merrill, 1963.

Beistegui, Miguel de, *Heidegger and the Political: Dystopias,* London: Routledge, 1998.

Benjamin, Walter, *Illuminations,* trans. Harry Zohn, London: Fontana/Collins, 1970.

Bruns, Gerald, L., *On Ceasing to Be Human,* Stanford: Stanford University Press, 2011.

Cadava, Eduardo, Connor, Peter and Nancy, Jean-Luc, eds, *Who Comes after the Subject,* New York: Routledge, 1991.

Calarco, Mathew and De Caroli, Steven, *Giorgio Agamben: Sovereignty and Life,* Stanford: Stanford University Press, 2007.

Canguilheim, Georges, *Ideology and Rationality in the Life Sciences,* trans. Arthur Goldhammer, Cambridge, MA: MIT Press, 1988.

Canguilheim, Georges, *A Vital Rationalist: Selected Writings of Georges Canguilheim,* ed. Francois Delaporte, trans. Arthur Goldhammer, New York: Zone Books, 1994.

Cassirer, Ernst, (1951), *The Philosophy of the Enlightenment,* trans. F.C.A. Koellin and J. P. Pettegrove, Princeton, NJ: Princeton University Press, 2009.

Castells, Manuel, *The Rise of the Network Society,* Oxford: Blackwell, 1996.

Clastres, Pierre, *Archeology of Violence,* trans. Jeanine Herman, New York: Semiotext(e), 1994.

Darwin, Charles, (1871), *The Descent of Man and Selection in Relation to Sex,* London: Appleton, 1992.

Darwin, Charles, (1859), *The Origin of The Species,* London: Gramercy, 1995.

Darwin, F., *The Life and Letters of Charles Darwin,* London: John Murray, 1887.

Davis, Mike, *Planet of Slums,* London: Verso, 2006.

Deleuze, Gilles, *Kant's Critical Philosophy: The Doctrine of Faculties,* trans. Hugh Thomlinson and Barbara Habberjam, London Althone Press, 1984.

Deleuze, Gilles and Guattari, Felix, *A Thousand Plateaus,* trans. Brian Massumi, Minneapolis: University of Minnesota Press, 1987.

Delson, E., Tattersall, I., Van Couvering, J. A., and Brooks, A. S., eds, *Encyclopedia of Human Evolution and Prehistory,* New York: Garland, 2000.

Dennett, Daniel, *Darwin's Dangerous Idea,* London: Penguin, 1995.

Derrida, Jacques, *The Animal That Therefore I Am,* ed. Marie-LouiseMallet, trans. David Wills, New York: Fordham University Press, 2008.

Derrida, Jacques, 'Eating Well', in Eduardo Cadava, Peter Connor, and Jean-Luc Nancy, eds, *Who Comes after the Subject?* New York: Routledge, 1991.

Derrida, Jacques, '*Geschlecht* II: Heidegger's Hand', trans. John P. Leavey Jr, in John Sallis, ed., *Deconstruction and Philosophy: The Texts of J. Derrida,* Chicago: Chicago University Press, 1987.

Derrida, Jacques, and Paule Thévenin, *The Secret Art of Antonin Artaud,* trans. Mary Ann Caws, Cambridge, MA: MIT Press, 1998.

Dyer, Gwynne, *Climate Wars,* Melbourne: Scribe, 2008.

Elliott, Brian, *Phenomenology and Imagination in Husserl and Heidegger,* London: Routledge, 2005.

Fagan, Brian, *Floods, Famines and Emperors,* New York: Basic Books, 1990.

Fagan, Brian, *The Long Summer: How Climate Changed Civilization,* New York: Basic Books, 2004.

Foucault, Michel, *Language, Counter-Memory, Practice,* trans. Donald F. Bouchard and Sherry Simon, New York: Cornell University Press, 1977.

Frankfort, H., *The Birth of Civilization in the Near East,* London: Williams and Norgate, 1951.

Frankfort, H., Frankfort, H.A., Wilson, J. and Jacobsen, T., *Before Philosophy,* Harmondsworth: Penguin Books, 1968.

Freud, Sigmund, *Civilization and Its Discontents,* ed. and trans. James Strachey, New York: Norton, 1961.

Freydberg, Bernard, *Imagination in Kant's Critique of Practical Reason,* Bloomington: Indiana University Press, 2005.

Friere, Paulo, *Teachers as Cultural Workers,* trans. Donoldo Macedo, Dalr Koike and Alexandre Oliveira, Boulder, CO: Westfield Press, 1998.

Fry, Tony, *Design as Politics,* Oxford: Berg, 2011.

Fry, Tony, *Design Futuring: Ethics, Sustainability and New Practice,* Oxford: Berg, 2009.

Fry, Tony, ed., *RUATV? Heidegger and the Televisual,* Sydney: Power Publications, 1993.

Fry, Tony, ed., *The Urmadic City,* Brisbane: Griffith University, QCA, 2011.

Fry, Tony, Kinnunen, Nora, Perolini, Petra and Will Odom, *Metrofitting: Adaptation, the City and Impacts of the Coming Climate* Brisbane: Queensland College of Art, 2009.

Futuyma, D. J., *Evolutionary Biology,* New York: Sinauer Associates, 1986.

Gadamer, Hans-Georg, *Truth and Method,* trans. Joel Weinsheimer and Donald G. Marshall, New York: Crossroad, 1990.

Geddes, Norman Bel, *Horizons,* New York: Dover, 1977.

Goodell, Jeff, *How to Cool the Planet,* Boston: Houghton Mifflin Harcourt, 2010.

Hanssen, Beatrice, *Walter Benjamin's Other History: Of Stones, Animals, Human Beings and Angels,* Berkeley: University of California Press, 2000.

Harman, Graham, *Tool Being: Heidegger and the Metaphysics of Objects,* Chicago: Open Court, 2002.

Harman, Graham, *Towards Speculative Realism,* Winchester: Zero Books, 2010.

Hegel, G.W.F. (1821), *Hegel's Philosophy of Right,* trans. T. M. Knox, Oxford: Oxford University Press, 1967.

Heidegger, Martin, *The Basic Problems of Phenomenology,* trans. Albert Hofstadter, Bloomington: Indiana University Press, 1988.

Heidegger, Martin, *Basic Writings,* trans. David Farrell-Krell, Routledge: London, 1978.

Heidegger, Martin, *Being and Time,* trans. John Macquarrie and Edward Robinson, Oxford: Blackwell, 1962.

Heidegger, Martin, *Being and Truth,* trans. Gregory Fried and Richard Polt, Bloomington: Indiana University Press, 2010.

Heidegger, Martin (1924), *The Concept of Time,* trans. William McNeill, London: Blackwell, 1992.

Heidegger, Martin, *The Fundamental Concepts of Metaphysics,* trans. William McNeill and Nicolas Walker, Bloomington: Indiana University Press, 1995.

Heidegger, Martin, *History of the Concept of Time,* trans. Theodore Kisiel, Bloomington: Indiana University Press, 1985.

Heidegger, Martin (1973), *Kant and the Problem of Metaphysics,* trans. Richard Taft, Bloomington: Indiana University Press, 1990.

Heidegger, Martin, *Parmenides,* trans. Andre Schuwer and Richard Rojcewicz, Bloomington: Indiana University Press, 1992.

Heidegger, Martin (1957), *The Principle of Reason,* trans. Reginald Lilly, Bloomington: Indiana University Press, 1996.

Heidegger, Martin, *The Question Concerning Technology and Other Essays,* trans. William Lovitt, New York: Harper and Row, 1977.

Heidegger, Martin, *What Is Called Thinking,* trans. J. Glenn Gray, New York: Harper and Row, 1968.

Heidegger, Martin, *What Is Philosophy,* trans. Jean T. Wilds and William Kluback, Albany: NCUP Inc., undated.

Heim, Michael, *The Metaphysics of Virtual Reality,* Oxford: Oxford University Press, 1993.

Herf, Jeffery, *Reactionary Modernism,* Cambridge: Cambridge University Press, 1984.

Hrynyshyn, James, 'Can Geoengineering Reverse "Irreversible" Climate Change?', *The Economist,* 28 Jan. 2009.

Intergovernmental Panel on Climate Change (IPCC), 'Climate Change 2007', Special Report on Renewable Energy Sources and Climate Change, Fifth Assessment Report, www.ipcc.ch/.

Jameson, Fredric, *Archaeologies of the Future,* London: Verso, 2007.

Jameson, Fredric, *The Prison House of Language,* Princeton, NJ: Princeton University Press, 1972.

Jones, Cheryl, 'Technical Innovation May Have Driven First Human Migration', *Nature,* 30 Oct. 2008.

Jünger, Ernst (1934), *On Pain,* trans. David C. Durst, New York: Telos Press, 2008.

Kamper, Dietmar, and Wulf, Christoph, eds, *Looking Back at the End of the World,* New York: Semiotext(e), 1989.

Kant, Immanuel, *Critique of Pure Reason,* trans. J.M.D. Meiklejohn, New York: Prometheus Books, 1990.

Kant, Immanuel, 'Idea for a Universal History from a Cosmopolitan Point of View', in L. W. Beck, ed., *Kant on History,* trans. L.W. Beck, R. E. Archer and E. L. Fackenham, Indianapolis: Bobbs-Merrill, 1963.

Kearney, Richard, *The Wake of Imagination,* Minneapolis: University of Minnesota Press, 1988.

Kintisch, Eli, *Hack the Planet,* New York: Wiley, 2010.

Kunzig, Robert, 'Geoengineering: How to Cool the Earth at a Price', *Scientific American,* Nov. 2008.

Latour, Bruno, *We Have Never Been Modern,* trans. Catherine Porter, Cambridge, MA: Harvard University Press, 1993.

Lawson-Tancred, Hugh, 'Introduction', in *De Anima,* Aristotle, Ch. 13, Book 3, London: Penguin Books, 1986.

Lee, James, R., *Climate Change and Armed Conflict,* London: Routledge, 2006.

Lemonick, Michael, 'A (Somewhat) Curmundgeneonly Take on Geoengineering', 5 May 2010. http://www.oneearh.org/author/michaelle-monick.

Leroi-Gourhan, André, *Gesture and Speech,* trans. Anna Bostock Berger, Cambridge, MA: MIT Press, 1998.

Levinas, Emmanuel, *Otherwise Than Being or Beyond Essence,* trans. Alfonso Lingis, Dordrecht: Kluwer Academic Publishers, 1978.

Lévi-Strauss, Claude, *The Savage Mind,* London: Wiedenfeld and Nicolson, 1966.

Luhmann, Niklas, *Social Systems,* trans. John Bednarz Jr and Dirk Baecker, Stanford: Stanford University Press, 1995.

Lyotard, Jean-François, *The Inhuman,* Stanford: Stanford University Press, 1991.

Magnus, Bernd, *Nietzsche's Existential Imperative,* Bloomington: Indiana University Press, 1978.

Marx, Karl, *Capital,* vol. 1, trans. S. Moore and E. Aveling, London: Lawrence and Wishart, 1977.

Marx, Karl, 'Economic and Philosophical Manuscripts of 1844', in *Early Writings,* trans. R. Livingston and G. Benton, London: Penguin Books, 1975.

McKie, Robin, 'Cold Comfort for Earth', review of Chris Stringer, *Homo Britannicu',* *Guardian Weekly,* 5–11 Jan. 2007.

McNeill, William, *The Time of Life: Heidegger and Ethos,* Albany: State University of New York Press, 2006.

Merleau-Ponty, Maurice, (1962), *Phenomenology of Perception,* trans. Colin Smith, London: Routledge, 1989.

Michaelsom, Jay, 'Geoengineering: A Climate Change Manhattan Project', *Stanford Environmental Law Journal,* Jan. 1998.

Minogue, Kirsten, 'Stone Age Toolmakers Surprisingly Sophisticated', *Science,* 28 Oct. 2010. http://news.sciencemag.org/science-now/2010/10/stone-age-toolmakers-surprisingly-sophisticated.html.

Mumford, Lewis, *The City in History*, London: Penguin Books, 1966.

Nietzsche, Friedrich, *The Anti-Christ*, (1895) trans. R. J. Hollingdale, London: Penguin Books, 1975.

Nietzsche, Friedrich, (1886), *Beyond Good and Evil*, trans. Walter Kaufmann and R. S. Hollingdale, London: Penguin Books, 1990.

Nietzsche, Friedrich, (1882), *The Gay Science*, trans. Walter Kaufmann, London: Penguin Books, 1974.

Nietzsche, Friedrich, (1879), *Human All Too Human*, trans. R. S. Hollingdale, Cambridge: Cambridge University Press, 1986.

Nietzsche, Friedrich, (1887), *On the Genealogy of Morals*, trans. Walter Kaufmann and R. S. Hollingdale, New York: Vintage, 1969.

Nietzsche, Friedrich, (1883), *Thus Spoke Zarathustra*, trans. R. S. Hollingdale, London: Penguin Books, 1973.

Nietzsche, Friedrich, (1901), *The Will to Power*, trans. Walter Kaufmann and R. S. Hollingdale, New York: Vintage, 1965.

Pecora, Vincent, P., 'Nietzsche, Genealogy, Critical Theory', *New German Critique*, no. 53, Spring/Summer 1991.

Rapoport, Amos, *House, Form and Culture*, Englewood Cliffs, NJ: Prentice Hall, 1969.

Richardson, John, *Nietzsche's New Darwinism*, Oxford: Oxford University Press, 2004.

Sahlins, Marshall, *Culture in Practice, Selected Essays*, New York: Zone Books, 2005.

Sallis, John, ed., *Deconstruction and Philosophy: The Texts of J. Derrida*, Chicago: Chicago University Press, 1987.

Sallis, John, *Delimitations: Phenomenology and the End of Metaphysics*, Bloomington: Indiana University Press, 1995.

Sartre, Jean-Paul, *The Psychology of Imagination*, London: Methuen, 1972.

Spencer, Herbert, *Structure, Function and Evolution*, ed. Stanley Andreski, London: Thomas Nelson, 1971.

Stiegler, Bernard, *Technics and Time 1: The Fault of Epimetheus*, trans. Richard Beardsworth and George Collins, Stanford: Stanford University Press, 1998.

Stiegler, Bernard, *Technics and Time 2: Disorientations*, trans. Stephen Barker, Stanford: Stanford University Press, 2009.

Stiegler, Bernard, *Technics and Time 3: Cinematic Time and the Question of Malaise*, trans. Stephen Barker, Stanford: Stanford University Press, 2011.

Stringer, Chris, *The Origin of Our Species*, London: Allen Lane/Penguin, 2011.

Thomson, Iain, D., *Heidegger on Ontotheology*, Cambridge: Cambridge University Press, 2005.

Toynbee, Arnold J., *A Study of History*, abridgement by D. C. Summervell, Oxford: Oxford University Press, 1987.

Van Camp, Nathan, 'Animals, Humanity and Technicity', *Transformations*, no. 17, 2009.

Van Camp, Nathan, 'Bernard Stiegler and the Question of Technics', *Transformations*, no. 17, 2009.

Vattimo, Gianni, *The End of Modernity: Nihilism and Hermeneutics in Post-Modern Culture*, trans. J. R. Snyder, London: Polity Press, 1988.

Virilio, Paul, *Speed and Politics*, trans. Mark Polizzotti, New York: Semiotext(e), 1977.

Warren, Mark, *Nietzsche and Political Thought*, Cambridge, MA: MIT Press, 1998.

Weiner, Norbert, *The Human Use of Human Beings*, Cambridge, MA: Da Capo Press, 1988.

Whitehead, Alfred North, *Process and Reality*, New York: Free Press, 1978.

Wittgenstein, Ludwig, *Zettle*, trans. G.E.M. Anscombe, London: Blackwell, 1967.

Wolfe, Cary, *What Is Posthumanism?*, Minneapolis: University of Minnesota Press, 2010.

Zimmer, Carl, *Where Did We Come From?*, Sydney: ABC Books, 2005.

Zimmerman, Michael E., *Eclipse of the Self*, Athens: Ohio University Press, 1981.

Žižek, Slavoj, *Living in the End Times*, London: Verso, 2011.

Index